Praise for *They're Not Gaslighting You*

"In a world where every argument is labeled 'gaslighting' and every difficult person is called 'toxic,' *They're Not Gaslighting You* pulls back the curtain on the dangerous overuse of therapy speak. Dr. Isabelle Morley challenges us to stop hiding behind clinical terms and instead face the real, messy work of understanding ourselves and improving our relationships. This book is for anyone ready to move beyond blame, embrace nuance, and reclaim the power of true emotional intelligence."

—**Laura Gassner Otting,** ABC contributor and *Wall Street Journal* bestselling author of *Wonderhell*

"A refreshing, clear-eyed look at the misuse of therapy speak that infiltrates our everyday lives. Morley shows how weaponizing psychological terms not only distorts our relationships but also undermines their therapeutic value. This book is a must-read for anyone tired of the modern obsession with labeling individuals."

—**Jessica Zucker, PHD,** psychologist and author of *I Had a Miscarriage* and *Normalize It*

"With honesty, humor, and sharp insight, Dr. Morley unpacks the rise of weaponized therapy speak and its damaging impact on relationships. More than just identifying the problem, she offers real solutions, making this book a vital resource for anyone who wants to use mental health language to foster understanding rather than division."

—**Israa Nasir, MHC-LP,** founder of @well.guide and author of *Toxic Productivity*

"In a world where psychological terms like 'gaslighting' and 'narcissism' are thrown around so casually, their true meanings get lost—and so do we. In *They're Not Gaslighting You*, Dr. Isabelle Morley cuts through the noise with clarity and insight, restoring the real definitions behind these powerful concepts. With her accessible and engaging style, she explores how misunderstandings of these terms impact our relationships and attachment dynamics. By distinguishing between true psychological harm and everyday conflict, Dr. Morley empowers readers to navigate relationships with greater awareness, trust, and emotional resilience."

—Deb Curtis, LICSW, cohost of *That Relationship Show* podcast

"Dr. Morley's book comes at the perfect time! As a clinician who works with survivors of relational trauma, and as a survivor myself, I find that many survivors struggle to identify their own experiences, largely due to the pathologizing and weaponization of many mental health terms. Many of my clients have had their abusers twist reality by using clinical terminology to cause confusion and harm, which can feel retraumatizing. Thank you for this work of validation!"

—Kaytee Gillis, psychotherapist and author of four books, including *Healing from Parental Abandonment and Neglect*

"This book is about the power of words, both in and beyond talking therapies. But power goes both ways, and it all depends on how words are used, the context in which they are spoken, and the intentions and competence of the user. If we acknowledge the healing power inherent in words, then we must also acknowledge their ability to do damage. Therapy speak has finally hit the mainstream, but with it comes much misuse—where once we ached for therapy to be acceptable, weaponized therapy speak has now become common vernacular! Nowhere are these weapons more destructive than in couples therapy (Isabelle Morley's specialty). Time for damage control. This is the reset Morley achieves with this delightful yet serious book. 'No, your partner is not a narcissist because he leaves his clothes on the floor!' Morley aims to return therapy speak to where it belongs—as a tool for self-reflection, empowerment, and growth, not externalized either to change others, or worse, to seek revenge. This book is a necessary corrective and an enjoyable read for all therapists and consumers of therapy alike."

—Andrea Celenza, PhD, author of *Transference, Love, Being: Essential Essays from the Field*

"They're Not Gaslighting You felt like a breath of fresh air! It cuts through all the noise of overused therapy buzzwords and gets straight to the heart of what really matters in relationships. It's honest, direct, and filled with the kind of clarity that stops you dead in your tracks. This book doesn't just offer insights—it equips you to trust yourself and build deeper connections. A perennial favorite in the making and an absolute must-read for anyone interested in healthier relationships."

—Rebecca Eudy, LMHC, AASECT, certified sex therapist and cohost of the *Love Lab Uncensored* podcast

They're Not Gaslighting You

Ditch the Therapy Speak and Stop Hunting for Red Flags in Every Relationship

- sociopath
- love bomb
- narcissist
- boundaries
- borderline
- toxic

Dr. Isabelle Morley

THEY'RE NOT GASLIGHTING YOU
Copyright © 2025 by Isabelle Morley

Published by
PESI Publishing, Inc.
3839 White Ave
Eau Claire, WI 54703

Cover and interior design by Emily Dyer
Editing by Chelsea Thompson

ISBN 9781683738268 (print)
ISBN 9781683738275 (ePUB)
ISBN 9781683738282 (ePDF)

All rights reserved.
Printed in Canada.

—Note—

In this book, I give examples to help explain and clarify the weaponized words. The personal examples are all real, with names changed to protect others' privacy (except my husband's—sorry, Lucas). The clinical examples are drawn from my work but are intentionally vague, with specific information altered so that they do not directly reflect any one client or couple. All identifying information, including gender, specific situations, and ages, have been changed. There are also vignettes in each chapter to help you understand each diagnosis or term. None of the vignettes are based on past or current clients. These examples are intended to be clear and accurate but not reflective of any specific person I have known or worked with.

Dedication

To Lucas:
Sorry for all the jar lids I don't put on,
and I love you.

For every messy human out there:
Even the best relationships are hard,
and you're doing great.

And for every survivor:
You deserve to have these terms protected,
and I hope you're healing.

Table of Contents

Introduction 1

1. How Therapy Speak Left the Therapy Room
and Became a Weapon 9

2. The Purpose and Limitations of Diagnoses 27

3. The Difference Between Abuse and Bad Behavior 37

4. Are They Gaslighting You, or Do They Just Disagree? 53

5. Do They Have Obsessive-Compulsive Disorder, or
Are They Just Particular? 73

6. Is It a Red Flag, or Are They Just Imperfect? 91

7. Are They a Narcissist, or Did They Just Hurt
Your Feelings? 109

8. Are They Love Bombing You, or Are They Just
Being Nice? 131

9. Are They a Sociopath, or Do They Just Like You Less
Than You Like Them? 151

10. Are They Bipolar, or Did Their Mood Just Change? 171

11. Did They Violate Your Boundaries, or Did They Just
Not Know How You Felt? 193

12. Are They Borderline, or Do They Just Have
Strong Feelings? 213

They're Not Gaslighting You

13. Toxic, Triggered, and Trauma Bonded 235

14. Being a Human in a Relationship Is Hard,
So Here's Some Advice.. 243

15. It's Time to Lower Your Weapons 255

Resources 261
Bibliography 263
Acknowledgments 267
About the Author 270

Introduction

Back in 2021, when I realized many of my clients and friends were wrongly diagnosing their exes as sociopaths, I wrote a blog article called "Is Your Ex a Sociopath?" Alongside my answer—"probably not"—I made a case for how people who make this claim are missing important information (such as the extent of their ex's suffering post-breakup) and are leaning on a diagnosis to make themselves feel better about the end of their relationship. To date, it's my second most-read blog post. (Fun fact: It was beaten by my analysis of the painful relationship between Shiv and Tom from the show *Succession*, a couple that could be a whole book in itself.)

It seems a lot of people wonder if their ex is a sociopath.

So, I kept writing blog articles that encouraged people to bring more nuance to their analyses of their relationships with others. Then, when the term *weaponized therapy speak* was born, journalists started asking me for my professional opinion on the problems with misusing therapy terms. A popular trend was looking at specific situations where celebrities were weaponizing terms to their benefit. The extent of this problem really hit me. I realized just how often clinical words and diagnoses had boldly left the therapy room and were now showing up in our everyday lives and conversations. The rise of social media, along with increased access to mental health information and therapy, made everyone an expert. Suddenly, there were red flags and triggers and people with bipolar disorder everywhere we looked. Our mothers-in-law were borderline. Our fathers had obsessive-compulsive disorder. Our friends were violating our boundaries. Our partners were gaslighting us during fights and love bombing us afterward. Our exes were narcissists, or sociopaths, or both!

My therapist friends and I went from talking about our concerns regarding our clients' issues to talking about their overuse (or misuse) of *therapy speak* about those issues. Forget a case conceptualization—there wasn't time for that! We were too busy trying to talk people out of their armchair diagnoses so that we could get to the actual work of therapy. It seemed like our clients had become so focused on analyzing everyone else, they had stopped wanting to understand themselves.

I started to get worried when I saw weaponized therapy speak make its way into my couples therapy sessions. Sure, in individual therapy, clients have always tried to diagnose or label people in their lives, but I'd never seen couples diagnose each other right in front of me, and certainly not with such conviction and self-righteous rage. Suddenly, I found myself in the position of pushing back against people's conclusions (which are not often well-received) and spending a lot of time teaching them the real definition of the words they were using. I also had to do damage control, helping both partners recover from the incorrect and often harsh terms they had volleyed at each other.

Then, I *really* got worried when I saw therapists misusing these terms, diagnosing people they'd never met based on their clients' stories. They were throwing out words like *love bombing, borderline, red flag,* and *narcissist,* and encouraging their clients to be increasingly vigilant in their relationships. I've heard more than one story of a therapist telling a couple in a therapy session that one of them was gaslighting the other, even though it was unnecessary, unethical, and just plain wrong. To keep their position as the expert in the room, avoid any possibility of negligence, and be the strongest advocate for their clients, therapists started adopting the same extreme measures and terms.

Introduction

This is an extension of a long-standing tendency. Sure, we've all wondered aloud to our therapists or friends whether our ex is a sociopath or if the person we're dating has crossed some boundaries, but that's where the use of these terms stopped. They stayed in the therapy room or in outside conversations; they weren't used as weapons in the actual relationship. I don't think we need to stop considering diagnoses or assessing behavior, but I do think we need to stop bringing these terms into our relationships.

When these terms are used to mislabel our loved ones or absolve ourselves of any possible blame, they create more problems than they solve. These words signal that there's something deeply wrong happening in a relationship—that we need to make some serious changes, that someone needs professional help, or that we need to get out of that relationship. They exist to show us when there is a serious problem *so that we can decide what to do about it.* They do not exist for the purpose of venting or validating our frustration, or much less to force change in someone else. If you've used them that way, you've already found out that it doesn't work.

As more people started overusing therapy speak, I realized a few blog posts weren't going to convince people that relying on clinical terms to solve their relationship problems wasn't helpful. And thus, this book was born, and it has two main goals. The first is to show that having a better understanding of mental health and relationships is a great thing, but weaponizing terms to diagnose or criticize people we love isn't. I want therapy to keep educating and empowering people, but real empowerment happens when people gain insight and develop the agency to make positive changes. Weaponized therapy speak may help people gain insight, but it makes them feel like they have license to tell *others* how to change.

The truth is that we can only change ourselves.

Sometimes, that involves speaking up in our relationships, pointing out bad behaviors, and asking for others to reflect on themselves and make changes. But that's not the only thing we can or should do. We should always start by looking inward and finding what *we* need to change about our own thoughts and behaviors, and then move on to improving our relationships. Weaponized therapy speak robs us of that opportunity to grow.

The second goal of this book is to protect the real meaning of these terms. The words that I see weaponized most often relate to abusive people or situations. Overuse or misuse of these words results in a "boy who cried wolf" situation, where real concerns are not taken seriously. For the one person in one hundred who is married to an actual narcissist wreaking havoc on their life, it's devastating to hear ninety-nine others complain that their husband is a narcissist because he leaves his clothes on the floor.* Even more concerning, as I'll explain later, is that abusive partners have enthusiastically adopted therapy speak to bolster their abusive control tactics. Clinical terminology has become a new means of twisting reality to their liking. I've seen abusive people accuse their partners of gaslighting *as a way of gaslighting them.* That's next-level stuff. This is a shocking and deeply serious development that we all need to be aware of. We need to protect these words so that they mean what they're supposed to, people who need help can get it, and abusive people aren't able to twist the words for their own aims.

How to Use This Book

If you've glanced over the table of contents already, you've probably spotted one or two chapters that you're eager to dive into. The nice thing about this book is that it's flexible. While you can honestly just jump into any chapter, I recommend starting with the first three chapters in their given order. This will set you up to get the most out of

---

* This is not an actual statistic.

Introduction

subsequent chapters on specific diagnoses or terms. Chapter 1 starts with an explanation of what weaponized therapy speak is, how it became so widespread, and the problems it causes for people and their relationships. Chapter 2 looks at the official reference guide that clinicians use to diagnose clinical disorders and talks about its intended purpose as well as its limitations. Then, chapter 3 looks at some key defining aspects of abusive relationships that help us determine if someone is abusive or just behaving badly.

After reading the first three chapters, go wherever you'd like! There's no need to read chapters 4 through 12 in exact order, as each chapter follows the same pattern:

- You'll begin by reading a vignette that shows an accurate scenario when the term applies.

- Next, you'll get to dive into the clinical definition for what the term *truly* means. (It's worth noting that some terms, like *red flag*, don't have an official clinical definition. In these instances, I'll just talk about their intended meaning.) I'll walk you through the diagnostic criteria (when it applies) and highlight the important features that help us distinguish between the actual clinical definition of the term and popularized misconceptions.

- Then, I'll share a vignette that highlights how the term is commonly (and incorrectly) used. (This is the usage you're probably more familiar with.) This will set us up nicely to explain what people mistakenly think the word means, when it is most misused, and the negative impact of its weaponization. I'll demonstrate why casual use of the clinical term doesn't help improve relationships or resolve conflicts and, in fact, can cause harm to you and your relationships.

- Finally, I'll give you some actionable advice to use if someone has made unfair accusations against *you* with the term or diagnosis.

They're Not Gaslighting You

I'll also provide advice for what to do if you suspect someone you know actually *does* meet the criteria for the term.

As I said, skip around all you like between chapters 4 and 12. Chapter 13 is a bonus chapter where I briefly review three additional commonly misunderstood and misused terms. Once you're done, I recommend reading the final two chapters so you can consolidate your understanding of this societal trend and feel empowered to either work on generally healthy relationships or leave abusive ones. There's also a resources section at the end with great books you can read if you want to take a deeper dive into any of these terms or learn more about how to create a healthy relationship.

As you're reading, you might think of someone in your life who could benefit from this book or certain chapters. In my ideal world, everyone would read this book; if we all gained the same knowledge about the line between normal and pathological behaviors, maybe we'd feel more compassion toward one another. However, I'm forced to acknowledge that we don't live in my ideal world, so perhaps the best you can do is bookmark certain chapters or paragraphs for your loved ones to read. It's easier to hear something you didn't know or don't like from someone you're not in a close relationship with, and I hope to be that person, educating you and others so that you can drop the weaponized therapy speak and start addressing issues more effectively.

I hope you find this book to be a resource you can return to, whether you need a refresher on these terms or are looking for specific guidance if you find yourself in the difficult position of being unfairly accused with one of these terms. I also hope that if you read this book and realize you're in an unhealthy relationship with someone who perhaps *does* have one of these disorders or is exhibiting these abusive behaviors, you feel encouraged to seek help and either change the relationship or leave it.

My biggest hope is that reading this book helps you learn to embrace how wonderfully flawed humans are. Our increased obsession

Introduction

with optimizing ourselves and our lives makes perfection seem easier to attain, but perfection is as impossible as it has ever been. Instead of making perfect relationships the goal, let's accept that everyone has emotional scars, unhelpful coping strategies, counterproductive defense mechanisms, and moments of selfishness or volatility, and this doesn't make everyone pathological. Despite our challenges, humans are amazing creatures that form powerful, meaningful bonds with one another. Our relationships, though imperfect at times, can give us immense happiness, a sense of belonging, security, and love. So, let's accept (even embrace!) the inherent messiness of the human experience as we learn how to drop the therapy speak and have compassion for the people we love. ∎

Chapter 1

How Therapy Speak Left the Therapy Room and Became a Weapon

Let me begin with a confession: I've had every mental health disorder in the book. Major depression, obsessive-compulsive disorder, generalized anxiety, posttraumatic stress disorder, attention-deficit/hyperactivity disorder . . . Hell, I even went through a few weeks of having narcissistic personality disorder (rough times, especially for my then-boyfriend). You name it, I've had it.

Of course, these disorders were all anxiously and inaccurately self-diagnosed when I was in graduate school earning my doctorate in clinical psychology. Luckily (or perhaps unluckily), I wasn't alone in this; my peers were psychological disasters too. Every time a professor taught us a new disorder, the whole class shuddered with the realization that it described each of us to a tee.

We didn't only diagnose ourselves as clinical messes. We also eagerly diagnosed everyone we knew. As our education progressed, we realized all the behaviors and feelings we used to see as frustrating but "normal" were actually symptoms of chronic mental and emotional disturbance. Nobody I knew was safe—as soon as I learned about a new disorder, someone came to mind who seemed to fit the picture. A cousin had borderline personality disorder, a parent was most certainly avoidant, a friend had attentional issues, and an ex-boyfriend was a psychopath.

They're Not Gaslighting You

How relieving to finally have an explanation for every single person in my life who caused me any degree of hurt or irritation!

I'm telling you this because the last thing I want is for this book to leave you feeling judged. Believe me, *I get it*. I've wondered if I meet the criteria for many different disorders and if my partners, family members, or friends also have clinical-level issues—and this doesn't mean that I'm a deeply disturbed individual. It means that I, like you, have often struggled to understand myself and those around me, and I wanted a convincing explanation for why life can feel so hard.

We all want to understand what's happening inside us and our relationships, and clinical terminology offers explanations that feel objective and reliable in situations when we're confused, hurt, and don't know where to turn or whom to trust. They might even give us a roadmap for fixing the issue and avoiding this type of painful situation again. Labeling or diagnosing something (or someone) can seem like a way to spare ourselves from future suffering. What we don't realize is that it can just as often work against us. Let's talk about why.

Enter: Weaponized Therapy Speak

Coming of age during a time of growing mental health awareness is great in some ways, but it has also fostered an unhelpful trend toward labeling, diagnosing, and pathologizing that I, as a young person and an eager student, often participated in.

It's comforting to have an explanation for what we're experiencing, as well as scripts (expected behavioral patterns for certain situations) and playbooks (healthy how-to guides) to help inform our responses to our experiences. Humans create these cognitive shortcuts to help things make sense in an otherwise chaotic and nonsensical world. They also seem to promise a way of avoiding pain: By identifying and categorizing people's bad behavior or traits, we can avoid such people in the future. However, in our attempt to understand our experience and inform our decisions, we began borrowing the language of therapy to label or accuse others. This is what we call *weaponized therapy speak.*

It's not a new phenomenon for people to use therapy terms casually, even flippantly, to describe themselves or other people. How long have we referred to someone as a "psycho" when they're acting irrationally or being mean? And to be honest, I don't see a huge problem with casually using these words in conversation to get a point across. We're not actually saying that person is a psychopath. We're merely condemning their behavior as aberrant or unacceptable. When we do this, we're misusing therapy speak, but we're not necessarily weaponizing it. While our diagnostic conjectures are clearly inaccurate, they're not supposed to be accurate—they're supposed to make a point.

The trend of weaponized therapy speak marks something very different. These days, clinical words are wielded, sincerely and self-righteously, to lay unilateral blame on one person in a relationship while excusing the other from any wrongdoing. Words that were originally meant to stay in the therapy room so we could understand our world better and figure out how to navigate it have become ways to force others to change. Our increased awareness of mental health issues and what constitutes abuse has caused us to conflate normal emotional or relationship challenges with deviant ones.

Many times, we use these words as protective measures to help us avoid abusive partners and reduce our risk of "wasting" time or emotional energy on family or friends who don't deserve it. But using these terms can also absolve people from taking responsibility for their actions in their relationships. They can say, "I had to do that because of my obsessive-compulsive disorder" or "We didn't work out because she's a narcissist," instead of doing the hard work of seeing their part in the problem and addressing the issues behind it.

As a couples therapist, I'm particularly concerned with how the enthusiastic but inaccurate embrace of clinical terminology has made it harder to sustain healthy romantic attachments. Nothing hijacks a

They're Not Gaslighting You

session like a client who accuses their partner of having a disorder and who turns to me for confirmation, while their partner (although it's almost never the first time they've heard it) anxiously waits for me to weigh in on if they really are a sociopath, or a ticking love bomb, or whatever term has been volleyed. Weaponized therapy speak turns our session into a Psych 101 lecture instead of what it should be: an exploration of the hurt that led to the accusation in the first place.

I'm most concerned, though, by the way that abusive people have adopted this trend. Eternal victims in their own minds, abusers have always been good at blaming their partners for every negative emotion they feel. Now, they have therapy speak to back that up. Their partner went out with a friend of the opposite gender? That's a boundary violation and toxic behavior. Their friend doesn't agree with their warped view of an event or their disproportionate reaction? The friend is an empathy-lacking narcissist who is actively gaslighting them. (This is actually a well-known abuse tactic we'll talk about in chapter 3.) Since most of us tend to instinctively defer to scientific or clinical language, it feels wrong to challenge or outright deny it, but giving consideration to this kind of accusation allows the abuser to spin a false narrative that gives them the relational upper hand. In one memorable session of mine, a client managed to accuse their partner of narcissism, gaslighting, love bombing, blaming the victim, lacking accountability, having no empathy, and being generally abusive, manipulative, and toxic . . . all within twenty minutes. The client's partner showed no evidence of being any of those things, but unless they fully accepted all these labels and acquiesced to everything my client said, it was unlikely these accusations would ever end.

Weaponized therapy speak isn't a problem with one population or during any one phase of life, and that's what makes this issue so important to address. It's become a near-universal behavior for teens and adults alike that's also been enthusiastically adopted by abusers. It's not something we only do as immature adolescents that we eventually grow out of. It's something we must actively choose to leave behind, and we won't choose to do so unless we're told why it's ineffective and how we could do things differently, which is exactly why this book exists.

Weaponization Pathologizes Normal Behavior

It's one thing to be too cursory in assigning labels to other people, which we often do in casual conversations with our friends when analyzing our relationships. These terms can, after all, be helpful ways of quickly understanding someone without launching into every detail and example. It's quite another thing to pathologize someone's pretty normal behavior (even if it's ineffective or hurtful) and shift all blame to them. And then there's the glee with which abusers have learned how to weaponize therapy speak to make themselves the victims, and that's the most concerning problem of all.

Let's look at romantic relationships to see how this plays out. For the vast majority of couples, a problem takes two people to create and two people to solve. Sure, one person may behave worse than the other, but how the other responds will also determine the outcome. By weaponizing therapy speak, one person in the relationship is attempting to place all the blame on their partner. They are essentially saying, "Sure, I'm in this relationship too, but I think this problem is because of *you*, not me, so I don't need to be involved in addressing it."

I'm certified in emotionally focused couples therapy (EFCT), which is a type of couples therapy based on attachment theory. I won't go too deep into it (that's a whole other book!) but EFCT helps couples identify and address their "negative cycle" so they can get unstuck from ineffective patterns of interacting when they're feeling hurt. It explores how painful feelings (such as rejection, embarrassment, inadequacy) come up when our partner is unhappy with us, and how we develop coping strategies to alleviate those feelings. Since these vulnerable, painful feelings often stem from early childhood wounds that can be pretty hard to tolerate, our coping strategies tend to involve defense mechanisms like minimization, denial, or rationalization. For example, if you feel like a failure for letting your partner down, you might immediately minimize your partner's feelings and tell them they shouldn't react so strongly to such a small issue. (For anyone wondering, this *isn't* gaslighting.) That makes them feel unheard and unimportant, so they get even more upset, which makes you dismiss their reaction as dramatic, and round and round it goes.

The negative cycle is worth understanding because when people are stuck in it, they can behave badly, sometimes badly enough that another person could reasonably justify a label or diagnosis. However, diagnosing someone when they are mid-conflict with the person they love—when they are behaving harshly as they attempt to shield themselves from intense emotional suffering—is not a fair assessment. If you saw me in the middle of a bad argument with my husband, Lucas, I'm sure you could pick out a label or two, but that label wouldn't be accurate because it reflects one tiny snapshot of my life without considering the context of the rest of our relationship. It would also be ignoring how Lucas, although wonderful, is also not perfect in arguments and was part of the reason the conflict escalated.

The Negative Cycle in Action

For a more concrete example, let's say your partner says it hurt their feelings when you were late to their work party earlier that night. You instantly feel shame for disappointing your partner, but to avoid this painful emotion, you become defensive and explain why you were late. You say that you cleaned the kitchen before you left since you know your partner likes coming home to a clean house. This helps you feel better and less at fault, but it also makes your partner think you didn't

How Therapy Speak Left the Therapy Room and Became a Weapon

listen to them, don't care about how they feel, and are now blaming *them* for the situation.

They fire back at you, giving more detailed reasons as to why your tardiness was hurtful and drawing on past examples of when you've been late. Heck, they even expand the issue by saying your poor time management is also why you can't seem to ever clean the kitchen in an efficient or timely manner.

This comment *really* spikes your shame, making you feel like a failure. You think your partner views you as this lazy, chronically late, inefficient person. But this doesn't feel fair to you because the thing they're mad about is so small (really, they're this angry that you were *ten minutes* late?) and you were only late because you were cleaning the kitchen, which was to make *them* happy, so you become more defensive. And, in addition to being defensive, you tell your partner that their way of bringing up issues is the real problem because they were way too critical and ruined a perfectly good evening. If they didn't leave their dirty breakfast dishes in the sink, you wouldn't have had to spend the extra time cleaning.

See how this escalates?

If I stopped you at this point and talked to both you and your partner separately, I'm sure you could pathologize each other's behavior. You could claim your partner is toxic and borderline because they're emotionally volatile and unforgiving. You could say their feelings are disproportionate to the problem, and their verbal assault is bordering on abusive.

But your partner could say that you are a narcissist who is gaslighting them by refusing to acknowledge their feelings, showing no empathy for the distress your tardiness caused, and shifting the blame to *them* (just like a narcissist would!).

You'd both be wrong, of course, but you can see how these conclusions could happen. And, if these conclusions are left unchecked, you then look for more evidence to corroborate them. This is called *confirmation bias*, and it's what happens when we have a preconceived belief about something and we filter incoming data to only notice information that supports our conclusion and overlook evidence that doesn't.

Weaponized therapy speak is our attempt to understand people and situations in our lives, yes, but it is also a strategy to avoid responsibility. It puts the blame solely on the other person and allows us to ignore our part. This trend has made normal behavior seem clinically problematic because it doesn't take into account that humans behave poorly when upset. We've always struggled to find the line between "regular bad" behavior and "clinically bad" behavior, particularly in our romantic relationships, and weaponized therapy speak has made it even harder instead of helping.

How the Internet and Social Media Made Us Think We're Experts

Historically, clinical language has been used by doctors to pathologize behavior; in other words, to draw the line between normal and abnormal functioning. (We'll dive into this more in chapter 2.) The intention was to identify emotions and behaviors that cause impairment in an individual's functioning, and the purpose of *that* was to formulate an appropriate treatment plan to help the individual. These terms were never meant to insult, accuse, or excuse an individual's behaviors. They're meant to be used by professionals to identify the issues their clients are experiencing so that they can get the right help.

Therapists undergo extensive training to use these clinical terms correctly and learn how to be judicious when assigning a diagnosis. Even after all that, therapists still participate in consultation groups or supervision to assess and treat their clients accurately. Diagnosis is a very powerful tool that can significantly impact someone's life—that's why it requires an objective perspective from a trained professional.

How Therapy Speak Left the Therapy Room and Became a Weapon

Even clinicians with decades of experience shouldn't attempt to diagnose themselves or the people in their personal lives, much less someone whose clinical "knowledge" is derived from a social media algorithm.

Although clinical terminology has previously only been accessible to mental health professionals, these terms have become mainstream with the rise in popularity of therapy and growing discussions around mental health. The internet started this trend by giving people access to articles about various mental health issues and self-reported accounts of disorders. Then social media arrived on the scene and further increased access. To be clear, the internet and social media have also helped reduce stigma about mental health, which is a really good thing. By normalizing mental health struggles and removing the shame that so often accompanies them, people were able to admit to illnesses and get help. Nowadays, people with depression don't have to suffer in silence; it's a medical problem they can disclose and seek help for. There's no denying that's a great change.

The unanticipated problem is that people are now over-pathologizing themselves and others. On social media, you'll typically find short posts or brief videos of specific symptoms that are relatable to almost everyone. For example, having a hard time focusing? You have attention-deficit/hyperactivity disorder (ADHD), just like the influencer you're watching! You watch a reel where they explain how they get distracted during tasks and jump from one thing to the next, starting but never finishing anything, and that experience resonates with you. Then you watch another video from them about how hard it is to start a difficult task, like cleaning, and *that* resonates too. Suddenly, you've self-diagnosed with ADHD. You start searching for more videos about symptoms. And now the algorithm has you all figured out. The app feeds you more ADHD videos, leading to confirmation bias, as you only see videos that confirm your suspicion instead of challenging it. (To be fair, there are probably very few of these anyway.)

Another interesting outcome of this increased access to knowledge is that our awareness about the "best" and "healthiest" ways to live our lives has led to high expectations. We demand potential or current partners disclose their mental health status, self-care routine, red flags they're working on, boundaries, attachment style, Myers-Briggs personality type, therapy history, transference issues, love language, and the list goes on. To keep up with this level of awareness, we need to read all the psychology self-help books and know all the right language. And lord help you if you don't know all of it, because that means you're not invested in self-growth.

In our attempt to be the most responsible and healed person possible, we've started over-pathologizing normal feelings and actions. Again, this misses the complicated, nuanced experience of being human. Trying to slot ourselves or others into discrete categories overlooks the reality that human behavior and emotion exist on a spectrum. We can act poorly but not be abusive. We can behave ineffectively without meeting the criteria for a disorder. Our relentless attempts to label ourselves (and others) have stopped us from recognizing and accepting how emotionally and behaviorally *messy* humans are—and while this messiness might not be helpful at times, it's also not pathological.

A decade ago, when I was a new clinician, I could not have predicted how many people would arrive at my practice already having a diagnosis that they gleaned from social media. Back then, Instagram was just a photo-sharing app and TikTok hadn't even been invented. In this pre-reel world, any information people had on mental health disorders came primarily from health care professionals. Now, influencers can convince viewers that they have a disorder or that their parent is exhibiting a clinically problematic trait that needs to be treated. Anyone can be considered an expert if they have a large enough platform. But despite their overuse, these clinical terms still carry the same power, and herein lies the problem.

The temptation to label and categorize is very understandable. There are many parts of being a human that are difficult, and if there's a chance something is a clinical issue that could possibly be solved instead of an unavoidable part of being a human, who *wouldn't* want that to be the case? But as I've explained, weaponized therapy speak stops you from recognizing your areas of growth, it hurts and alienates the other person, and it creates a culture of finger-pointing and pathologizing.

Therapists Are Part of the Problem

As more and more people enter therapy with preconceived conclusions about themselves and their loved ones, an interesting and unexpected development has occurred: Clients are recruiting their therapists to confirm their diagnoses instead of working with a trained expert to figure out what's happening in their relationships.

No longer is therapy a forum for curious, collaborative exploration; instead, people want a therapist's rubber stamp on their preestablished conclusions. The therapist, as the expert, bears witness to the diagnosis instead of being the one to decide it. This puts therapists in a difficult position: Do they challenge the unsubstantiated diagnosis and risk invalidating their client, leading to a therapeutic rupture and possible early termination of treatment, or do they go along with the client's self-diagnosis even if it may be inaccurate? There is risk in either path. Some therapists opt for the second route and then gently, over time, encourage their clients to consider other explanations for their symptoms or to seek psychological testing to confirm (or deny) the diagnosis.

When clients come to therapy having diagnosed their loved ones, this put therapists in a particularly difficult situation. If the therapist disagrees with the diagnosis, the risk of rupture is even greater since, to the client, it feels like the therapist is invalidating them (even "gaslighting" them) and taking the other person's side. Clients can feel blamed by their therapist for the relationship's troubles when they want the therapist to blame the other person instead.

The fact is, it is irresponsible for therapists to make a diagnostic conclusion about another person they haven't met. (It would also be a violation of their ethics code.) Nevertheless, the increase in weaponized therapy speak has spawned a concerning trend where therapists are feeling freer to label or diagnose clients' friends, partners, and family—people they have never assessed or treated.

I've encountered many clients in my couples work who tell me that they and their individual therapists have determined a diagnosis for their partner. For example, I worked with a married couple who were stuck in some very unhelpful patterns, leaving both partners feeling attacked, lonely, and angry. After years of arguing and battling to be "right," they were admittedly not good at navigating conflict. In a one-on-one session with me, the wife disclosed that in her individual therapy, she and her therapist had diagnosed her husband as a narcissist. That's why he would get so defensive whenever she brought up a request or complaint, she explained. Her therapist, hearing only the wife's side, was the one to suggest the diagnosis. But I'd witnessed the manner in which the wife would raise these "complaints," which was often through character assassinations ("You're so irresponsible because your mom babied you your whole life!") where she'd also bring up ten other things he did "wrong." Her approach made his defensiveness a lot more understandable. Her therapist heard a very different version of events ("I asked him to order more paper towels, and he said it's not his job to keep track of it!") and jumped to an inaccurate conclusion.

Unfortunately, this therapist is not a rare exception. I hear stories like this often. And I can understand how it might happen. Early in my career, I can't tell you how many times I consulted with one partner in a couple and left the consultation thinking, *Good lord, their partner sounds like an absolute monster. I don't know why they haven't left already,* only to meet with their partner for a consultation and hear a very different but

How Therapy Speak Left the Therapy Room and Became a Weapon

equally reasonable perspective that made me feel embarrassed for vilifying them in my mind. Now, after years of couples work, I know better.

I know that . . . people can share valid perspectives and memories of how their partners have hurt them, but their partners usually have equally valid points of view and wounds they've suffered.

I know that . . . we can draw many conclusions from just one interaction, and the lens through which we see our partners can greatly influence which conclusion we arrive at.

I know that . . . a therapist is more likely to reinforce a client's negative view of their partner when that client is in what couples therapy researcher John Gottman calls *negative sentiment override.* When clients are in this frame of mind, everything their partner says or does confirms that negative view, and the way they talk about their partner reflects this view as well.

While *I* now know this, therapists who don't can easily fall prey to thinking that a client's partner sounds very troubled and needs serious help. What the client may need, however, is a therapist who gently encourages them to consider possible extenuating factors that impact their partner's behaviors, look for evidence that challenges their conclusions, and build more empathy and perspective-taking skills. They may need a therapist who shifts the focus from what the client's *partner* is doing wrong to what the *client* has control over so they can be a part of positive change. For example, maybe the client's partner gets too angry when unfolded laundry is dumped on the bed, but the client's cold and dismissive response each time certainly doesn't help.

Therapists who don't do couples work may not have the benefit of seeing both sides of the story. They may be so focused on building rapport and validating their clients that they neglect to help their clients consider a more balanced and forgiving analysis. But a gentle reminder for all my fellow therapists reading this: We should be giving the benefit of the doubt until proven otherwise (with some really good evidence). We should stop assuming the worst about the people in our clients' lives and instead assume they may have an equally valid perspective that we're not hearing. We should watch for abuse but not immediately assert that it's there. Math will back me up here—statistically speaking, most people's partners aren't abusers or sociopaths or narcissists; they're just complicated humans who act badly sometimes. And while I'm not great at math, knowing that sociopaths are only 6 percent of the population, at most, makes it pretty clear to me that not every single ex is one.

Now, I'll also note that it can be an important part of the therapeutic work for therapists to make observations or offer explanations about the people in their clients' lives. For example, maybe a client doesn't realize that his mother's obsession with cleanliness suggests that she has a clinical phobia of germs. His entire life, he had thought he was a dirty, careless kid who made their home practically unlivable. In this case, it can be very powerful to help this client see how the angry encounters he had with his mother in childhood, where she admonished him for leaving traces of toothpaste on the bathroom sink, were evidence of her mental health struggles—and not his failure for being a "bad kid." However, confidently diagnosing his mother with obsessive-compulsive disorder and spending time analyzing and blaming his mother is less helpful (and, again, unethical).

This speaks to a core tenet of therapy: Therapists must strive to help their clients understand how people have impacted them so that *they* can gain insight and then take responsibility for making changes in their own lives. The point isn't to blame others and then stew in self-righteous anger. That doesn't help anyone. There's a way to recognize how others have affected you, both positively and negatively, and then be empowered to take action.

I fear that the rise of weaponized therapy speak is pulling us away from this model, relying on finger-pointing at others instead of allowing us to take responsibility for our own part. By labeling the other as the sole issue, be it a family member, coworker, friend, or partner, we ignore our own opportunity to make our relationships better.

Why We Should Practice Caution with These Terms

When the diagnoses and terms discussed in this book are truly present in a relationship, it indicates that significant harm is happening within that relationship. However, when these terms are misused or overused, it minimizes their meaning and the painful experience that survivors have lived through. That's why a central goal of this book is to defend the true meaning of these words, allowing you to accurately assess dangerous situations and take the necessary steps to protect yourself. It also encourages all of us to remember that these words exist for a reason: to explain truly aberrant experiences that cause distress and destruction.

And listen, some people *do* suffer from relationships with abusive partners, narcissistic friends, or parental figures with real personality disorders that make them emotionally volatile, overly demanding, and generally difficult to have a relationship with. These are the people who meet the criteria for a diagnosis and who do need to self-reflect and change because they're hurting those around them. If you know someone who has had a close relationship with a true narcissist, or you've experienced this yourself, then you know the damage is far worse than people realize. It's not an annoying argument about whether you're coming home for the holidays or their tendency to favor your sibling; it's pervasive emotional abuse that destabilizes you, takes away your self-esteem and self-trust, and controls your life.

However, the vast majority of partners and friends are not sociopaths, narcissists, or abusers. They're just *flawed*. They're insecure, demanding, controlling, emotional, or any number of adjectives, but these traits alone aren't pathological. They're people doing their imperfect best to navigate their relationships.

AN EXTRA WORD OF CAUTION

If it's tempting to diagnose our partners, it's even more tempting to diagnose our exes. Sometimes, seeing an ex more clearly through a diagnostic lens is very helpful and appropriate. If you were married to a narcissist, you know how disorienting and damaging it is, and being able to label their behavior (and read books and find support from others) can be a critical part of healing. A great therapist can help you determine if an ex exhibits traits of a disorder that could explain the hard or abusive parts of your relationship. However, most exes don't meet the criteria for a clinical disorder. In this case, calling them bipolar or borderline might help you feel better and affirm that the breakup wasn't your fault. But it might be untrue and prevent you from doing some important self-reflection in how the relationship went south.

For better and for worse, everyone seems to know more about clinical terms these days and has either used them or been incorrectly labeled with them (sometimes both). As you read through certain terms in the chapters that follow, you may realize that you have used them wrongly at one time or another. If that happens, I encourage you to be curious and reflective but not berate yourself. This is a trend we've all fallen prey to, and it's okay if you realize that you've weaponized therapy speak in the past. You're in good company. I'm right there with you. The good news is that by reading this book, you will gain a better understanding of when and how to apply these powerful and sensitive terms. For situations where they don't apply, you'll learn helpful tools for addressing conflict and navigating ongoing issues without letting the harsh use of clinical terms ruin a potentially great relationship.

Humans are wonderfully imperfect, which makes emotional pain inevitable even in the best relationships. Self-reflection and self-growth

How Therapy Speak Left the Therapy Room and Became a Weapon

are all we can do; improving is a continuous process throughout our lives. So, be kind to yourself as I guide you through these commonly misused and misunderstood terms to help you better understand yourself and those around you. ◾

Chapter 2

The Purpose and Limitations of Diagnoses

Clinical diagnoses are helpful ways of not only describing the human experience, but also giving us a line (if a somewhat arbitrary one) between what is normal and abnormal. When we can identify an abnormality, we can use our knowledge to address it and reduce someone's suffering. Before mental illness was understood, people suffering from abnormal thoughts, feelings, and behaviors were given very little empathy or support—they were just called "crazy" and hidden from society. So, let's look at a brief history of how mental health disorders came into being, which will allow us to be better, more critical consumers of them.

Back in the old days (think 1800s), curiosity about how the mind could become "sick" and impact a person's ability to function was uncharted territory. Doctors, only just beginning to recognize disorders of the mind, were coming up with some pretty ludicrous hypotheses and treatment plans. But while these ideas may not have always been done well, these pioneering researchers did bring focus to helping people struggling with mental health issues.

Most of us today are familiar with Sigmund Freud, at least by name. An Austrian neurologist who paved the way in researching mental health, leading to his reputation as the so-called "father of psychoanalysis," Freud laid the foundation for a modern era in which mental health is not only recognized but valued by society. Still, he had some *wild* ideas. For example, he proposed that women were so pained by their status as the "inferior sex" that they endured a variety of psychological symptoms as a result. Without much competition in his field, Freud's theories held significant sway. Thank goodness for all of us that, eventually, more scientists took up researching mental health and creating evidence-based explanations for psychological challenges. Otherwise, postpartum disorders might be written off as "penis envy," and we'd still be taking prescribed cocaine to alleviate our troubles. (Freud quite enjoyed cocaine and, for a while, fervently recommended it as a treatment. What a time to be in medicine!)

Freud's greatest gift to the field was the conviction that abnormal thoughts, feelings, and behaviors have rational explanations behind them. In his wake, doctors and academics spent decades identifying, categorizing, and defining mental health disorders which they compiled and turned into the *Diagnostic and Statistical Manual* (DSM) in 1952. The first edition of the DSM was a valiant attempt, but like the clients it described, the manual had . . . issues. Both the DSM-I and the DSM-II (released in 1968) were based solely on Freud's psychoanalytic principles and thus lacked biological explanations and reliable measurement tools. Admittedly, it's a tall order to take observations and self-reported symptoms and turn them into discrete diagnoses, and the criteria listed by the DSM aren't clear enough to always lead to the same conclusion; two different clinicians could arrive at two different diagnoses when evaluating the same client. Although subsequent versions of the DSM have attempted to rectify this, it's an ongoing process. We are currently on the DSM-5-TR (fifth edition, text revision—if you're wondering what that means), which was released in 2022. It remains the definitive standard for mental health providers to assess and treat their clients.

You may be wondering, who writes the DSM now? The answer is the DSM Task Force, a diverse committee of experts—clinicians, psychiatrists, and researchers—assembled by the American Psychiatric Association. There are also advisers and organizations involved, and the task force accepts public feedback, but it's mainly these core members who are in charge of sorting through modern research and adjusting diagnoses accordingly. For the record, you couldn't pay me to be a part of this task force—the job sounds like a nightmare. (They wouldn't pay me anyway; it's all volunteered time.)

The DSM Is Imperfect, Just Like Us

While the DSM serves an incredibly important purpose for clinicians—providing explanations for painful or challenging psychological experiences that can help chart a path forward—it is far from perfect or exhaustive. Even with the task force working hard to ensure the disorders listed represent the most recent, scientifically valid findings, the DSM always presents room for improvement; no sooner is a revised edition released than both clinicians and clients begin to eagerly await a new one that accounts for their unique struggles.

Even the manual itself acknowledges that it shouldn't be the sole basis for treatment planning. Nevertheless, clinicians use it because it offers a shared language for understanding clients (particularly helpful when consulting with colleagues) and, perhaps more importantly, because insurance companies require a diagnosis. If not for these things, perhaps we would lean less heavily on this manual. So, while it's necessary and very helpful, let's also acknowledge a few of its flaws.

As mentioned, the DSM lacks strong interrater reliability, which essentially means that two clinicians, when given the same client, could arrive at two different diagnoses and thus offer different treatment recommendations. This is obviously problematic. At the same time, it's somewhat inevitable, given the overlap in symptoms across many disorders.

The DSM also lacks good validity, meaning that the diagnoses we may arrive at aren't always accurate. While we do have scientifically valid ways of measuring disorders, our measurements are based on standard deviations (the bell curve you may recall from high school statistics class), making them a lot less neatly defined than, say, medical conditions like diabetes, which has an exact number associated with the disease. If you have a fasting blood sugar level of 126 mg/dL or higher on two separate tests, you have diabetes, but how strong and persistent do your fears of abandonment have to be before you have borderline personality disorder? This reflects how mental health disorders can range in severity, and a careful and nuanced understanding of this is essential for diagnosis.

However, the DSM is based on the medical model, in which symptoms, or even experiences, are classified into discrete categories. Critics argue that human behavior and emotion do not fit into delineated groups and that there aren't natural or distinct boundaries between psychological disorders, which tend to exist on a spectrum. Categorizing a psychological problem with a single label is useful in guiding treatment and getting insurance coverage, but it may not help us determine what caused the problem, what treatment will help, and what the prognosis is for recovery.

For example, to be diagnosed with major depressive disorder, you need to have five or more of nine possible criteria, such as insomnia, fatigue, and loss of appetite. These criteria exist on a spectrum and vary

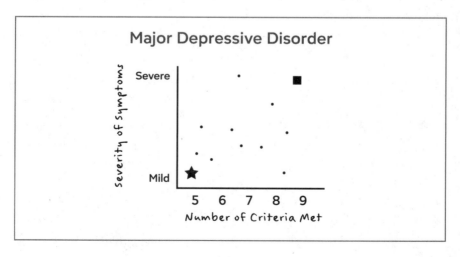

The Purpose and Limitations of Diagnoses

in severity. A person who meets the minimum criteria and has mild symptoms (the star symbol on the graph) will look incredibly functional compared to someone with meets all nine criteria with severe symptoms (the square symbol), but they both have major depression. See why these categories aren't be-all and end-all definitions?

Not to pile on here, but it's confusing how two people with the same disorder can have completely different presentations of said disorder. Since there are those nine criteria for major depressive disorder in the DSM-5-TR, two people can have this disorder with almost no overlap in terms of symptoms. One person might stay in bed sleeping all day, find no joy in life, lose weight because they're not eating, and hate themselves, while the other might feel keyed up and irritable, struggle with concentration, suffer from insomnia, and gain weight because they're over-eating. Both have depressed mood, but their symptom profiles look markedly different. This is important to remember for later chapters since it shows how the symptoms of a single disorder can present on a wide spectrum. A person with narcissistic personality disorder who meets every single criterion and exhibits severe symptoms will look quite different from someone who meets the minimum criteria and has a mild presentation.

Finally, and most importantly for the purpose of this book, the DSM has a history of pathologizing normal behavior. For example, homosexuality was considered a mental disorder until the DSM-III removed it as a diagnosis in 1980. That means for almost three decades, a doctor could diagnose someone with homosexuality and encourage or force them to seek treatment to "fix" this disorder. Clearly, this manual isn't infallible. It's easy to wonder what other normal variants of human preferences, emotional states, and behaviors are still incorrectly classified as disorders.

For example, the current DSM has a diagnosis called prolonged grief disorder for people who experience notable symptoms of grief a year after the loss. To qualify for a diagnosis, clients only need to meet three of eight criteria, such as yearning for the person who's gone, feeling a part of themselves has died, experiencing emotional pain or numbness related to the death, and feeling lonely. But wouldn't we expect people to feel this way after losing someone they care about? This diagnosis allows people who are struggling with their grief to get their therapy covered by insurance, but that doesn't mean it's problematic or pathological.

This, again, illustrates how important it is to be clear about the DSM's purpose: to help clinicians understand and help their clients. Even when clients find relief in a category or label that explains their experience, that label is not intended to explain everything they are going through. Although diagnoses are used to understand and inform treatment planning, clinicians are taught to not cling to those diagnoses too tightly, nor to see them as a permanent definition of that client.

How the DSM Led to Weaponized Therapy Speak

Not to point fingers, but I partly blame the DSM for the current state of weaponized therapy speak. The DSM, in its effort to be a guide for clinicians who need to identify and treat mental disorders, has also become a framework through which "armchair experts" can pathologize the human experience. This is why many clinicians, even while using the DSM, take issue with its approach to mental health. They feel its medicalized approach prompts people to see themselves as being more unwell than they actually are and encourages health care providers to provide treatment that may not truly be necessary. We already struggle to find the line between hard but normal emotions versus emotional experiences that are aberrant and require treatment, and the DSM's framework makes it easier to confuse the two.

This happened to me. Back in my graduate school days, I developed intense anxiety. Keep-you-up-at-night, ruminating-about-things-that-can't-be-changed, heart-racing kind of anxiety. It was prompted by a

The Purpose and Limitations of Diagnoses

recent breakup with my then-boyfriend Noah, the increasing demands of graduate school, and some growing pains with my family. At the time, I was seeing a wonderful therapist who supported me and challenged me—my first (of many) great therapy experiences. During one early session, I said I thought I needed medication. She listened, nodded, and said it was an option if I wanted to try it, but she also said my anxiety made sense given my stressors, and she thought I could work through it.

She was absolutely right. Could I have started medication and found relief? Probably. But my anxiety was in response to hard things in my life; it wasn't a chronic disorder that I couldn't manage. I'd only had a few sessions, but the DSM said I met the criteria for a disorder that could be treated with antianxiety drugs, so I was ready to jump into a medication consult. Fortunately, my therapist didn't pathologize my experience beyond what it was. She was understanding and gentle in helping me reframe my experience as difficult, yes, but normal.

This story isn't to encourage people to tough it out and avoid meds. I think medication can be absolutely necessary and very helpful for many, many people. At the same time, many people, after getting a diagnosis, lean too far into it. They find new signs and symptoms that fit a particular disorder when, in truth, their experiences are not aberrant or even problematic. A common example I see is people who think they have ADHD because they procrastinate and finish projects right before the deadlines when, in theory, they could have done it sooner. This, in itself, isn't ADHD. It's actually not even a problem unless it's causing significant distress or impairment—for example, you can't function at work, your relationships are falling apart, or you can't maintain a healthy lifestyle with good hygiene and a regular eating and sleeping schedule.

Your bad habits are not always symptoms of a disorder, even if they are listed in a book. The same is true of your bad experiences.

We all know that person (or maybe we've been that person) who consults "Doctor Google" every time they have a mysterious rash or suffer from inexplicable stomach pain. In search of answers for their mystery symptoms, these folks spiral down the rabbit hole of the Internet, diagnosing themselves with rare diseases and one-in-a-million chronic conditions, only to discover that an over-the-counter cream or a few days of rest fixes the problem.

Having a human body and mind makes us vulnerable to all sorts of passing pains, physical and psychological. If we focus narrowly enough on the problem, we can find all sorts of evidence that we're sick. Actual doctors even have a name for it—it's called *symptom spotting*. (Incidentally, it runs rampant among medical students.)

Interestingly, when it comes to psychological issues, we tend to turn our overfocused lens on others rather than on ourselves. Did your boyfriend have a few nights where he couldn't fall asleep and now he's acting intensely irritable? Yep, it's depression; sleep changes and irritability are criteria for that. Or it could be bipolar disorder; maybe the insomnia and mood changes are early signs of hypomania or mania. Or perhaps he has ADHD; that's why he keeps staying up too late when he knows he should have gone to sleep. Or anxiety—definitely anxiety! He couldn't sleep because his anxious mind wouldn't turn off and he's so keyed up. But wait, that *is* hypomania, isn't it?

You can see how easy it is to pathologize very normal experiences. However, one night of poor sleep does not a disorder make, just as one instance of insensitive behavior does not qualify someone as a sociopath. This is why we need lots of data and an independent professional's analysis before making any diagnostic call.

A Quick Word on Personality Disorders

There are almost three hundred disorders in the DSM-5-TR. There are anxiety disorders, depressive disorders, developmental disorders, sleep-wake disorders, and of course, personality disorders. This category (like the DSM in general) is slightly controversial and often misunderstood, so let's do a quick background on what it means.

The Purpose and Limitations of Diagnoses

We classify someone with a personality disorder when they feel or behave in ways that contradict social norms and cause issues with functioning (meaning it impairs their ability to work, maintain relationships, or take care of themselves). People with personality disorders struggle to accurately see and understand themselves and others. They find it difficult to adapt to their environments and to new demands, relying on unhealthy coping strategies when their inflexibility causes them trouble. People who meet criteria for these disorders don't know how to accurately identify and manage their intense feelings. They exhibit maladaptive patterns of behaviors, particularly in their relationships, which tend to be emotionally charged, unstable, conflict-ridden, and even abusive. As a result, they struggle to maintain healthy, consistent relationships with those close to them. With acquaintances or more peripheral relationships, they can sustain healthier interactions.

You'll read about three personality disorders in this book: narcissistic personality disorder, sociopathy (which is actually called antisocial personality disorder), and borderline personality disorder. You'll be interested to know that these particular disorders are all grouped under the same subcategory of *dramatic and erratic* personality disorders. There is also an *anxious and fearful* subcategory (including the dependent, avoidant, and obsessive-compulsive personality disorders) and a *suspicious and eccentric* subcategory (including the paranoid, schizoid, and schizotypal personality disorders).

Here's the tricky part: Just like all disorders, personality disorders exist on a spectrum, and all of us exhibit some mild symptoms or behaviors consistent with at least one of the ten disorders. For example, we have all acted selfishly without thinking about how it might hurt someone we love, been suspicious of our partner's whereabouts without good reason, or used unhelpful coping strategies to soothe extreme distress. But doing such things now and then in our relational histories, or doing them often in just one relationship, doesn't mean we have a personality disorder. These diagnoses are reserved for people who exhibit a persistent pattern of maladaptive behaviors in most or all of their close relationships.

The temptation (and danger) of using personality disorders to understand people in our lives is that it means *they* are the entire problem in our interpersonal conflicts, that they don't know how to be a healthy person in a relationship. Again, this is true *for some people*. True narcissists don't know how to have healthy relationships, and the relational problems they encounter are of their own making. People with borderline personality disorder don't know how to ease the abandonment fears that cause emotional volatility in their lives. Sociopaths don't have sufficient empathy or commitment to social contracts—to those implicitly agreed-upon "rules" of society—to engage healthily with others. But most people, even if it looks like they meet some of the criteria, simply don't qualify for the diagnosis.

Put Down the DSM and Slowly Back Away

The DSM was never intended to be a self-help book. It's time we take a step back from our zeal for integrating clinical terms into our daily lives. We have a newfound reliance on diagnosis as a mandatory precursor to understanding and change. We emphasize the importance of "naming" things as a necessary part of growth. But the truth is that we *don't* need to label someone to understand them or work on improving our relationship with them. We can see them more clearly by exploring reasons for their actions in light of who they are instead of seeking evidence for what issues we fear they have. In short, we can deprioritize the label and focus more on the individual. Which, as it happens, is most of what clinicians are trained to do. ∎

Chapter 3

The Difference Between Abuse and Bad Behavior

Relationships are amazing and fulfilling. They can also be complicated and distressing. They give us meaning and connection, yet they can also be the source of our most intense pain and loneliness. This is particularly true of romantic relationships, which may be why I have made them the focus of my career. They present conundrums that, when solved, bring people intense happiness and meaning. But they can be tough conundrums to solve because even the best relationships have really hard times, phases of severe disconnection, and long periods of resentment, to a point where partners sometimes feel divorce is inevitable. The fact that this is all normal makes it hard to find the line between typical relationship challenges and abnormal situations that qualify as abuse.

I can sympathize with people struggling to figure out whether or not their relationship is abusive. When I was younger, I certainly thought I was in abusive situations. Later, upon reflection, I recognized that they were complicated, and I got hurt, but these relationships and my partners weren't *abusive*. We were simply young and messy and trying to navigate how to be true to ourselves while also being good to each other. But it is absolutely imperative that we differentiate abusive relationships from generally healthy relationships where people act badly sometimes.

Abuse can destroy a person's self-trust, self-esteem, self-worth, and even sanity. An abusive person can cause unimaginable damage to another's sense of self and ability to trust others. I've seen it happen in

They're Not Gaslighting You

real time, and I've seen the aftermath of an abusive relationship as the survivor starts to repair themselves and their life. It's some of the most painful work I've done with my clients because abuse erodes almost every part of them. It takes away their identity and sense of reality, alienates them from people who love them, and activates their fight-or-flight response so that triggers for intense anxiety are everywhere. So, you can imagine why it's upsetting to see someone casually throw around the word *abuse* or any affiliated terms like *gaslighting* and *love bombing* when they're not accurate. Doing so diminishes their meaning and how awful they are when they do happen. For all these reasons, abusive relationships need to remain in a category of their own.

It's also vital to recognize that one bad action does not constitute abuse. It's a series of those bad actions repeated throughout the relationship, along with other abusive actions, that we can see over time (more on this later). But when we're hypervigilant about spotting abuse, we jump to that word at the first sign of bad behavior. And listen, this makes sense to me. The idea of being caught in an abusive relationship is terrifying. We all know how painful and destructive they can be, and no one wants to be damaged by an abusive partner. However, in our attempts to ensure we don't get stuck in one, we're sometimes seeing abuse when it's not actually there.

Interestingly, it's only been a rare handful of times when I've had a client accurately diagnose their partner as abusive, and it's usually only after the relationship ends. More often, I'm the one telling a client that their partner is engaging in a pattern of abusive behaviors. That's because people in these types of relationships have a hard time seeing it for what it is. This is a direct result of how abuse works; it's an insidious, crazy-making, self-doubt-inducing process that slowly chips away at a person's sense of reality and ability to trust themselves. Abusive people convince their partners that *they* are the problem. That's why those partners rarely come to me with awareness of how bad their relationship is, and even worse, they usually think it's their own fault.

38

The Difference Between Abuse and Bad Behavior

A closer look at what abuse is, and what it isn't, will set us up to understand how to accurately use terms related to abuse.

Defining Abusive Relationships*

In abusive relationships, abusive partners try to gain power and control.

Abusive partners are insecure and sensitive and need to have power and control to feel better about themselves and the relationship. Any perceived slight or offense leads to explosive reactions from them, and instead of trying to change their reactions (the healthy thing to do), they try to stop their partner from ever doing things that might upset them. All the abuse tactics I'll talk about are different ways to gain the upper hand in the relationship, which allows the abuser to control the narrative and dictate their partner's life.

Abuse is often a slow build, but sometimes it can happen seemingly out of nowhere. This is one of the hard things about understanding and defining abuse—it can present very differently from one relationship to another. For many partners in abusive situations, there are small moments of abuse that tend to worsen over time until one day, a person wakes up in a full-blown textbook abusive relationship and doesn't really know how they got there. It's the "frog in the pot of boiling water" scenario. However, other couples seemingly have a healthy relationship until a flip is switched, and suddenly, one partner engages in abusive behaviors. People in this situation can be so shocked and confused that they stay in the relationship despite knowing the change is unacceptable, sometimes hoping that the partner will return to being the person they were before.

---

* If you think you're in an abusive relationship, please seek support from the National Domestic Violence Hotline, a support group, or an individual therapist.

They're Not Gaslighting You

A key component of abusive relationships is isolation.
Abusive people slowly isolate their partners, removing sources of support who could challenge the abuser's impact. In doing so, survivors are cut off from family and friends who might serve as reality checks, countering the abuser's narrative and reinforcing that the survivor is not to blame for the abuser's actions. Abusive partners can accomplish this in many ways, such as claiming that their partner's friends or family are bad influences or don't want them to be happy. The isolation factor is important because, once isolated, a person becomes much easier to control and much less likely to speak up about what's happening and reach out for help. It also explains why abuse is scary to us; it's hidden away behind closed doors, shielded from evaluating eyes who might be able to identify it for what it is.

Healthy relational behaviors can make people vulnerable to abuse.
Most of us know that the healthy approach to relationship conflict is to be empathetic and consider our partner's perspective, apologize for our role when things go awry, and commit to change. However, these skills can make people easy prey in abusive relationships. Abusers slyly get their partners to adopt the abuser's distorted perspective, take on all the blame, and identify themselves as the ones who need to change. The traditional foundation of relationships—trust and an assumption of good intent—is dangerous in abusive ones. The very qualities that make someone a great partner can make them vulnerable to being controlled by an abuser.

Good relationships are easy to leave, while abusive relationships are very hard to get out of.
This seems counterintuitive, but it's true. In a good relationship, you feel safe discussing problems and ending things if it isn't working for you. When your self-esteem hasn't been destroyed, you feel a baseline assurance that you'll survive without the other person and find someone new.

The Difference Between Abuse and Bad Behavior

Good relationships can even be ended mutually or on amicable terms; this is never the case in abusive ones. People in abusive relationships are afraid to voice their unhappiness, let alone leave, fearing for their emotional or physical safety. Plus, the pillars of their lives have been slowly chipped away so that they don't have the social support, financial means, or self-esteem to leave. They think that no one else would ever love them. We imagine it would be easy to walk away once we recognize an abusive situation, but in reality, it's much easier to leave a healthy relationship.

The Cycle of Abuse

In the late 1970s, American psychologist Lenore E. Walker identified a fairly consistent cycle in relationships with physical violence. This cycle consists of four phases: building tension, incident, reconciliation, and calm. The cycle starts when tension builds and the abusive partner gets progressively snippier and more irritable. The victimized partner can't seem to do anything right and walks on eggshells, hoping to avoid an explosion. However, they can't avoid it because eventually they'll do something that will set off the abusive partner, and an abusive incident will occur. During this period, the perpetrator will engage in a range of abusive actions, all attempting to control their partner. Following the incident, the perpetrator may feel bad or fear that their partner will leave and thus start apologizing and trying to reconcile. They can be overly apologetic, kind, generous, and self-blaming in their efforts. They convince their partner that they regret it and won't do it again. Following this, there is harmony, and things feel somewhat positive and stable. This is the only good time in an abusive relationship, and it doesn't last, as tension inevitably starts to build again and the cycle repeats.

Emotional abuse can present slightly differently from physical abuse, with less distinct phases, but it's equally important to identify because it almost always precedes physical violence, and it can have a devastating psychological impact on survivors. In fact, many survivors report that

They're Not Gaslighting You

emotional abuse has a more deleterious effect on them than physical abuse. Emotional abuse includes subtle manipulation tactics, such as gaslighting and love bombing, that confuse a partner into questioning their own reality and ultimately believing the abuser's narrative.

As shown in the following graphic, there are many kinds of abuse, including physical, emotional, financial, and sexual. Some behaviors are universally abusive, but many require the larger context of the relationship to determine whether abuse is taking place. There's a lot to know about abuse, and if you're eager for a deeper dive, check out the resources section at the end of this book to learn more.

When we weaponize therapy speak by referring to someone's behavior as "abusive," it's typically in the context of (what we mistakenly believe is) emotional abuse. After all, the line of physical violence is easily seen once crossed, and we all know it's unacceptable to physically harm one's partner, regardless of circumstance or excuse. But if our partner is trying to convince us that we're overreacting and that our memory of an event is inaccurate? That's much harder to spot. And as our awareness of emotional abuse has grown, we've become more vigilant in trying to identify these moments. After all, we don't want to wake up six months or two years or ten years down the line and realize we've been emotionally torn down, manipulated, and controlled by our partner.

Abuse can be obvious or subtle, and there are some actions that fall under the umbrella of abuse that many people resort to during fights, but not as an abuse tactic. This is why labeling bad behavior with terms like *gaslighting*, or even calling them abusive, can be difficult to do correctly.

Before we move on, I want to tell you something important. You don't need to definitively know your relationship is abusive, or define how abusive it is, in order to end it. If you're in a relationship that is harming you and you don't want to be in it, that's a good enough reason to leave. I will make a case for why even good relationships are challenging and require hard work, but it's always your choice whether you stay in a relationship and do that work. Maybe your partner is

The Difference Between Abuse and Bad Behavior

PHYSICAL ABUSE
- Hitting someone with items
- Punching or slapping
- Restraining someone
- Blocking someone from leaving
- Choking or strangling
- Driving recklessly with someone in the car

EMOTIONAL ABUSE
- Mocking and sarcastically imitating
- Getting irrationally jealous and suspicious
- Humiliating, especially in public
- Engaging in name-calling and put-downs
- Intimidating or threatening someone
- Gaslighting

FINANCIAL ABUSE
- Restricting someone's spending
- Controlling credit cards
- Denying access to bank accounts
- Racking up shared debt
- Withholding financial support

SEXUAL ABUSE
- Forcing sexual contact without consent
- Engaging in unwanted touching
- Coercing or threatening someone into sexual acts
- Taking advantage of someone while they're intoxicated or unconscious

undeniably abusive, maybe they're not, but it doesn't matter. If you want to leave, you should leave.

How Can We Tell?

So how do we distinguish abusive partners from those who are behaving badly but can change? There are two "tests" that can help answer this question: Abusive partners won't take responsibility and abusive partners won't change.

1. Abusive Partners Won't Take Responsibility

Abusive partners usually think their partner is the sole bad actor in the relationship. The abusive person blames their partner for "making" them feel all their terrible feelings (e.g., jealousy, anger, insecurity) and for how they respond to those feelings (e.g., isolating their partner, throwing things in anger). They truly believe that if their partner would just do what they want and stop upsetting them, the relationship would be fine. And it's this mentality that slowly seeps into their partner's brain. The partner starts thinking, *I'm always the source of conflict, I keep doing things wrong. If I can just be better, these issues will go away.* They start to walk on eggshells and self-monitor and sacrifice, in hopes that this will make their abusive partner happy.

This is why survivors of abusive relationships rarely recognize what's happening to them in the moment. They lose touch with their own reality, get pulled into the abuser's twisted perspective, and become convinced that they're the ones to blame. Abusers are adept at making their partner feel at fault for the relationship's issues, a tactic known by the acronym DARVO: Deny, Attack, Reverse Victim and Offender. They deny any wrongdoing, attack their partner's credibility and character, and make themselves into the victim while painting their partner as the true offender. With this strategy, abusers are known to weaponize therapy

The Difference Between Abuse and Bad Behavior

speak too. They will claim that their partner violated a boundary when the partner stayed out later than expected with friends. They will accuse the partner of gaslighting them simply because the partner disagrees with them. When an abuser uses these terms incorrectly, it's for the purpose of controlling their victim's behavior and perception of reality. (This is a big reason why weaponizing therapy speak is so problematic.)

An abusive partner never accepts responsibility for their actions unless they're in the love-bombing stage of the relationship, and even then, it's not lasting or genuine. Abusers feel entirely justified in how they act, claiming that their partners "made them do it." But here's a fact that I want everyone to take away from this book: *Bad behavior doesn't justify bad behavior.* I don't care if the victimized partner *did* lie, call the abuser mean names, cheat on them—you name it. It doesn't mean the abuser has carte blanche to do whatever they want in retaliation. We don't get a free pass to seek revenge when we've been hurt or wronged, but that's how abusive partners think. They respond to their partner's supposedly unacceptable behavior (which is usually perfectly normal behavior) by acting worse, all the while saying that they wouldn't be so angry and wouldn't have to act in such cruel ways if their partner would shape up.

2. Abusive Partners Don't Change

Abusive partners feel justified in their emotions and actions because they blame their partner for everything. This, as you might imagine, makes them very hard to work with in therapy. I can spot these clients pretty quickly because they refuse to take any responsibility or self-reflect on how they are part of the problem. Now, most people feel justified in their feelings and behaviors, but they are also capable of accepting how those things may have impacted another person. Abusive partners have convinced themselves that they have nothing to apologize for and are not at fault in any way, and my gentle prodding to help them see differently doesn't work.

Some abusive partners will carefully admit fault for something minor or put on a show of being empathetic, but it's not genuine, and you can tell. You can feel the manipulation happening. But they're only saying the right things and appearing to participate in therapy so they can vehemently point that out if they're ever accused of not making an effort to change. ("What! I went to couples therapy, didn't I? Nothing is enough for you!") Sometimes, showing up to therapy and offering lip service is just another strategy to keep their partner under their control.

There have been a few times when I've seen abusive partners have brief moments of realization, where they seem to accept how destructive and problematic they're being. But those moments don't last. A minute later, or in an hour or a week, they return to their stance of being the victim and justifying their actions by blaming their partners. Insight doesn't stick because they don't have the ability, willingness, or emotional tolerance to recognize how unacceptable their actions are. Sometimes, these partners will declare they'll start individual therapy and change their ways, but they never do. Again, it's just lip service to keep their partner from leaving.

Good People Behave Badly Sometimes

Identifying abuse becomes even more complicated when we accept the truth that good people can behave very badly without being abusive. This is a reality that I teach people all the time, especially those who have latched onto a clinical label that isn't accurate. Good partners who have empathy and a conscience can, at times, behave very badly. They can even act in ways that fall under the umbrella of abuse, but that doesn't mean they are abusive in an irredeemable way. Partners who behave badly but aren't abusive aren't trying to gain power and control, can experience genuine remorse, want to work on changing, and then *do* change.

The Difference Between Abuse and Bad Behavior

Abusive partners can't (and don't want to) do these things. They lack insight and awareness, any remorse is shallow and short-lived, and despite the occasional proclamation that they want to change, they rarely or ever take steps to do so. They might acquiesce to therapy to appease their partner, but they won't meaningfully or productively participate. In contrast, people who behave badly without being abusive are great candidates for therapy. They may not fully realize how problematic their actions are, but once told, they feel regret, and they work to improve.

Once these types of partners feel heard and accepted in therapy, they can be de-escalated and self-reflect on how they are contributing to the relationship's problems. First, they need someone to say, "Hey, I understand why you feel so angry when your partner doesn't consider your feelings. I see how painful it is to feel unprioritized, and I understand why you would start shouting so they don't ignore you." They need to know their feelings aren't crazy and that their behaviors, while not helpful or healthy, aren't crazy either. Then these types of partners are able to do the work. They can recognize how shouting at their partner makes their partner feel scared or angry or shutdown, and how this makes communication impossible. An abusive partner will never get to this point. They will get stuck at the validation stage, and when I try to move them into self-reflecting and accepting responsibility, they will go back to pointing the finger: "Well, if my partner stopped making me feel angry, then I wouldn't have to shout at them!"

We generally see well-adjusted people behaving badly during fights when they're overwhelmed, panicked, and desperate. I've seen people do things like dismiss or lie to their partners, not out of a desire to gain power and control in the relationship, but in an attempt to defend themselves and end the conflict. It is essential to understand this difference when evaluating a person's behaviors because people who are acting out of desperation to connect, not control, are people who can have insight and can change. But, if weaponized therapy speak is used, it will end dialogue and make them more concerned with defending themselves from the unfair label than with reflecting on and improving their behavior. They certainly won't take the risk of being vulnerable and admitting fault if they think it will reinforce their partner's diagnostic suspicions.

For example, in my mid-twenties, I briefly dated someone who was very jealous. I was of the age of using code names when referring to a crush, so in honor of that sacred tradition of my youth, we'll call him Pepper. When we were just flirting, Pepper was fine, but the second we said we were "together," he became insanely jealous. He'd get angry if he saw me talking to another guy and then send an anxious and, at times, accusatory message. It really upset me. However, I felt very safe with him despite this bad behavior because he didn't act abusively in any other ways. I knew he was deeply insecure and wasn't actually trying to control me; he was simply panicked that I would leave him because he didn't feel secure about us. But, instead of voicing that in tough moments, he got angry whenever he felt our relationship was being threatened. We'd talk about it later, and he'd recognize his jealousy was a defense against his insecurity. He really wanted to behave better, but I didn't want to do that work with him. If I had liked him more, I could have stayed and gotten to the other side of it with him. Instead, I ended things with Pepper because I didn't feel a strong enough connection to want to do that work with him. He behaved badly but wasn't abusive.

Why do generally well-adjusted people engage in such bad behavior? The answer is pretty simple: Being in conflict or feeling insecure with the person you love, the person with whom you have your strongest and most important emotional attachment, is incredibly dys-regulating. Fighting can make the entire relationship feel unstable and thus can trigger painful feelings such as despair, desperation, or panic. When our most important relationships feel insecure, *we* feel insecure.

As you probably know, these types of feelings are hard to tolerate and manage. They are big and devastating, and we try to get rid of them in whatever ways possible. Sometimes, that includes acting unaccept-ably, such as screaming to get our point across, denying or minimizing

The Difference Between Abuse and Bad Behavior

someone's complaint so they'll see it isn't such a big deal, or stonewalling them and going completely silent in hopes that they'll drop the issue and we can go back to normal. Most of us don't do these things to gain the upper hand, to get power and control. We do it to stop the fight and reestablish harmony.

Obviously, these tactics don't work. Engaging in unhealthy behaviors usually worsens arguments instead of resolving them. Nevertheless, the primal part of our brains kicks in and acts out when we feel panicked, causing us to rely on unhelpful strategies that we learned from our caregivers or found effective at other points in our lives. And we use these strategies because we don't know other ones that will work. If we're feeling unheard, why not say it louder and with more emphasis on how serious the problem is? If we're scared that we hurt our partner and afraid they'll leave us, why not try to explain how they're overreacting so they'll calm down and stay with us? If their anger feels too big and scary to tolerate, why not exit the conversation and hope our partner lets it go? It's not illogical or crazy to use these strategies, it's just ineffective.

I used to do all sorts of ineffective things with Noah, my high school relationship that limped along for eight years. When he would hurt my feelings, I would sometimes full-on stonewall him, refusing to speak to him for a little while. This was at least half-consciously dramatic. From everything I saw on television, when your boyfriend upsets you, the thing to do is ice him out (I blame Marissa from *The O.C.*). But I was also overwhelmed with my feelings and didn't know how to effectively address the issue with him. Stonewalling him wasn't my attempt to gain power and control; it was part drama, part self-protection. I wasn't an abusive partner. I was a messy newcomer to relationships, as we usually are in our teens and twenties, trying my best to navigate my feelings while following bad examples from television and making plenty of other blunders along the way. Stonewalling was immature and an unhelpful way of coping, but it wasn't abuse. (I'll just add, in my defense, that he did break up with me on prom night, so save a little compassion for eighteen-year-old me who was trying her best to cope with some pretty legitimate drama.)

When someone you love does something that falls under the umbrella of abuse, like slamming doors or refusing to speak during a fight, sometimes it's because they're panicked and trying to connect. These are the people who usually feel regret and guilt for how they acted post-argument. They also tend to feel hopeless and desperately want disagreements to go better. Abusive partners, on the other hand, will either love bomb after a fight or they'll blame everything on you and take no responsibility for their actions. In short, you need to look at the full picture of the relationship before you decide that it's abusive.

All Relationships Are Hard

Given our general hypervigilance about being taken advantage of or getting stuck in abusive relationships, it makes sense that we'd quickly label bad behavior as abusive as a way of protecting ourselves. There's no way we'll be taken advantage of if we're constantly on the lookout, right? Unfortunately, this doesn't work how we'd like it to.

First of all, our hypervigilance leads us to identify normal actions as abusive. If we're terrified of being controlled, we'll see an assertive boss as a dictator trying to take away our autonomy. If we're worried we won't be listened to, we'll think that a friend who disagrees with us is gaslighting us. If we're panicked about losing ourselves in a relationship, we'll perceive our spouse's request to skip a social event to spend more alone time together as an attempt at isolation. Our fears and fixations can become self-fulfilling prophecies, where we find what we're looking for.

Second, real abuse is hard to spot because abusers are skilled at slowly taking over our perception of reality so that we feel at fault, disoriented, and alone. When we point out their jealousy, they turn it around and ask why we're so obsessed with protecting our relationship

The Difference Between Abuse and Bad Behavior

with a coworker. When we voice a desire to spend a weekend with our family, they remind us that our parents were rude to them during the last visit and act hurt that we'd put them through that again. Every time we get close to naming the problem, it gets spun into *our* problem. And even if we are able to accurately spot the abuse, pointing it out to an abusive partner generally doesn't go over so well. The abuser will just get angry and turn it around on us somehow so that we end up apologizing for hurting them and ruining their life.

If we're looking for a partner who will always do the right thing, even in the hardest moments, we're only setting ourselves up for disappointment. As I mentioned before, really good people can behave really badly, but this bad behavior usually isn't repeated, systematic, or part of an effort to gain power and control. Being on the lookout for missteps and immediately labeling them as abusive won't stop the other person from behaving badly. It just means we'll be arguing about the inaccurate use of a term instead of addressing the more important issue of how that behavior made us feel.

If we don't know the difference between abusive behavior and normal problematic behavior, we're at risk for either accepting abuse (thinking that it's just a hard time) or, alternatively, throwing away a perfectly good relationship because we can't accept any flaws or mistakes. In either scenario, we suffer. But what if we took all our newfound knowledge and, rather than shouting it from the rooftops every time we feel hurt or misunderstood, kept an eye out for worst-case scenarios while also maintaining compassion for the imperfect people we love? This would put us in the best position to both avoid bad situations, such as marrying a sociopath, and work on improving relationships that are worth saving. ■

Chapter 4

Are They Gaslighting You, or Do They Just Disagree?

In my sessions with therapy clients, I spend more time than I'd like providing the accurate definition of gaslighting. Disagreeing with someone, thinking your loved one is objectively wrong, arguing about what *really* happened and what was *actually* said, trying to find your way to the one and only "truth"—these are things that most people do. They are not helpful or effective, but they also are not gaslighting. So, let's set the record straight on this popular, commonly misused term.

Nikola Is Gaslighting

Nikola and Eric met at a mutual friend's party and moved in together after dating for about a year. Nikola is charismatic and passionate, which drew Eric to her right away, and Nikola felt the same gravitational pull toward him. But now, just over a year later, things between them have grown tense. Eric goes out with friends more than Nikola likes, leaving her feeling abandoned and unprioritized, especially when she doesn't get invited along. They fight about this a lot.

Tonight, Eric played in the finals of a club basketball tournament and didn't invite her to watch. It might have been fine if he hadn't gone out to a local bar with his team after the game. When Nikola found out he was hanging out with friends at a bar only a few minutes away from where they live, she was livid.

Eric had no idea she'd be upset about this. After all, it's pretty normal to go out with friends after a big game, isn't it? They live together, for crying out loud—he sees her every night, even if it's not for as long as she wants. When the post-game drinks are done, Eric walks into the living room expecting Nikola to be asleep, only to find her sitting on the couch fuming.

"Hey, you're still up! I thought you'd be asleep. Are you okay?" Eric asks tentatively. He knows Nikola is about to explode.

"How can you ask me that? You know I'm not okay. I saw where you were all night," she responds. They shared their locations a few weeks into dating at Nikola's insistence, and Eric sorely regrets it because it seems to fuel a lot of conflicts for them. Nikola says it makes her feel better knowing where he is, but she seems to be mainly concerned with catching him being places he "shouldn't."

"Yeah, I was out having dinner after the game. Sorry, I should have texted you that I was going out, I just figured you knew I was out for the night," Eric says.

"I'm honestly so confused right now. You didn't invite me to the game, and then you intentionally didn't invite me to hang out after, even though you *knew* I was only a few blocks away. What's going on with you? Is this basketball team some special little secret I can't be a part of? Why are you acting like this isn't a big deal? Don't downplay how messed up this is." Nikola's anger is only growing with the realization that Eric doesn't understand how bad this is.

"Listen, I'm sorry you feel left out, but I honestly didn't think you'd want to come," Eric says, getting frustrated. "You haven't come to the other games I invited you to, so it feels unfair that you're angry about this one all of a sudden."

Are They Gaslighting You, or Do They Just Disagree?

"Okay, that *really* sets me off," Nikola bites back. "You have literally never invited me to a game before. You tell me when they're happening, but I can tell you don't want me to come, so I never do. You've been weirdly sneaky about this basketball thing. It's really shady. I'm seriously shocked that you think you've been inviting me. That's messed up, Eric."

Now Eric is confused; he has *definitely* invited her before. He can think of at least four distinct times. He recalls even texting her about coming tonight, didn't he? But she seems really convinced that he never did.

"I swear I did invite you, Nik, a couple of times even. I think I texted you about it once. Let me find the message to show you—" Eric starts, but Nikola quickly interjects.

"Don't do that, Eric. Don't try to find evidence for why I'm wrong and you're right. It's always like that with you, needing to steamroll and one-up me. I can't believe you're acting like you aren't wrong about this. Would I be upset right now if you'd invited me to come watch your games and hang out after? That makes no sense, Eric! Why would I be upset right now if you'd included me? I'm upset because you leave me out, like you leave me out of everything in your life, and I'm sick of it. And it's honestly scary to me that you could intentionally exclude me from something like this and then be angry with me for being upset. This is straight up gaslighting. You're just trying to defend yourself, but stop lying and just accept that you messed up."

Nikola's voice rises with each sentence. She's outraged by his attempt to avoid responsibility for this. She remembers him mentioning that she should come watch him play but she pushes that thought aside—he clearly didn't invite her with enough enthusiasm for her to feel welcome. Plus, Eric needs to learn that he can't go out and do things without her all the time. This is the perfect time to get that point across so that he'll change.

55

They're Not Gaslighting You

Eric is second-guessing himself at this point. *Did* he invite her? He could have sworn he wanted her to watch him play and asked her to join, but maybe he didn't. After all, why would she be so upset right now if she'd been invited before?

"I don't understand you, Eric." Nikola breathes out a huff of frustration. "You tell me you love me, and we move in together, but then you gaslight me and do things like this that are so insanely mean, and then you act like they aren't awful! I don't know if this is just your bad memory or if you honestly think you've been inviting me, but you haven't. So please don't pretend that you've been a great boyfriend, okay?" She can tell she has the upper ground in this conversation, and she's going to solidify her position so that Eric doesn't do something like this ever again.

Eric feels confused and sheepish. Nikola must be right. He didn't used to think he had a bad memory, but she keeps pointing out times when he's forgotten or misremembered things, so now he really can't count on his memory of events.

"You're right, I'm really sorry. I don't mean to exclude you at all. I should have asked you to come," Eric says.

"And you should have asked me to come like you really wanted me to come. Not just because I'm some obligation in your life. Or you should have come home right after instead of ditching me for your friends. There were lots of things you could have done," Nikola replies.

She's unwilling to accept his apology, let alone offer an olive branch by recognizing that he didn't have malicious intent and that she may have been too harsh. Her anger dissipates, knowing that Eric has seen the error of his ways and knows he's wrong.

But Eric isn't wrong. He *did* invite Nikola to several games—four, to be exact. Each time, she scoffed at the idea of sitting in the "gross gym with bad lighting," so this most recent time, he didn't bother. He does have a text message to her saying, "Hey babe, I know you had a

long day but if you want to stop by the gym at 7:30 I'd love to see you."
He'd later show this to Nikola, still reeling from her version of reality,
but she counters this evidence by saying he knew she was tired from her
day and wouldn't come, so it wasn't a "real" invitation. Nikola continues
to gaslight Eric by turning this around, making it more evidence for
her case—that Eric didn't really want her to come and always picked
the worst days to invite her when he knew she'd say no. Eric is at a loss.
He thought he was trying to include her, but now he believes Nikola's
impassioned version of events.

Defining Gaslighting

Gaslighting is an abuse tactic where a person is made to question their
experience and sense of reality, eroding their self-trust and forcing them
to accept the other person's narrative. When an abuser engages in gaslighting, they convince the victim that their recollection is wrong, that
their experience of reality can't be trusted, and that they can't be trusted
to differentiate fact from fiction—despite the victim having evidence or
a clear memory of what occurred. To accomplish this tactic, the abuser
will often express confusion, concern, or incredulity that the other person
could possibly have such a wrong impression of reality. These emotions
make the abuser appear less malicious (they're "concerned," not angry,
after all) and encourage the other person to question their experience.

I've worked with people who have been gaslit. I've even seen it
happen in session, in front of my eyes. It's frighteningly hard to spot
even when it's clearly unfolding in the present moment, and that's
because abusers are incredibly skilled at promoting their perception as
the truth and weaving their partner's perceptions as lies. You'd think this
would be hard to do, but remember from chapter 3 that healthy relational skills, like empathy, trust, and perspective-taking, can make people
vulnerable to abuse. For example, people who have perspective-taking

They're Not Gaslighting You

skills are willing to reconsider the other person's point of view and make room for their version of events, which leaves the door open for an abusive person to commandeer the narrative. Humans are hardwired to connect, and abusers can take advantage of this to control and manipulate others.

A defining factor in gaslighting is that it involves outright deception. Oftentimes, the person who's engaging in gaslighting *knows* they are spinning a story that isn't accurate. They know their version isn't the truth; they just want other people to believe it is. These gaslighters are often fully aware they're manipulating people, and some enjoy the "craft" involved in it, as well as the sense of superiority and control it affords them.

Other times, gaslighters don't even realize what they're doing. They are simply so deeply entrenched in the belief that their perspective is always correct that they instinctively challenge others' realities. Their unshakable conviction inspires self-doubt in the other person. Once the perpetrator is seen as the "sane" one who remembers things right, they can spin any story as truth to get a desired outcome. They can excuse their own bad behavior, make others blame themselves for conflicts, and so forth. If they should be confronted with evidence of their own error, like Nikola was, they still feel justified in their deception if it gets them power and control in their relationship.

Finally, gaslighting isn't usually a one-time thing. People who use gaslighting to gain power and control use it regularly. They subtly but persistently dominate the narrative and convince others that their experience is plain wrong. It can become more nuanced and complex over time, where lies feed into new lies, making it incredibly hard for others to see the truth through the layers of deception. An abusive person will repeatedly use this strategy until others lose all self-trust and the abuser gains full control over the narrative. In short, gaslighting is truly scary stuff.

The Evolution of the Term

Perhaps the best description of gaslighting comes from the term's origin: a 1944 movie aptly titled *Gaslight*. In the movie, a husband named Gregory spends his nights searching for his wife's hidden jewelry, lighting gas lamps in their attic to help him search. In doing this, the other lights in the home flicker. His wife, Paula, notices the lights but Gregory convinces her she's imagining it. Paula can see the lights flickering before her very eyes, but her husband still persuades her that it's in her head. His manipulation continues and worsens throughout the film until, eventually, Gregory makes Paula think that she is deteriorating so much that she is unfit to leave the home. Paula can't trust herself, her perception of reality, or her memories of events. This is exactly what happens to people who are gaslit—they believe themselves to be unreliable narrators because of the abuser's manipulation and come to rely on the abuser's assertions of fact.

About twenty-five years later, the film's title showed up as a verb in an article written by two British doctors that was published in the academic journal *The Lancet*. The article provided case studies of gaslighting and showed how this tactic could lead to people being wrongfully committed to mental institutions. The psychological community tackled the phenomenon as well, exploring the forces at play with both the gaslighter and their victim.

Despite the concept being discussed in clinical literature, the term *gaslighting* didn't take off in popular usage for another thirty years. But starting in the mid-2010s, there came an outpouring of articles, books, blogs, social media posts, and reels all about gaslighting—people trying to define it, identify it, and help others avoid it. The term's usage has continued to expand as content creators, expert and non-expert alike, strive to pinpoint early signs or lower levels of gaslighting so that people can escape it before it destroys their self-trust. This is very understandable; no one wants to be the victim of gaslighting, and we'd all like to catch it before it catches us, so to speak. The problem is that these "lower level" instances of gaslighting can also be examples of normal behavior, and we won't know either way without a bigger picture of the relationship, which can require more time and data.

Meg *Isn't* Gaslighting

Cece and Meg have been together for almost four years. While they're overall very happy together, the past few months have been hard. They need to move into a larger apartment, and this decision has caused a lot of conflict that seems to seep into the rest of their lives. Even small choices, such as where to go to dinner, can lead to tension and frustration. The problem is that Cece wants to move farther out of the city and get a larger home where their dogs will have a yard and she and Meg can think about starting a family, but Meg loves being nestled in the city and walking the dogs around the bustling streets. Meg wants a family one day too, but she doesn't think it's in the next five years. They're still young, after all, so why move to the 'burbs so soon?

They keep sending each other listings for different homes, trying to find some middle ground of city versus suburban that meets both their needs. Cece has gotten a little passive-aggressive in the process, sending subtly mean messages alongside each listing. She sends a city apartment smaller than their current one to Meg with the message, "Look what our money can buy here lol." Meg can tell by the inclusion of the period after "lol" that Cece is angry.

Meg comes home on a Friday after having a tense text conversation with Cece earlier that day and is ready to confront the issue. Cece wanted to go to an open house for a beautiful Victorian home and sent Meg a message confirming the plan for tomorrow, but Meg said she didn't want to go. When Meg walks through the door, Cece is already home, sitting with their small dog on the sofa while the bigger one

Are They Gaslighting You, or Do They Just Disagree?

sleeps on the floor at her feet. Cece looks up from her book and says "Hi" with little enthusiasm.

"Hey, let's talk about today," Meg starts, hoping this conversation won't go south. "I know there's so much stress about moving and we want different things, and I feel like the way we're talking about it hasn't been working. I can tell you're upset about the open house. Can we talk?"

"Yeah, you're right, this really isn't working," Cece replies. "I know we want different things, but it feels like you won't even consider moving farther out of the city. I *am* considering options in the city. And then we planned to go to this open house, and suddenly you changed your mind, and that sucks." She's angry but also near tears.

"I didn't realize you were so serious about that open house. I didn't say I'd go to it, though. I said we should start finding houses to check out in person, but I don't think I said yes to *that* one," Meg answers.

"You did say yes to that one. I remember sending it to you and standing right here in this room talking about going to it. I said it's this Saturday at 10:00 a.m. and you said okay! That's why I'm upset, I feel like you pulled the rug out from under me," Cece says.

"What? I didn't say yes to seeing it, Cece. I said yes to finding houses we both liked and visiting them. Sometimes you just hear what you want to and then get mad at me when you realize it's not what I actually said," Meg answers.

"Stop gaslighting me! Don't tell me what happened. I remember *exactly* what you said! You told me yes to this open house and then changed your mind, and I'm upset about it. I'm allowed to be upset about it; don't invalidate my feelings!" Cece says, her frustration growing.

Meg feels surprised and nervous. She didn't think she was gaslighting Cece, which is exactly what she says. "I didn't mean to gaslight you. I just remember this differently. I don't remember saying I would go to this open house, so that's why I don't understand why you're this upset."

"Yes, you *are* gaslighting me because you're trying to convince me that what I clearly remember happening didn't happen. But you can't gaslight me because I'm positive I'm right," Cece answers coldly. She gets up and walks out of the room. Meg is standing alone in the room, feeling repentant and put down.

As you can see from Meg and Cece's exchange, they disagree about what happened in the conversation about the open house. They both remember it very differently, and they think the other person's recollection is just plain wrong. While Meg was asserting her perspective as right, she wasn't gaslighting Cece. There was no attempt to make Cece doubt her sanity or gain control over Cece by controlling the narrative. Meg wasn't trying to make Cece lose trust in her perception of reality or mental well-being. Most importantly, this exchange wasn't part of a larger pattern of abusive behaviors in their relationship. Meg is a loving and supportive partner. She doesn't try to gain power or control over Cece, she doesn't isolate Cece from family and friends, and she wants Cece to feel happy and fulfilled in her life. This one exchange, although ineffective and frustrating for them both, wasn't abusive. Cece's accusation of gaslighting quickly shut down the conversation, labeling Meg as a terrible partner and allowing Cece to exit the conversation as the victor.

The Weaponization of Gaslighting

As with any psychological buzzword, the meaning of gaslighting has become diluted as use of the term has expanded. For example, one influencer claimed that their parent gaslit them because they didn't agree to let the influencer use the family vacation home over the Fourth of July weekend. As a result, their twenty-five thousand followers now believe that a mere difference in recollection constitutes gaslighting. There are so many details that matter when assessing an action, but that nuance is usually lost in social media. Without nuance and

Are They Gaslighting You, or Do They Just Disagree?

context, a term like *gaslighting* gets expanded to include all sorts of everyday relational conflicts. Not only does this make true accusations of gaslighting seem less serious than they are, but it also inflates the seriousness of normal conflicts, to the point that even a soft challenge of someone's opinion can be viewed as abuse.

I find gaslighting to be one of the harder labels to deal with in my clinical work for three reasons:

1. **Accusations of gaslighting are incredibly common.** I hear accusations of gaslighting at least once a week, and yet it's only been accurate about five times in my entire clinical career. Boyfriend didn't agree with what time you were meeting for dinner? Gaslighting. Spouse said you didn't tell them to pick up milk on the way home, but you swear you did? Gaslighting. Friend says you overreact to small things and make it hard for them to be vulnerable with you, but you think your reaction was fine? Gaslighting. See how easy it is? The expansiveness of the term makes it easy to apply to many challenging interpersonal interactions, and so people use it often.

2. **People cling to their gaslighting claim.** The bigger reason I find this term scary is because it's really hard to walk people back from it. While people are more willing to hear a professional opinion about a DSM diagnosis like narcissistic personality disorder, they are less interested in evaluating whether gaslighting actually occurred. After all, who decides what gaslighting means? It's a term born from a film that was adopted by psychologists to describe an abuse tactic and, over time, it has evolved as many voices, expert and layperson alike, have contributed their ideas to what it means. In short, people can feel like they know as much about the word as their friendly

neighborhood psychologist. That makes it very hard for me to talk them out of it.

3. **Challenging the claim could be perceived as gaslighting.** As a clinician, perhaps the scariest line to walk is the one where I attempt to talk clients down from their assertion of gaslighting *while also* making sure my attempt isn't perceived as another case of gaslighting. If I tell a client I'm not sure their father-in-law was gaslighting them, my client could think that I, too, am trying to invalidate their perception of reality. Many therapists are nervous about this; the last thing any of us want is for a client to feel that we're siding with an abuser. And because clients are already sensitive to being unheard or invalidated, it can make them vigilant about it occurring in therapy.

I also find that when we misuse and weaponize gaslighting, it usually involves one of the two following scenarios.

1. We Think Disagreeing Is Gaslighting

People think disagreeing is the same as gaslighting, and this is just plain wrong. The truth is, people can have many different realities of the same event because people can have entirely different memories of that event. Even in the healthiest relationships, people disagree about what the "truth" is all the time, with perfectly valid reasons on both sides. This is because different information feels relevant to different people depending on their histories, sensitivities, and values, and thus their experiences and memories aren't always the same.

So, when couples argue about who's right, they typically aren't trying to convince their partner of a falsehood to gain power and control in the relationship or avoid the consequences of their inappropriate actions. There is no malicious intent, just the desire to figure out the ultimate

Are They Gaslighting You, or Do They Just Disagree?

truth. As I've said, this isn't an effective thing to do in a relationship (we'll discuss why in just a moment), but it's a natural human tendency.

There is no way to get people on the same page with the one right, "true" recollection. And that's fine. It really is. People don't need to remember things the same way or agree on the "truth" about everything, unless, of course, they make that a necessary part of their relationship. (I strongly recommend against doing that, or you'll be fighting until the end of time.)

If two people in a relationship *do* decide that different (but equally valid) memories of an event can't exist simultaneously, then someone has to be convinced that they're wrong. Oftentimes, the person who's called wrong will claim that they're being gaslit by the other. This *isn't* gaslighting, though. While it's often ineffective and unhelpful to try to convince someone that they're wrong, chances are it's not an attempt to make the other person doubt their sense of reality or dismantle their self-trust. It's just an attempt to make them concede that their experience wasn't accurate since both parties have tacitly decided that they need to pick one of their experiences as right.

If you think I haven't fallen into this trap in my marriage, you are sorely mistaken. Lucas and I, especially when we were younger, often fought about who was right. "I didn't say that!" "Yes, you did!" "You rolled your eyes!" "I swear I didn't roll my eye. You're so sensitive!" It's the most infuriating, unending, unhelpful trap to get stuck in. As we discovered, once you make the quest for Ultimate Truth a part of your relationship, it makes every conversation a chance to score a point, which means you argue even more about who is right and wrong. It was the most beautifully freeing day when Lucas and I accepted that we were both right and we were also both wrong, that we had different experiences and different perspectives, and that it really didn't matter who knew the truth. What mattered was that we learned to validate each other's experiences even if we disagreed with them. There are plenty of days when I still think Lucas is 100 percent wrong about his memory or experience of an event, but I can still validate and accept the way he feels about it.

2. We Think Lying Is Gaslighting

Along with conflating disagreeing with gaslighting, many of us incorrectly think that lying is the same as gaslighting. Although admittedly not great to do, lying is not always gaslighting. Sometimes people lie because they're ashamed, defensive, scared, or in denial. They're not lying to manipulate the narrative and control the other person. They're lying because they want to get out of relational trouble that would cause them distress.

You know who's lied when confronted with an unfortunate truth about their behavior? Me. The guilt of having erred enough to hurt someone I care about brings up fear that the other person will be angry with me and, at times, I have impulsively (and often unconsciously) lied. I'm not even worried about being abandoned (be it by a partner or friend). I'm just desperate to avoid a conflict because I am, as I like to say, a people pleaser in recovery. Whenever I catch myself lying, I immediately admit to the wrongdoing *and* the denial of it. But in that split second between my saying, "I didn't say that!" and my acknowledging, "Actually, you're right, I did say that," the other person could call me a gaslighter. However, in these moments, I'm not trying to make them think they're crazy or control reality to my liking. Rather, I am filled with immeasurable regret and acting desperately. We can all agree that lying isn't a good thing to do, but it also isn't automatically gaslighting.

People disagree all the time, and this is okay. Whether it's two different memories of a conversation, two different perspectives on an event that happened, or two different interpretations of how something was communicated, you don't need to find out who's "right." In fact, I encourage you not to do those things since they lead to discord without resolution. Instead, accept that people have different realities and memories and that sometimes a person you love will disagree with your reality and memory. They may even argue that they're right and you're wrong, which is annoying and unproductive, but not in itself abusive. Also, sometimes people lie. They do so because they're embarrassed, guilty, or panicked, not because they want to make you doubt your reality. Unless you're dealing with someone who's consistently pushing their narrative and trying to make you feel crazy for yours, they're not gaslighting you.

So, You've Been Accused of Gaslighting

It's possible that you will be accused of gaslighting when you disagree with someone during an argument. If you simply deny the accusation and throw it back in the person's face, you could reinforce their fears and make them more convinced you are engaging in abusive behaviors, which is the opposite of what you want to happen. Instead of defending yourself, here's what you should do.

Validate Their Experience

The best thing you can do to counter the accusation of gaslighting is to actively *not* gaslight the other person. To do this, validate their experience. (See the box that follows for more detail.) Tell them they're not crazy. Tell them you get their point, even if you see it differently. Tell them that their perspective makes sense to you and, more importantly, that it matters to you.

You could say, "I want you to know that I really understand your perspective on this. I see things differently, but your experience is valid, and it makes sense. I'm not trying to convince you that you're wrong and I'm right, and I'm sorry if I came across that way."

WHAT IS VALIDATION?

Validation is another word that suffers from frequent misuse. People demand validation, but what they're really asking for is agreement. And if someone doesn't agree, they call it toxic.

Here's the thing, though: Validation is *not* the same as agreement.

People get stuck thinking that if they validate someone's perspective, it's synonymous with agreeing with that perspective and saying the person is "right." However, the fact is you can validate someone's feelings and experience to the end of time without agreeing with them.

Maybe you think it's completely unjustified and unfair that they're upset. Fine. You can disagree in your head but still validate how they *feel*: "Hey, you're not crazy. I see why you'd feel that way. It makes sense to me. I'd probably feel that way too if I were in your shoes, experiencing our interaction the way you did. I care about your feelings."

Nowhere in there did I say, "You're right about this. I'm wrong. Your perspective is accurate. Mine doesn't matter. I'm sorry for being awful."

Consider putting a bookmark here and rereading this box often because validation is a critical relationship skill that you'll need to understand and use.

Recognize How It Felt to Them

Tell the person that you understand why your argument made them feel invalidated. Again, you don't need to agree that the *way* you were arguing was actually gaslighting or invalidating; you just need to validate how it felt to them. You could say you know it hurts to feel like someone you love is telling you your memory or experience is wrong, and you're sorry they felt like you were doing that.

For example, try saying, "I bet it felt really awful to have me challenge your experience and make you feel like it wasn't right or valid."

Try Again

When the person feels heard and validated, you can try explaining your perspective again. You can remind them that you're not trying to deny their experience, but you'd like to explain how you see things and help them understand your perspective without making them feel like they can't have their own different but equally valid perspective. (Warning: Don't embark on this step until you think they're de-escalated and feeling connected to you, or it will backfire.)

Explain Gaslighting

I don't mean to make you an educator in all your relationships, but it's helpful to clarify the term *gaslighting* so they understand what made you upset and so it doesn't get misused (or used against you) in the future. Explain that gaslighting is an abuse tactic intended to make a survivor doubt their reality and rely on the abuser's narrative, allowing the abuser to gain power and control. Clarify that it's more complicated and nefarious than simply disagreeing and fighting about what's right. Ask them not to use this term unless they really mean it.

If This Doesn't Work, Pause the Conversation

If you do these steps and the other person won't let go of the accusation, it may be time to pause the conversation. This, too, has to be done with care because you don't want to give them ammunition to claim you're stonewalling them (another abuse tactic).

For example, you could say, "I really want to figure this out with you, but I can tell we're stuck, and I'm worried we can't navigate this right now. I don't want you to feel like I'm denying your experience, and I'm not sure how I can make sure you know I see and accept your reality as

They're Not Gaslighting You

valid even though I see things differently. Can we take a few hours to cool down and try this again?"

When Nothing Works

Sometimes, nothing will help the person feel heard and safe in a conversation. This could be for many reasons. For example, maybe they have a significant trauma history, which makes it hard for them to trust people.

There are also times when you can't get through to them because they have some learning and growing to do before they can healthily engage in relationship challenges. (Even parents can fall into this category.) People who can't work through difficult moments, who hang onto the self-righteous upper hand, and who are unwilling to accept an apology or olive branch will be difficult to work with to get to the other side of an argument.

Still, other people refuse to yield their stance unless you completely capitulate, and *this* enters abusive territory. If they demand that *you* give up your perspective and admit to being completely wrong in order to end a fight, this is a problem, particularly if it happens repeatedly.

You've got a few choices here. You can let it go, or you can let *them* go. You might be dealing with someone who's not going to engage in mature conversations or reconsider their use of gaslighting, and you can decide to accept that and maintain a relationship with them, or you can decide to distance yourself or leave the relationship. I'd recommend trying the previous steps a few times before walking away—after all, it can take a while for people to change. But in the end, it's your choice to make.

So, You Think Someone Is Gaslighting You

By now, you should have a pretty good understanding of what gaslighting is and isn't. You've likely realized that many times when you thought you were being gaslit, you were actually having a normal disagreement.

Are They Gaslighting You, or Do They Just Disagree?

However, maybe you've realized that someone you love has been gaslighting you, and you need to figure out what to do. Here are some general guidelines to follow.

Talk to a Therapist

Speak with a professional about your relationship. You need someone with expertise in these matters to help you figure out if there's the possibility that things will improve or if the person is, in fact, abusive. If it's your partner you suspect of gaslighting, see if they'll go to couples therapy; maybe a qualified professional can help them see their behavior more clearly. If they resist this and refuse to acknowledge wrongdoing, you may want to consider leaving. Being in a long-term partnership with someone who gaslights will be unhealthy and ultimately crazy-making.

Note: If you're ever worried for your safety, you should not risk following any of the additional guidelines outlined here. You may be dealing with a person who will continue using gaslighting (and perhaps other abuse tactics) to get their own way during fights. If that's the case, you need to really think about whether you can stay in this relationship.

If You're Dealing with a Well-Adjusted Person, Validate Their Feelings

If you know your loved one is a generally well-adjusted person who's mishandling this conversation, you can work with this. Validate their experience and tell them you understand where they're coming from. This will help them calm down and be more receptive to hearing what you'll say next, which will be harder for them. Now, tell them that you're willing to accept their version of reality and validate their different experience, *and that you need them to do the same for you.* Encourage them to consider letting go of needing to be absolutely "right" and make room for both of you to have valid points of view.

This might be more effective after a short break. In the heat of a fight, it's hard to be self-aware and take responsibility. Maybe they can hear your concerns about gaslighting a few hours or days after the argument. Perhaps when they're less upset, they'll be able to reflect on how they handled the disagreement. If they refuse to do this, then you've got your answer.

Draw a Boundary

If you're dealing with an abusive person or someone who lacks the ability for insight, you probably won't have success getting them to change their stance. If they continue gaslighting you, it's time to exit the conversation. They won't want to stop until they've convinced you to admit you're wrong, but you're allowed to draw a boundary by disengaging from the topic. Tell them you're not discussing this until they can accept your different perspective. Don't continue engaging in the back-and-forth about who's right or wrong. It won't be productive.

Consider Leaving

If you're being continuously gaslit, this probably isn't a relationship you want to stay in. This is especially true if they're employing other abuse tactics or the overall climate of the relationship is unhealthy. It's not possible to build a good relationship with someone who refuses to acknowledge your perspective or reality. Having to always say, "Fine, you're right, I'm wrong," every time you disagree won't make for a healthy relationship characterized by open communication. And if you find this person *is* abusive in other ways, then it's really time to go. Find a therapist, recruit support from others in your life, and take care of yourself. ∎

Chapter 5

Do They Have Obsessive-Compulsive Disorder, or Are They Just Particular?

From requiring your friends to take their shoes off before entering your home to micromanaging a family holiday, people are increasingly claiming that their preferences are a sign of their obsessive-compulsive disorder, or OCD, especially in the context of their relationships. One of the only weaponized terms deployed in both directions, OCD empowers us to demand that people acquiesce to our desires or, conversely, to disregard others' requests by writing them off as "compulsive" and unnecessary. It's easy to frame desires and predilections as OCD symptoms but, as you'll see, this overlooks some critical components of the disorder.

Maya Has Obsessive-Compulsive Disorder

Maya hates going out because there are germs everywhere. She can't see them, but she can feel them lurking on every surface and floating through the air. But she has to go out sometimes, like right now. She and her daughter, Liz, need to grab a few quick things at the store for dinner—Maya promised to make enchiladas, Liz's favorite—and then she can return to where it feels safe. As soon as Maya steps inside the store, she knows it's going to be bad. The store isn't dirty per se, but something feels *off*. Liz can sense her mom tensing up and touches her arm.

"It's okay, Mom. We'll grab the tortillas and onions, and then we can go home," Liz says gently.

Maya nods anxiously and takes a deep breath. She tries coaching herself through it, like she always does. *It's fine, just like Liz said. People do this all the time. Germs are everywhere, but they're not dangerous. You can wash your hands at home and sanitize everything you buy like you always do, and it will be fine like it always is. You can do this.*

Entering the store, Maya quickly grabs a sanitizing wipe before Liz picks up a dirty basket.

"Don't pick it up until I wipe it down!" Maya snaps at her daughter. Liz recoils and her cheeks burn red. She knows her mom is stressed and didn't mean it, but it always stings to be reprimanded.

Liz waits for the mandatory wipe-down, then takes the basket from her mom, hoping that if she is the one to hold it, then her mom won't get so upset. However, Maya's anxiety skyrockets at seeing Liz hold the basket. Despite having just cleaned it, she hates thinking about the germs she could have missed.

As they walk down the first aisle, Liz sees her favorite snack and grabs it. Maya didn't get a chance to wipe it down first. Now, she can all but see the germs crawling up her daughter's arms.

"Bathroom, right now," Maya says tensely. Liz's heart starts beating quicker, and she nods. She knows what's about to happen. "And leave the basket over there, near that aisle. I don't want you close to it."

Maya feels relieved at seeing soap and paper towels fully stocked by the restroom's sink. Liz, knowing what her mom needs, steps up to the sink and diligently washes her hands while humming "Happy Birthday" twice. Then Maya takes her turn. She washes as meticulously as a

Do They Have Obsessive-Compulsive Disorder, or Are They Just Particular?

surgeon going into the operating room, using plenty of soap, counting to at least forty seconds, scrubbing the top and bottom of each finger, getting under the nail, then rinsing everything off. She wipes her hands and pauses. It doesn't feel quite right. She can feel the germs at the bottom of her hands. She must have missed that spot.

So, Maya does it all over again, this time for over a minute, paying extra attention to the base of her palms. But again, even once her hands are dry, Maya can't stop thinking about microscopic murderous germs. Now she feels them on her wrists.

"You washed really well. There are no germs now. Let's just grab our stuff and go home and see Dad," Liz says gently, not wanting to upset her mom further but wanting to get out of the bathroom.

"Don't interrupt me!" Maya barks at her. "Jesus, now I have to start again."

Maya turns back to the sink and washes farther up her arm so that her wrists are clean. This time, she doesn't even dry herself off before succumbing to the anxious thoughts about germs crawling up her arm. She goes right back into pre-op mode, washing her arms now, almost up to her elbows. Even as she does it, Maya knows she's in trouble. She knows her compulsions are time-consuming and frustrating, but she can't help it. At home, she can spend hours doing this until it feels right, but at the store she can't do that, especially not when she has Liz with her. Maya feels like crying because even though she's washed so high up on her arms that her shirt sleeves are now wet, it still doesn't feel right. She doesn't feel clean. Her brain is relentlessly thinking about germs on her body, and nothing will get rid of that thought except for washing, over and over, until it stops.

Liz stands quietly in the corner, near tears. She tried to help by holding the basket and nudging her mom to leave, but everything she did made her mom angry. She feels like the worst daughter in the world. Why did she ask for enchiladas tonight? It ruined everything.

75

Defining Obsessive-Compulsive Disorder

In previous editions of the DSM, OCD was listed as an anxiety disorder, but it now is in its own separate category of "obsessive-compulsive and related disorders." The change was a result of new research that showed OCD and some similar disorders, like hoarding and skin-picking disorder, share certain features that warranted a distinct category. Again, this shows the evolving nature of this diagnostic manual and why we should not rely on it as gospel.

In this chapter, we'll just be talking about OCD, which is characterized by uncontrollable and intrusive thoughts (obsessions) as well as behaviors intended to resolve or satisfy these thoughts (compulsions). We'll talk about the common presentations of OCD in a moment, but first, let's look at the core symptoms that are needed for a diagnosis of OCD:

1. **Obsessions:** Recurrent, intrusive thoughts, urges, worries, or images that keep coming to mind. The person with obsessions attempts to control or neutralize them by engaging in a variety of compulsive behaviors (see next).

2. **Compulsions:** Repetitive behaviors that someone feels driven to perform in response to the obsessions. This can include overt actions (like washing hands or checking locks) as well as mental actions (like counting or repeating specific words silently). The compulsions are not always realistically connected to the feared outcome the person is trying to prevent (e.g., counting as a way to prevent someone from breaking into the house).

3. **Time-consuming or cause significant distress:** The obsessions or compulsions take up an inordinate amount of time or prevent the person from functioning in their day-to-day life. For example, they can't work or spend time with friends because they're so caught up in obsessions or compulsions.

Do They Have Obsessive-Compulsive Disorder, or Are They Just Particular?

In the media, there are a few common presentations of OCD that probably come to your mind: people who can't stop washing their hands, engage in repetitive behaviors like locking doors or flipping light switches, or line things up so they are perfectly symmetrical. This isn't too far off the mark. OCD does indeed present in a few predictable types, including contamination fears, the need for symmetry and order, checking, and the need for things to be "just right." Less well-known compulsions include counting, repeating mental activities (like silently reciting words or phrases), touching certain things in a certain order or number of times, and having forbidden thoughts. The last category might surprise you (unless you know someone with OCD). Many people with this disorder struggle with very scary intrusive thoughts of a violent, sexual, or blasphemous nature, such as the thought that they might impulsively hurt or abuse themselves or others. Understandably, the idea of *not* engaging in compulsive behavior to alleviate or neutralize these obsessions can feel life-threatening.

People with OCD can have varying levels of insight into the issue. Some are fully aware that their obsessive-compulsive beliefs are excessive and not true, whereas others believe that their obsessions are reasonable and that the corresponding compulsions will prevent their dreaded fear from coming true.

OCD can be hard to determine since we all have some degree of needing order, cleanliness, or reassurance. Don't we all enjoy a tidy home with things put in their place? And who hasn't checked the stove or the curling iron five times to ensure it's turned off before you leave the house? Furthermore, we all get intrusive thoughts at times. For example, most commuters can relate to having a sudden thought like *What if I swerved the wheel right now and crashed the car?* or *What if I jumped off the train platform onto the track?* We don't want to do those things, but in situations where our brains subconsciously sense risk, we become

They're Not Gaslighting You

randomly and acutely aware of whether or not we have control over our bodies and could unintentionally cause harm to ourselves or others.

The key thing to remember, as I've said several times already, is that the obsessions and compulsions of true OCD are distressing, time-consuming, and impairing. They aren't a one-off thought of swerving your car off the road or a monthly compulsion to double- and triple-check that you paid the rent. They're persistent, anxiety-provoking, engrossing symptoms that feel out of a person's control even when they want to stop them. This is the line that we often use to separate "normal" human experience from the psychological disorder.

Imagine that I told you that you couldn't wash your hands before going to bed. It's possible you might be slightly annoyed by it since nobody likes being told what to do. (This is a psychological phenomenon called *reactance*; it refers to our desire to regain freedom when it's threatened or taken away, something the parents of teenagers will be very familiar dealing with.) But even if you were annoyed, you'd probably go along with it and fall asleep just fine. For a person with OCD who has obsessions about contamination, however, this would feel catastrophic. They would be so consumed by thoughts of germs and the urge to wash their hands that they wouldn't be able to sleep.

I have a weird example of something that I do in my head that could seem like a compulsion, but in fact, isn't. For as long as I can remember, I've had this cognitive habit of grouping letters together into fours. My mind takes a phrase and organizes it into clusters of four letters. There's something inexplicably pleasing to my brain about having phrases and sentences divisible by four. (And I'm someone who actually hates math, so I truly can't explain this.) For example, if someone said, "How was your weekend?" my brain very quickly, almost without my awareness, would do this: *howw- asyo- urwe- eken-d*. In this instance, my brain would be unhappy—it doesn't like when the groups aren't all an even four—so it would then quickly rephrase it to "how was the weekend,"

Do They Have Obsessive-Compulsive Disorder, or Are They Just Particular?

which can be rearranged as *howw-asth-ewee-kend*. Four letters in each group, and as an additional perk, there are four groups too. That's my brain's favorite scenario.

Why does this happen? I have no idea. When did this start? Again, no idea. How often do I do it? A lot, more than I'm even aware of, all throughout the day. I've wondered about it at times, and speculated that it's my brain's way of keeping me engaged in whatever I'm doing. But it doesn't worry me. It's simply an odd cognitive habit that doesn't cause me distress, take up my time, or impair my ability to function in any way. Moreover, this habit isn't a compulsion because I don't feel like I *have* to do it, and it isn't linked to any intrusive thought I'm trying to shake. It's just a very strange, useless, yet weirdly gratifying thing my brain does.

That said, it certainly sounds OCD-esque, doesn't it? To anyone unfamiliar with the DSM criteria, I could certainly make a convincing claim to having the disorder: "I'm so OCD, I have to organize and rephrase sentences until the letters are grouped into fours. I'm constantly doing it and can't stop." But if I said this to a mental health expert, they would assure me that this habit is not OCD—it isn't linked to any obsession, it's not time-consuming or distressing, and even though my brain can't really stop doing it, it's not getting in the way of living my life. In contrast, a person with OCD can't simply stop, even when they want to.

As you know from previous chapters, all these disorders are extremes of normal human behavior, which is why it's so easy to see ourselves in every single one of them. But someone with OCD isn't merely preoccupied with a thought. They are tortured by painful, intrusive, anxiety-inducing thoughts that they can only control by engaging in repetitive, time-consuming, frustrating behaviors. These are two very different experiences; conflating them can reduce empathy for people suffering from this disorder.

They're Not Gaslighting You

Juan *Doesn't* Have Obsessive-Compulsive Disorder

Juan is frustrated. Beyond frustrated, actually. He's asked his wife, Jess, to line up her shoes at the door for who knows how long—years, maybe?—and she still doesn't do it right. He's told her that putting her work flats on the top of the shoe rack makes the most sense (heck, he's even explained why it makes sense), and that she needs to put wet or dirty shoes on the bottom rack. But when he glances at the rack by the door, he sees that yes, once again, she's put her wet sneakers on a middle shelf, and they're dripping a little bit of water down onto the racks below.

It irks him to see the dirty water getting on her other (previously clean and dry) shoes, and he's honestly at a loss. First of all, how does Jess not see how this makes no sense? Doesn't she notice her wet shoes making the other ones dirty? Doesn't it bug her to see her boots crumpled down in order to fit on the middle shelf? And second, if she really doesn't care about it (which he still can't fathom), why doesn't she at least get how important this is to *him*? It almost feels intentional the way she continues to shirk the system they've discussed so many times. Is she trying to make him angry with this? He gets annoyed about this, and she knows it! He keeps telling her, but she doesn't seem to get it.

Juan can distinctly remember a conversation about four years ago, before this issue made him as mad as it does now. At that time, he told Jess, "I know I harp on this, but it's my OCD. I really need our shoe rack organized in a way that keeps our shoes clean and tidy." He's used that same phrase to explain why he wants Jess, before coming inside, to wipe off her shoes on the little shoe-cleaning device he bought online. It shouldn't be so hard to understand that he wants to leave the dirt outside, where it belongs. They have a white rug in their living room, for goodness' sake! If it gets dirty, he knows she won't be the one getting out the steam cleaner. She's never used it before; she doesn't even know

Do They Have Obsessive-Compulsive Disorder, or Are They Just Particular?

where they keep it. The last time this happened, he was running late for a meeting and had to leave the dirt in the entryway. He took care of it later that night when he got home, but he would have appreciated not having to clean it up in the first place.

Juan exhales an annoyed sigh and walks to the shoe rack. Maybe Jess can tolerate this disaster, but he certainly can't. With great irritation, he moves the shoes around so they're where they should be on the rack. He also grabs a towel and wipes down the lingering drops of water on the shelves below where her sneakers used to be.

At last, all is as it should be . . . but Juan is still irritated. He hates seeing a perfectly reasonable system ignored. The shoes could all be dry and clean if Jess just put things away right. Juan takes a deep breath and tries to let it go. They've had this conversation so many times, and he knows bringing it up will start a tiff, but he can feel that this is going to bug him for the rest of the night.

Juan likes the shoe situation to be tidy—that much is clear. He has a system that makes sense, and he's repeatedly told Jess that he wants her to comply with it. To Jess's credit, she does put her shoes on the rack the way he wants 99 percent of the time, but sometimes she's in a rush or she's tired or forgetful, and Juan never misses that 1 percent when she forgets. This drives her crazy because she really does try to put her shoes away the "right" way, even though it's something she personally doesn't care about, but Juan can never cut her some slack when she forgets. He claims this is all the result of his OCD. However, his internal dialogue about it, as well as the time he was able to leave the dirt where it was without experiencing significant distress, shows that his preference has nothing to do with alleviating intrusive thoughts. His desire to arrange the shoe rack a certain way isn't a compulsion; he just really likes the shoe rack clean and organized. By claiming he has OCD, he's making Jess's occasional noncompliance an issue of not supporting his mental health when, in reality, it's an issue of different personalities and preferences. The disorganized shoe rack may cause him stress, but it doesn't prevent him from functioning.

The Weaponization of Obsessive-Compulsive Disorder

Everyone has quirky or particular requests that others find unnecessary. These are *preferences*, and not compulsions. For example, there's always one person who cares about dishes being done more than the other person, who wants the dishwasher organized *just right*, and one person who walks around the house turning lights off and closing kitchen cabinets. And there are other specific preferences, like goodbye rituals (a kiss and nose boop every time for good luck!) or vacation preparations (with a detailed itinerary planned down to the minute). Our loved ones might have strong feelings about how things are done and feel stressed when they're not done that way, but that's not OCD.

My husband, Lucas, hates it when lids aren't properly put on jars. You know, when a lid is half on and still loose or haphazardly tightened and askew? I, on the other hand, could not care less. I am the only perpetrator of putting lids on wrong in our house. I barely screw on the top to the pickles, peanut butter, medications, water bottles, or food storage containers. I don't even realize that I do it because I care so little about it.

This drives Lucas absolutely crazy (and I know some of you are screaming inside your heads in solidarity with him right now). He has asked me a thousand times to be more careful, and I try—I really do. But I only care about doing it right because I care about Lucas. I'm just not programmed to put tops on correctly. My only consistent improvement is that I now make sure the tops of medication bottles are sealed after Lucas pointed out that if the ibuprofen fell, our eight-pound toy poodle, Clifford, could die if he ate them. This made me more careful

Do They Have Obsessive-Compulsive Disorder, or Are They Just Particular?

about it, and then once we had kids, I doubled down on my carefulness. (Before you align too much with Lucas, just know he's the person who leaves drawers open all over the house.)

Lucas could claim that his need for lids to be put on correctly is "his OCD" and make my failure in this area a disrespect to his mental health. In contrast, I could claim that his insistence on this matter is just him "being OCD" and refuse to comply because I think it's unreasonable and excessive. We'd both have effectively weaponized a mental health disorder to get our way, and we'd both be wrong about how we used it.

As I mentioned at the start of this chapter, every other term in this book is weaponized in a one-directional way. For example, no one inaccurately claims to be a sociopath as a way of justifying their behavior. From what I've observed, OCD is the only psychological diagnosis that's weaponized in both directions. People claim their preferences are because of their OCD when they want people in their life to comply, or people claim someone they know has OCD when *they* don't want to comply. Unlike the condition itself, people tend to use the term *OCD* in a very flexible and versatile way. That may be because we view OCD as more of a disease than other disorders; there's less stigma because we perceive it as something outside of control. And unlike personality disorders, like borderline or narcissism—where we tend to take more notice of how the afflicted person is affecting those around them—we tend to think that people with OCD are suffering more than they are making others suffer.

Regardless of how it's being weaponized, there are a few important reasons to not misuse this term.

1. It Minimizes Real OCD

Quipping that someone has OCD when they don't minimizes the experience of those who *do* have this disorder. It can also lead to misunderstandings, judgments, and resentment when people incorrectly believe that someone with OCD is simply "allowing" their particularities or fears to dictate what others can do. But OCD isn't about being particular or extra safe. It's an incredibly time-consuming, stress-inducing, distressing disorder that can make it impossible for people to work, maintain relationships, or even leave their homes.

2. It's Controlling

People who incorrectly claim to have OCD use it as a cover for being picky, bossy, or controlling, which allows them to dictate other people's behavior. When someone says they need things done a certain way "for their OCD," it's hard to imagine challenging them, even if their demand seems over the top. We live in a time of normalizing and supporting those who struggle with disorders, and it feels wrong to challenge someone's self-proclaimed diagnosis.

Ironically, the best course of treatment for OCD (along with medication) is exposure and response prevention, in which the person suffering must learn to tolerate their obsessions without giving into the compulsions that typically alleviate these intrusive thoughts. In doing so, the person learns new ways of coping with the obsessions and unlinks the obsessions and compulsions. Thus, giving into a person's obsessive demands is actually not helpful for their recovery.

Real OCD is rarely embraced as an excuse to control others. Quite the contrary, in fact: People with OCD often feel great distress or embarrassment when they feel compelled to ask others to make allowances for their compulsions. Many choose to withdraw from the world so they don't have to impose their uncontrollable impulses on those around them. They attempt to hide their symptoms instead of readily announcing them. And remember, those with OCD who request that others comply with or accommodate their compulsions aren't having a

Do They Have Obsessive-Compulsive Disorder, or Are They Just Particular?

good time with it. They're in great distress, and asking for accommodations is the only way they know to alleviate their suffering.

3. It's Dismissive

Telling someone that they have OCD when they make a request that you don't like is a great way to dismiss them through unnecessary pathologizing. This is not something I recommend doing in your relationships. If you tell someone that they're OCD because they're asking you to do something you feel is excessive or unnecessary, you're shutting them down by insinuating they're neurotic, overreacting, needy, or controlling. This won't be helpful to your relationship, to say the very least.

So, You've Been Accused of Having Obsessive-Compulsive Disorder

If you have a rigid preference or an ongoing anxiety that others don't seem to share, you may have been called OCD. Depending on how someone voiced this term with you, it may have hurt to hear. Before jumping into anger or defensiveness, here's what you should do.

Take a Deep Breath

Being told you have a disorder is a hard thing to hear, even if it's not true. Clearly, though, your requests or preferences have concerned or upset someone to the degree that they think you meet criteria for OCD—even if they're wrong, that's worth looking at. No matter the situation, you always want to respond thoughtfully instead of react impulsively. Giving yourself time to breathe, re-center, and return to a calm emotional baseline will help you be intentional in how you respond to their accusation.

Self-Reflect

If someone has weaponized OCD with you, perhaps they *do* have genuine concerns about your mental health. Take a moment (or several) to reflect on your emotions and behaviors. Do you think you're struggling with obsessions or compulsions as defined earlier in the chapter? Or have you just been controlling and bossy about how things are done? How much flexibility do you have in loosening up on your demands or preferences? Would doing so cause you significant distress? For example, would you experience physical symptoms of anxiety (like a racing heart or sweating) or upsetting intrusive thoughts (like "What if my spouse gets in a car accident because I didn't flip the light switch seven times")? And hey, while we're self-reflecting, does your family have a history of anxiety or OCD? If you do, that's a strong indicator you might have this disorder since OCD has a genetic component.

If You Think You Do Have OCD, Seek an Assessment or Therapy

If you decide that there's a chance you might have OCD, it's time to get a qualified professional's assessment and support. We can't self-diagnose, so even if you meet every single criterion and are pretty darn sure you have OCD, it's still important to have a professional make the official call. Starting therapy (and medication, if necessary) will also be helpful.

If You Think You Don't Have OCD, Talk to Them

Perhaps you decide that the person's OCD accusation doesn't hold water. Sure, you have strong preferences about certain things, but it's not because you have OCD. Instead, maybe you're a perfectionist and struggle with other people not holding themselves to your high standards, or maybe you have anxiety and an organized environment makes

Do They Have Obsessive-Compulsive Disorder, or Are They Just Particular?

you feel better. There are lots of alternative explanations for the same kinds of behavior.

If this is you, then it's time to talk with the person who suggested you have OCD. This conversation has two goals. First, you want to explain how their inaccurate armchair diagnosis made you feel. Hurt? Judged? Disregarded? Let them know the impact of that word. Second, you need to understand how your actions are impacting them because clearly something you're doing appeared problematic or aberrant enough for them to jump to an OCD hypothesis.

Admittedly, the second part is harder to do since it may make you feel judged all over again. It's easier if you first reassure yourself that you didn't do anything objectively wrong while also acknowledging that your behavior negatively impacted someone. This allows you to approach the conversation from a place of curiosity. What are you doing that's hard for this person? Did they suggest OCD because they're concerned about you or because they're feeling controlled, criticized, or frustrated? Are you being too rigid about your preferences? Are you snapping at them to do things "your way" all the time?

Keep Talking (Maybe with a Professional)

This won't be a one-time conversation. You'll need to have continuous talks about expectations and how you handle disagreements. If you want something done a certain way and the other person strongly disagrees, what will you do? How will you ensure you don't feel criticized by each other all the time? Which preferences are flexible and which are nonnegotiable? Depending on how these conversations go, you might want to elicit the support of a therapist, who can help you talk effectively about all this with your loved one while also helping you identify the recurring emotional and behavioral cycle that led to the accusation.

So, You Think Someone Has Obsessive-Compulsive Disorder

You may be in a relationship with someone who is a step beyond having strong preferences or quirks, and maybe you're wondering if they do, in fact, have OCD. While it can be difficult to treat, this disorder is much easier to address than, say, a personality disorder like narcissism. Plus, people with OCD are more likely to be willing to seek help and be treatment compliant because they are in distress as a result of having the disorder. So, if you think a loved one has OCD, here's what to do.

Educate Yourself

My brief explanation of OCD barely scratches the surface of all there is to know about this disorder. I strongly recommend reading more about OCD, including its many types and presentations, to gain a better understanding of this disorder. I've included some suggested titles in the resources section at the end of this book. As you educate yourself, be open to your suspicions being either confirmed or denied.

If You're Not Convinced It's OCD, Address the Issue

If it turns out the person probably doesn't have OCD, it's time to shift your focus. If you genuinely thought they had a clinical disorder, there's clearly a problem afoot here. Their preferences may have become inflexible demands that are leading you to feel controlled or bullied, so you need to talk to them. Explain how you might do things differently and why there needs to be room for everyone to have some autonomy. Tell them you're willing to do things their way for issues that are really important to them (as long as you're okay with that) but that you need to have independence and freedom of choice too.

If You Are Convinced It's OCD, Approach the Person Gently

If you have concerns that the other person's behavior is becoming distressing or causing them problems, it's good to share that. However, the way you share these concerns is critical. Be kind, gentle, and non-pathologizing when you tell them you've noticed they're having a hard time. Ask them about their experience, such as what thoughts they can't shake or how they feel when they're stuck in a repetitive compulsion. Try to understand them and show them you care.

Don't Blame Them

Being in a relationship with someone who has OCD can be really hard, particularly if it's a severe case. But it's important to remember that people with OCD live in great distress, and if they could magically stop having obsessions and compulsions, they certainly would. Don't blame them for being unable to stop doing whatever compulsive behaviors you've observed. Don't get annoyed that they keep thinking the same obsessive thoughts. At least right now, these things are out of their control.

Encourage Them to Seek Help

As I mentioned earlier, the recommended treatment for OCD is a type of therapy called exposure and response prevention, often in combination with medication. Encourage the person to start getting help if they haven't already. If they're resistant, gently explain the impact of their behavior on both of your lives. Don't make them, as a person, seem like the problem—instead, make OCD the problem that you're both working to address.

Be Supportive in the Process

It can be very scary to consider giving up the compulsions that have been useful in keeping obsessions at bay, and your loved one might be nervous or avoid starting therapy because of this. Offer to be a support in any way they need (if you are able and willing, of course). Help them find a clinician or write down their symptoms so they know what to tell their therapist or prescriber. Offer to drive them to their appointments. Do whatever small part you can in reducing barriers to them getting help.

Know That It's Okay to Distance Yourself or Even Leave

I hope that you know this already, but I'll say it anyway: If this person refuses to get help, it's okay for you to downgrade the closeness of this relationship or leave it altogether. Although it can feel mean to leave someone struggling with a disorder in a time of heightened unwellness, you need to take care of yourself first. If being in this relationship is detrimental to your mental health or well-being, then it might be time to go. ◼

Chapter 6

Is It a Red Flag, or Are They Just Imperfect?

Red flags are a euphemism for the kinds of behaviors that precede early signs of abuse—in other words, they are indicators that another person is not a great choice for a relationship. They are signs that we often miss or choose to ignore when we are assessing a new relationship or are infatuated with a new person, but that we see more clearly in hindsight after the relationship has taken its toll. Since the term encompasses a wide range of behaviors, it can be hard to define or refute. In this chapter, we'll look at the common uses of the term and learn how to be cautious when applying it.

Christy Has Red Flags

Sonya is sobbing as she tells her husband what happened at work: Her boss, Christy, admonished her during an all-staff meeting. A colleague's mouth actually dropped when Christy said, "Sonya seems unable to complete her one given task again, so can someone step in and save us?" Sonya couldn't believe it. Her boss had asked her to assemble a deck for a client meeting with only a day's notice, and she did it. It was a great deck, in fact. But one slide had one typo, which Christy caught while Sonya was going over it in the meeting, and Christy suddenly lashed out.

It's far from the first time that Christy has behaved in ways that are beyond unprofessional. When Sonya interviewed for the job, Christy

They're Not Gaslighting You

was late—not just a few minutes, but a full half hour. Sonya sat outside her office waiting and when Christy showed up, bag of leftover takeout in hand, she didn't apologize. With a glance at Sonya, she said, "Oh, you're still here for the interview? Give me a minute then." Sonya sat another eight minutes until Christy called out from her office, "Come in!" She didn't acknowledge her tardiness, much less apologize for it.

The interview, when it finally happened, was only fifteen minutes long. Christy didn't have many questions and seemed a bit annoyed that Sonya wanted to know about the position and work culture: "Wow, you seem really anxious about this place. You don't have to work here, you know. It's just your standard job with your standard people." Thinking she was coming across as needy or insecure, Sonya stopped asking questions. When Christy casually hired her on the spot, Sonya—who was nervous about returning to the work force after having been on maternity leave—eagerly accepted it.

Things didn't get better from there. Christy insisted Sonya start the next week—"or don't bother, we need someone ASAP"—but didn't send an employment contract for another month. Sonya worked without getting paid or having any proof she actually had the job. Whenever she asked about it, Christy would dismiss her concerns: "Calm down, Sonya. HR is getting your package together. They're busy with other things too."

Christy was always asking for things at the last minute and then getting angry at Sonya when she couldn't get them done. Christy would send late-night emails and expected Sonya to respond. In her second week, Sonya showed up to work on an optional Monday holiday only to find the front door locked because no one had told her they took it off. When she asked Christy for a list of holidays, Christy brushed her off, saying, "It's just the normal holidays like every company."

Sonya's husband, who is worried about how Sonya's mental health and self-esteem have plummeted since starting at this job, listens to her recount the most recent situation with Christy. Then he grabs her hands and says, "Sweetie, you need to quit. This job isn't worth your happiness. Christy has shown so many red flags, starting with the very first day when she was late to your interview without caring. You keep giving her the benefit of the doubt, but she's just not a good person, and you shouldn't work with her."

Sonya sniffles but straightens up. Her husband's right. Christy has behaved unprofessionally and uncaringly since the day they met. She never apologizes, she's sarcastic and harsh, she embarrasses people, she's demanding, and she's just not nice. For some reason, seeing these behaviors as red flags—all pointing in the same direction—help Sonya feel sane again. She's not a terrible employee; Christy is a terrible boss.

Defining Red Flag

A red flag is an action or behavioral pattern that indicates someone will exhibit toxic or unhealthy dynamics in a relationship. Red flags are warnings that someone may be emotionally unsafe in some way— unreliable, untrustworthy, even abusive—and you'd do best to steer clear. This definition is not a clinical term, and despite much searching, I couldn't pinpoint when we started using it to specifically talk about romantic relationships. Whatever its origin, it has since been used to describe the warning signs in all sorts of relationships. Since it covers a lot of ground, "red flag" can't be defined very specifically, but we can look at examples to help us understand it better.

Some common red flags that someone might exhibit include:

- Avoiding conversations about the relationship's status or saying, "We don't need labels"

- Steamrolling you in conversations or gaslighting you

- Telling you not to go out or be friends with certain people

They're Not Gaslighting You

- Texting or flirting with other people, especially if it's being kept secret

- Yelling, slamming doors, or stonewalling

These are just a few examples of behaviors that might forewarn of harmful relational habits:

- An inability or unwillingness to commit

- Resistance to considering your perspective

- Controlling or manipulative behavior

- The presence of multiple relationships without your knowledge or outright infidelity

- Emotional volatility or withdrawnness

Red flags are indicators that someone may actually meet the criteria for a personality disorder, such as narcissism or sociopathy, or that they're using abuse tactics like gaslighting or love bombing. When red flags involve abusive behaviors—behaviors that are manipulative, controlling, or in any way unsafe—we should pay close attention. The tricky thing here is that an abusive person will often not present as abusive early on in a relationship. They can be quite skilled at concealing their problematic behavior, and it is only with repeated bad experiences, outside insight from others, and lots of reflection that we see them as abusive. This is when it's helpful to get input from a therapist, trusted family member, partner, or friend who is willing to express their concerns about the relationship.

To accurately see and heed red flags, we need a full picture of someone's behavior. One warning sign is not enough data from which to draw a conclusion. Red flags are most concerning when they come in multiples—when several signs point to the same deduction. For example, if your partner snaps at a server when their order is wrong, that could be a red flag. But perhaps your partner just flew back from a

Is It a Red Flag, or Are They Just Imperfect?

hellish work trip and got two hours of sleep the night before, and they feel awful about their behavior when they get home. But, on the other hand, perhaps your partner also has bad road rage, has admonished four servers in your presence, and has started raising their voice at you during bad fights. In this case, the red flags are starting to add up and suggest your partner has an anger problem that might make them a poor relationship partner.

The Evolution of the Term

In the eighteenth century, red flags were used in war to signal that danger was afoot or to signify an intent to fight. They have since been used to indicate the presence of a flood or fire or to provide warning of other impending dangers. Naturally, it makes sense that we've adapted this term for signs that a relationship is heading into dangerous territory.

Relationship red flags have also led to the popularization of relationship green and beige flags. While I won't be discussing those in detail here since they aren't weaponized, it's worth explaining that green flags are signs someone is a good person to be in a relationship with—someone who is secure, loving, and well-adjusted. A person exhibits green flags if they are open to having hard conversations without becoming reactive (good emotion regulation skills), check in with you before doing something that could upset you (respecting your boundaries), or apologize when they've hurt you (taking responsibility).

Beige flags are harder to pin down. They're not glaring signs that would raise an alarm. They're not good or bad things. They're weirdly neutral quirks or peculiarities. For example, someone could have a beige flag if they peel a banana from the bottom instead of the top. Is it unusual? Yes. Is it a problem? No. Another beige flag could be a person who always wears sunglasses even on overcast days. Again, it's not bad or harmful; it's not an indicator of anything concerning about who they are as a person. It's just strange or silly. There has been talk of whether people should be "paying more attention" to beige flags, but I hope we don't keep walking down that path. Everyone has quirks and preferences, and they don't need to be overanalyzed.

Amit *Doesn't* Have Red Flags

At twenty-one years old, Amit is finally ready to date. The only son of an immigrant family, he was taught that academic success should come first and romance should come way after. He worked hard in high school, achieving good grades and getting awards, and was admitted into a prestigious college, all without ever going on a single date. But now, at school a few states away from his family, Amit wants to meet people and try a relationship.

When Amit meets Phoebe in Intro to Bio, he nervously asks her out. He doesn't quite know the "rules of engagement," but he asks her to dinner, which is what people on TV always do. She says yes. When he's heading out to meet her at her dorm room, Amit's roommate stops him. "You can't get there this early, Amit. She'll think you're clingy. A big part of dating is seeming like you're unavailable. Get there a little late," his roommate says. So, Amit waits awhile, then arrives at her dorm fifteen minutes after their agreed-upon time.

Phoebe seems a little stressed, which makes Amit nervous. Did she change her mind? But she says, "I sort of thought you weren't going to come." Amit answers with what his roommate said to tell her: "Oh yeah, I had a lot of other stuff going on." They walk to the dining hall, grab food, and generally have a good, albeit nervous, time together.

Amit walks her home and says he had a great time, and she agrees. "Can we do this again?" he asks, to which she says, "Definitely." He walks home on cloud nine, already excited to see her next week in class. However, when he sees her in class, Phoebe brushes past him and sits down far away from where they usually sit. He gives her space, thinking

Is It a Red Flag, or Are They Just Imperfect?

maybe she didn't see him or is having a bad day. Amit tries to catch up with her on the way out, but she quickly slips away.

The same thing happens during their next class together. Amit doesn't have her phone number, so he decides to stop by her dorm room to see if anything's wrong. He knocks on her door and waits outside, trying to take deep breaths to calm down. When Phoebe answers, she looks mad.

"What are you doing here, Amit?" she asks tersely.

"Hey, how are you? I tried catching up to you yesterday in class. I wanted to see if everything's okay," Amit answers.

"I'm fine," Phoebe says.

"Okay, good, I'm glad to hear that. I wasn't sure if you were upset, it seemed like you were avoiding me," Amit probes, unsure what's going on in this conversation.

"Yeah, I guess I was just treating you how you treated me. Obviously, you're not interested, and it's kind of weird that you're here right now," she responds.

Confused, Amit asks, "What do you mean, I'm not interested? I had so much fun with you last week."

"It's just red flag after red flag with you. You show up late to our date, you don't kiss me goodnight or get my number, you don't friend me on Instagram. You act like it's okay to do all of those things, and then you randomly show up at my door, which is super strange," Phoebe says.

Amit didn't realize those were the expectations. He didn't even get a social media account until the summer before arriving at college; his parents thought it would be a distraction. "I'm so sorry I did this all wrong, Phoebe. I don't have experience with any of this, and I didn't realize I was hurting you. I don't know how to do this stuff," Amit says anxiously.

"Yeah, I know you're newer at this, but you saying that is just another red flag, and this time, I won't ignore it. Like, if you know you're bad at dating, why wouldn't you put more effort in instead of ignoring me? It just doesn't add up. Thanks for the date and everything, but I don't think we're a good fit," Phoebe says with finality, closing her door.

Amit is stunned and very sad. He had no idea he was sending Phoebe the message that he didn't care or wasn't trying. Amit feels awful as he walks home, kicking himself for not following her on Instagram. He knew there would be a learning curve for dating, but he didn't realize it was so easy to demonstrate red flags.

Phoebe, meanwhile, is sad. She liked Amit a lot. He wasn't like other guys, who seem only interested in hooking up and avoiding emotional conversations. Amit really listened to her when they went out, and she felt like they had a special connection. But when she told her friends how she felt sad that he didn't kiss her or worried that he didn't follow her on Instagram, they immediately pointed out these were red flags. He probably *was* just interested in hooking up, they insisted, or maybe he's not interested in her at all. He wasn't putting in any effort, after all. Phoebe's friends insisted she pay attention to all the red flags and drop him. She did, but it doesn't feel like the right choice.

The Weaponization of Red Flags

The term *red flag* is intended to represent concerning behaviors that suggest a person will be unhealthy, toxic, or potentially abusive in the relationship. But because it covers such wide territory, it can be a convenient term to use when we experience something we don't like from another person. Is your partner always leaving a wet towel on the floor after showering? Red flag—they're irresponsible and will expect you to clean up after them. Is your friend bad at texting to let you know when they're behind schedule? Red flag—they're selfish, inconsiderate, and don't value your time. It's all too easy to weaponize this term in a relationship, in hopes that it will shame the other person into changing.

However, there are four main problems with relying on red flags.

Is It a Red Flag, or Are They Just Imperfect?

1. We Often Only See Red Flags Clearly in Hindsight

This is the most frustrating part of red flags: They offer early warning signs that we'd like to heed, but we often miss them. If there are a lot of red flags, perhaps we can piece together a picture of a problematic person before getting too involved with them, but usually we need to experience these bad behaviors and patterns over time before we can correctly identify them. That's why a single red flag isn't very helpful unless it's truly egregious, like physical violence. More helpful would be to look for undeniable red flags or multiple instances of red flags.

It's worth noting that truly abusive people are adept at convincing us that their bad behavior is perfectly normal, even a sign of their love. For example, they might insist they're "protecting" us from a bad friend by telling us not to text that person. If you have missed red flags such as these because they were well-concealed or because you were being a good person and giving someone the benefit of the doubt, don't beat yourself up and try not to be excessively vigilant with people moving forward. You simply can't accurately deduce a person's character from one situation or behavior. Instead of seeing one behavior you don't like and jumping to the conclusion that it's a red flag, look for *patterns* of behavior, which will help you get a more accurate picture of the person you're dealing with.

2. We Find Red Flags When We're Looking for Them

The second problem with looking for red flags is that hypervigilance leads to discovery. You'll remember from chapter 1 that this is called *confirmation bias*, when you've made a conclusion and then look for all the evidence that supports that conclusion while overlooking any evidence that might counter it. For example, if you're constantly looking for indicators that your partner is cheating, you can infer unfaithfulness from all sorts of otherwise normal or innocuous behaviors. A simple mix-up about when you're getting together could be a sign that they were with someone else and *that's* why they were late. A phone dying (yes, that does sometimes happen) could be construed as their attempt to turn off their location so you can't see that they're in a hotel room with someone else. Now, if there are quite a few of these instances, they could possibly be red flags and are worth having a conversation about, but only with the understanding that perhaps they're simply benign mistakes that don't suggest anything beyond forgetfulness.

3. When We Label Things as "Red Flags," We Avoid Vulnerability

When we use the blunt label of *red flag*, we are stamping an action as bad or harmful without explaining why it hurt us or what we're worried it suggests. Like all weaponized therapy terms, it's a way of saying we want someone's behavior to change without being vulnerable about its impact on us.

If there's a change you want in the relationship, it's far more effective to share why the behavior was upsetting to you and explore how to address the underlying fears or feelings that it brought up. Something like "When you leave me on 'read' for hours, I feel unimportant and a little embarrassed. Can you answer or even give my text a thumbs up so I don't feel that way?" or "I worry you don't feel as proud of me when you talk a lot about how great my brother is doing in life. I know this probably isn't true, but I just wanted to tell you." If you do this and the person still reacts badly—if they're defensive, dismissive, or cruel, or even truly gaslight you—you've got some real data on who they are and will be better informed for what to do next.

Is It a Red Flag, or Are They Just Imperfect?

4. We Forget All Humans Have Issues

The truth is that we *all* have red flags. Humans are inherently flawed and error-prone. We make mistakes, and we behave badly even when we know better. The point isn't to find a person with no issues but, rather, to find someone whose issues we're willing to work with. Red flags that are indicative of abuse should be flashing signs we pay attention to, but if we notice signs that someone is imperfect and makes mistakes, we should give them a little grace.

If Lucas had been scouting for red flags when we first met, he would have found a handful. I was in graduate school, still figuring out how to be vulnerable in romance, and finding my footing as a sort-of independent adult. For example, I didn't want to talk about our finances because it gave me anxiety. I had a negative bank balance, thanks to student loans, so the idea of talking about a retirement savings account was not first up on my financial to-do list. But Lucas, who had been working for a few years and was already established with things like a savings account and a 401k, wanted to talk about our financial picture and make plans for our future. He could have looked at my hesitance to engage in such discussion as a huge red flag. *Unwilling to discuss her financial situation? She probably has secret credit card debt or is perhaps hiding her assets so that I can't get to them, or maybe she doesn't really want a future together and doesn't think a financial talk is necessary.* Instead, my avoidance of this topic irked him, but he realized it was about my own money stress and that I didn't feel like I was in a place in life to plan a financial future—not some warning sign that I was an unwilling or unfit partner.

This example shows how hard it is to see red flags in the moment they occur. If I *was* hiding money or not invested in sharing a future, I probably would have behaved similarly, and Lucas might have generously given me the benefit of the doubt only to find out I'm a cruel and conniving person who was playing him the whole time. But remember, I didn't show other signs of being cruel or conniving—in other words, there weren't more red flags to build a case against me. Lucas accepted that I was a flawed human being doing my best, even if it was falling short of what he wanted during that time.

I kid you not, right now, as I'm sitting in a local restaurant writing this chapter, I can overhear a man nearby telling his date that his ex had red flags. His first example? She wasn't posting about him on Instagram. (I'm not *trying* to eavesdrop, but he is speaking very loudly.) From what I've heard him say, the ex sounds like a perfectly normal person who was pretty open about not wanting to be exclusive in their relationship. But he's now decided he's found other red flags that are indicative of her pathological commitment issues as opposed to, say, clear signs of her lack of commitment to *him*. From an outside perspective, not posting about him doesn't qualify as a red flag; it's just a good indicator that she isn't as invested in the relationship as he is. He's pathologizing her to avoid feeling rejected.

People aren't perfect. Individually, we're messy, and in relationships, we're much messier. We all make mistakes, sometimes repeatedly for our entire lives. Instead of labeling all unwanted behaviors as red flags and expecting change or running away altogether, try a new approach: Identify why those behaviors hurt you and share that with your loved one instead.

So, You've Been Accused of Having a Red Flag

I'm not sure what you did, but whatever it was, you've upset someone enough that they've labeled your behavior as a red flag. First, take a deep breath, acknowledge your feelings about it, and find a place of calm. You don't want to react in a way that will give them more opportunities to red-flag you. Instead of getting angry and weaponizing a term against them, try these steps instead.

Clarify the Issue

Before diving any further into the issue, make sure you understand what they're saying. What did you do that upset them, and what do they think this behavior is a red flag *for*? For example, if you were uncomfortable with them going out for after-work drinks with a coworker you think likes them, do they see this as an indication that you'll be a controlling partner? If your sibling is mad that you didn't ask how their presentation went, do they worry you're not interested in their life? Ask clarifying questions until you have a full understanding.

Validate Their Feelings

Take a moment to validate the person's feelings. Explain to them that you see how your actions were concerning or upsetting to them, and you can understand their desire to point this out to you so that it doesn't keep happening. Even though using the term *red flag* communicated a problem in a more accusatory and less vulnerable way, try to see it as their attempt to alert you that something you did hurt them.

If You See Their Point, Work on the Underlying Concern

If someone you love waves a red flag, whether it's justified or not, it's a sign that you did something that concerned them. Once you've clarified the issue and you know what the underlying concern is, you can start to address it in a way that works for both parties. Maybe your partner has had bad experiences with partners who have been jealous and controlling. Maybe you *have* been acting jealously and you need to self-reflect. Either way, commit to developing an awareness of the issue and work to change it; doing so will go a long way. This could include having more frequent conversations about the concern, reading a self-help book, or going to individual or couples therapy.

If Someone Is Using the Term Totally Inaccurately, Assert Your Autonomy

You might be dealing with someone who's weaponizing the term *red flag* to control you. Abusive people, after all, are skilled at using weaponized therapy speak to get their way. If this is the case, you don't want to humor them by saying you'll work on the issue. Instead, open a conversation about how to ensure you can both have autonomy and make your own decisions while respecting the other person's needs. This might be a conversation best had in couples therapy. Don't let the use of a buzzword shame you into giving up your independence or needs in the relationship.

If They Repeatedly Weaponize the Term, Consider Your Options

If you find yourself being repeatedly accused of red-flag behavior, the other person might need to do some self-work. If they truly think you're a walking red flag, they should consider leaving you, not continuously point out your allegedly abusive behavior. While we all act in ways that hurt or annoy our loved ones, being continuously told that your actions are red flags suggests this isn't the right relationship for either of you.

So, You Think Someone Has a Red Flag

In this book, you'll learn about narcissists, sociopaths, and a variety of abusive behaviors like gaslighting and love bombing. This may lead you to realize that someone in your life has shown a red flag or two. If you notice one in the moment, here's what to do.

Is It a Red Flag, or Are They Just Imperfect?

Clarify the Issue

This is the same first step as in the previous section, but this time, you're clarifying the issue with yourself. Real red flags, particularly those indicative of abuse, can be hard to accurately see, especially when an abusive person is making you think you're crazy or overreacting. It's also easy to let someone's misstep balloon in your mind, causing it to feel worse and more intentional than it was. In either case, taking time can help you see it with more balance. Think through what they did and why it hurt you. Consider if boundaries were crossed or if it's part of a pattern of behavior pointing to the same conclusion. Talk to a therapist or friend to help you see the situation clearly.

If it's an undeniable red flag—that is, if the person crossed one of the universal uncrossable boundaries (see chapter 11 for a list)—then you need to be on high alert with this person. They might not be someone you should stay in a relationship with. However, if the person's mistake wasn't at that level, continue on to the next step.

Tell Them Why You're Upset

Now that *you* know why you're upset, tell this to the other person. (Note: You don't need to use the actual term *red flag*, which rarely encourages open dialogue.) If they do something that really hurts you, explain why: "When you refused to pick me up from the airport, it made me feel insecure and worried that our friendship isn't as important to you as it is to me." Point out if there have been other things that made you feel this way, and share your desire to change this pattern.

If They're Receptive, Keep Communicating

If the person understands your feelings and wants to work on things with you, then great! It's a sign that they are a pretty emotionally healthy person who cares about making a relationship work. They may have acted a certain way because of their own fears or insecurities, and it may take time to work through these issues. In this process, they might exhibit more red flags; if and when they do, your job is to calmly communicate your feelings and concerns. If it's your romantic partner, try couples therapy to expedite the relationship growth process. Be communicative and compassionate, and remember that you have red flags too.

If They're Defensive, You Can Keep Trying

When confronted with the knowledge that we've hurt someone, many of us become defensive. We hate the idea of hurting the person we love and since we usually didn't intend to hurt them, we start explaining why our actions weren't that bad and why they shouldn't feel upset. It comes from a place of inadequacy, self-criticism, and remorse. If the other person responds like this but you can tell they care about your pain, this may be a good time to give them some grace in the form of empathy and time. Wait a few hours or even a few days, then try the conversation again. Try reading a book about attachment styles, the negative cycle, and effective communication (check out the resources section). Try couples therapy if it's your partner. If this person is willing to do this work with you, this flag probably isn't as red as you feared.

If They're Not Receptive or Outright Mean, Tread Carefully

If, on the other hand, you tell someone your concerns and they are dismissive, minimizing, mocking, or gaslighting, or they provide any other harsh or abusive response, then you might be dealing with someone who isn't in a great place to be in a relationship. If you ask them to work on changing some interaction patterns, but they refuse or blame you for being the root of all the relationship's issues, it's time to consider other options. It's very hard to work on a relationship when the other person refuses to engage, and it's impossible to work on things when the other person is abusive. Depending on how important they are in your life and

Is It a Red Flag, or Are They Just Imperfect?

how much interest you have in staying connected with them, you can decide to have new boundaries and more distance with this person, or you can end the relationship with them. ◼

Chapter 7

Are They a Narcissist, or Did They Just Hurt Your Feelings?

We all love to hate a narcissist. They're cruel, annoyingly fragile, impossible to work with, and seemingly ubiquitous. There are a fair number of narcissists out there, but not nearly as many as people may think. This disorder is one of our favorite ones to volley at people, *particularly* our exes, but before we conclude that anyone who hurts is a narcissist, let's learn what that actually means.

Cal Is a Narcissist

Aubrey couldn't believe her luck when she met Cal. First of all, he was stunning. With dark brown hair, a permanent smile, bright blue eyes, and an easy laugh, he was the definition of a catch. Cal glowed in the attention of women, which is why it felt even more amazing that Cal turned his bright eyes to Aubrey and picked her out of everyone. He flirted with abandon and by the end of the night, Cal had put his name in her phone as "Cal (Future Hubby)," which Aubrey was secretly elated by. She'd been looking for a serious relationship, and then this Adonis falls right into her lap!

Cal was so flattering—Aubrey had never felt more special and adored in her life. He complimented her constantly and said things like "Jesus, how did I manage to find and keep such an angel? You're so beautiful, babe." But then he'd make a joke right after, saying, "But obviously I'd have to leave you if you got into a car accident and it wrecked your face. Just kidding, just kidding! Just drive safe so we don't find out." At the time, this felt silly and loving to Aubrey. She didn't look too hard at the fact that Cal actually seemed to care a lot about her looks and that he probably wouldn't be with her if she wasn't conventionally attractive.

Cal liked to be "fancy." He insisted that their dates be at the nicest restaurants. One night, he "didn't have time" to change after work and made Aubrey wait around for an hour in a store while he looked for the perfect shirt. He nudged her to buy some new clothes too since hers "didn't fit great" and were "kind of low quality," according to him. Cal quickly said, "No offense, babe, but you could just be looking so much better. We gotta show off that body!"

As much as Cal cared about how Aubrey looked, he was even more preoccupied with his own appearance. He could spend well over an hour getting ready to go out. He got upset if Aubrey wasn't effusive enough in complimenting him. He still flirted with other women, even in front of Aubrey, and couldn't seem to stop himself from garnering others' admiration. Aubrey wasn't the jealous type and didn't mind if he innocently flirted, but even *that* made Cal angry that Aubrey wasn't more possessive of him. Aubrey felt at a loss; no matter how hard she tried to make him happy, Cal kept getting offended and angry.

At first, Aubrey's friends were obsessed with Cal. How could they not be? He was gorgeous, charming, and flirty. But that quickly changed. Aubrey had some pretty down-to-earth friends who didn't care about status or reputation, which was all Cal wanted to talk about—wealthy people he knew, plans he had for an ingenious start-up, and the ways in which he was much smarter than everyone else he knew. Cal looked down on people he didn't consider his equals, and Aubrey's friends quickly fell into that category. He told Aubrey he wouldn't go out with them anymore and that she needed to upgrade her friend group. Cal said they'd hold her back from achieving her potential. Whenever she hung out with her friends, Aubrey hid it from Cal because she knew it would piss him off. Eventually, she began seeing them less and less just to avoid the risk of getting caught and enduring another fight.

Aubrey noticed other patterns emerging too. Not only was Cal almost always getting offended by people, including her, but he thought that the world was unfair and that everyone was out to get him. He was self-righteously angry at least once a week. His attitude would vacillate between believing he was the victim of others' attempts to thwart his success to believing that he was so amazing that no one could compare to him. Aubrey also found out that Cal had a litigious streak, loving to threaten to sue people who had wronged him; he'd even entered in some legal battles with landlords, bosses, and neighbors in the past. He kept changing lawyers each time, though, claiming they didn't do a good enough job and he deserved better representation. Cal joked that *he* should be a lawyer since he always had better ideas and strategies than anyone he'd hired. Aubrey didn't point out that the lawyers never seemed sad to lose Cal's business.

After about six months of dating, Cal asked Aubrey to pay his rent. She didn't feel super comfortable with this, but he played the victim and guilt-tripped her, pointing out her salary was three times his and that while *she* had the luxury of a savings account, not everyone did. One night, when Cal was drunk, he said he was jealous Aubrey made more than he did, and he felt like *he* actually deserved to make more because he was better at his job. Jealousy was an emotion he was no stranger to. Aubrey's heart would drop whenever there was a handsome man nearby who would get more attention than Cal because she knew Cal's mood would darken.

Aubrey stayed with Cal longer than she should have because after every crazy-making fight, there would be an amazing period of time where things felt better again. He'd compliment her, make a bigger effort to support her, shower her with physical affection, and talk about getting married and having kids. The breaking point was when Cal insisted they move in together (way before Aubrey felt ready, which he knew) and said he expected Aubrey to foot the entire cost of the place, which would be a lot since he also insisted they needed to live in the nicest part of the city in at least a two-bedroom apartment. Nothing was enough for Cal, no matter how much Aubrey paid for or how much she complimented him. He always needed more validation, admiration, and money.

One day, when Aubrey spent time with one of the friends Cal had tried to ban from her life, her friend gently said that she had noticed a bad pattern in Cal's behavior. She suggested that Aubrey consider if Cal might be a narcissist, given how he acted with her and, it sounded like, in all his previous relationships. Aubrey, still reeling from the latest fight and tempted to forgive Cal, who had been sending sweet messages with promises of a better relationship, went home and read about narcissistic personality disorder. Suddenly, everything made sense, and Aubrey knew she couldn't go back to Cal.

Defining Narcissistic Personality Disorder

Narcissists are infamous in our society, and understandably so. They cause significant harm to those who have a close relationship with them, but they are also very hard to spot at first. We're all living in fear of falling into the clutches of a narcissist, who will lure us in only to turn our lives upside down. But what are the actual DSM criteria for this personality disorder?

When we call someone a narcissist in the clinical sense, we're really saying they have narcissistic personality disorder (NPD). This is one of the ten personality disorders in the DSM and is in the subgroup of *dramatic and erratic* personality disorders. Also in this category are antisocial and borderline, which we'll be looking at in subsequent chapters. As with all personality disorders, NPD becomes clear in early adulthood, when someone is persistently self-aggrandizing, demands admiration

Are They a Narcissist, or Did They Just Hurt Your Feelings?

from everyone around them, lacks empathy, and is easily wounded when people don't fawn all over them. To qualify as a clinical narcissist, a person must meet five or more of the following nine specific criteria:

1. **Grandiosity:** Have an inflated sense of self-importance. Think of someone who talks up every accomplishment (to the point of fibbing about them), needs people to shower them with accolades, and wants to be seen as superior because of their self-proclaimed (but possibly not real) talents and achievements.

2. **Fantasies of being amazing:** Are obsessed with being successful, being seen as attractive to those around them, gaining significant power and wealth, and generally being better than everyone.

3. **Belief that they are special:** See themselves as unique and better than other people. They think they should only spend time with other high-status, special people and not waste their energy on people who are "less than."

4. **Need for admiration:** Are consumed by their need for a steady stream of attention, validation, and admiration. They angle to get what they see is well-earned praise and reverence.

5. **Sense of entitlement:** Believe they inherently deserve certain privileges or benefits and that people should automatically comply with their requests or expectations. They become intensely wounded or angry when people don't do this.

6. **Exploitation of others:** Readily and unremorsefully exploit others as they strive to reach their goals.

7. **Lack of empathy:** Struggle to recognize and care about how other people feel, especially when they have wronged someone. (Note: They might have some small capacity for empathy, but their feelings for themselves usually overshadow it.)

8. **Intense envy:** Are constantly jealous of what other people own or have accomplished. They also think people should be jealous of them and how great they are.

9. **Arrogance:** Have an exaggerated sense of self-importance, look down on others, and believe they deserve special treatment.

It's important to reiterate that a diagnosis of NPD requires that someone's symptoms be pervasive, inflexible, and stable over time—*and* these symptoms must cause significant difficulties in their work life, social life, home life, and other important areas. In other words, you can't have NPD for just one year or in just one relationship; it's persistent across time, relationships, and settings.

However, this doesn't mean someone with NPD can't present as a well-adjusted person in certain contexts or early on in relationships. Indeed, their self-aggrandizement might initially seem like confidence and ambition, which many people find attractive. They can sell their fantasies of success as attainable plans, which makes them seem capable and prosperous. For a very short period of time, they can appear like the most self-assured, driven, appealing person you know. Ironically, they are the opposite of these traits, but it can take us a while to weed through the fiction to get the facts, especially given that narcissists choose to engage differently depending on the person and situation. For example, a narcissist will be kind and engaging with someone of high status whom they want to be associated with but will treat someone of perceived lower status with disdain and disrespect.

This is an important point to emphasize because this is how people get stuck in relationships with narcissists. People with NPD seek relationships with individuals whom they consider "equal" to them, someone who is attractive or wealthy, or who has some other trait that the narcissist thinks will then reflect upon them favorably. Narcissists foster that relationship until the other person inevitably disappoints them or falls

Are They a Narcissist, or Did They Just Hurt Your Feelings?

in their esteem, then proceed to treat that person incredibly poorly. This shocking change is a common pattern: Narcissists idealize new people, putting them on a pedestal, only to devalue them, knock them off the pedestal, and discard them. People are often left confused and stunned at the extreme shift in treatment.

Narcissists are fragile. They don't appear that way, but they are. They are incredibly sensitive to being slighted, overlooked, misled, or unprioritized. They often have a history of serious trauma, which forced them to project this image of self-esteem as a form of self-protection. This is why they need to amplify their self-worth by exuding an air of grandiosity, seeking admiration and praise from others, and convincing themselves everyone is jealous of them. An emotionally secure person, for example, could be passed over for a promotion without flying into a rage because they have a stable sense of self-esteem. A narcissist doesn't have that foundational core, so any slight, real or perceived, cuts them to the bone, and they retaliate with anger and indignation.

Narcissists also leave a trail of destruction behind them. Parents with NPD can cause irreparable damage to their children, whom they consider extensions of themselves. They demand that their kids reflect well on them by doing exactly as they say and achieving what they want so they can feel vicarious accomplishment. Narcissistic bosses are the ultimate professional nightmare. They are overly sensitive to feedback, take credit for others' work, demand significant productivity without showing much gratitude, and blow up at employees over the smallest infractions.

And then there are narcissistic romantic partners, who cause their loved ones to feel small, insignificant, and uncertain of their own reality. When narcissists abruptly shift from adoring their partner to devaluing them and ending the relationship, it leaves the other person reeling. Healing from a narcissistic relationship is a lengthy, painful process. The good news is that there are many resources to help people identify, leave, and recover from a relationship with a narcissist. If you think your partner truly is a narcissist, I encourage you to look into some of the

Mark *Isn't* a Narcissist

Nathan is fuming. He just hung up on another infuriating conversation with his father, Mark. Once again, Mark asked when Nathan would be coming home. It's the same thing every few months and Nathan's getting really sick of it. Nathan has an amazing job and he's eager to rise through the ranks at the company, but he can't do that if he's taking days off to travel all the time.

"I can't, Dad. I keep telling you this. It's not easy for me to fly home all the time, and I don't want to take any time off right now," Nathan said irritably.

"But you haven't been home in a year. Don't play the time-off card. You just went to Tahoe for a week with your friends. Clearly, you'll take time off for some people but not your parents," Mark answered.

"They were *work* friends! It's networking. We talked business every single day. And you don't get to control how I spend my free time. My life doesn't revolve around you!" Nathan shouted back.

"Is it that crazy to want to see our kid? Hell, we'll fly out to see *you* if that's the problem! You always said you prefer coming to us since you can see your high school friends. We don't care where it is, Nathan, we'd just like to see you! I didn't raise a son who treats his parents like this," Mark yelled back.

"You are such a narcissist! My life is *my* life! I don't have to come see you or have you come see me. Just because you're my parent doesn't give you the right to control my life!" Nathan hung up the phone.

Nathan never fought with his dad like this before graduating from college, but he can't understand why his dad keeps asking so much from him. Nathan feels pressured to compete with his "work friends" and keeps passing up on things he'd usually love, such as holidays at home and trips with high school friends, because he doesn't want to miss anything at work. Promotions require good connections. Doesn't his dad understand that Nathan can't miss these opportunities to network? Nathan doesn't know when his dad became so self-centered and controlling.

A few weeks ago, Nathan's friend pointed out that his parents are really pushy about stuff and are maybe trying to live vicariously through him, like narcissistic parents often do. Nathan was happy to find an explanation for why conversations with them feel so tough.

Meanwhile, on the other end of the call, Mark sadly puts his phone down. He misses his son. Nathan is a great kid who has always been independent, but since graduating from college (which was across the country) and starting a new job in finance on the opposite coast, he's almost never around. Mark understands that Nathan is starting his own life, and he won't be spending every long weekend with his parents, but he didn't think Nathan would be as absent as he is. Nathan has become really caught up in this competitive finance world, and Mark sees a new version of his son, one that has him worried.

The Weaponization of Narcissism

The word *narcissist* is right up there with *gaslighting* in terms of how frequently it's used. We have overly embraced this term to label those who hurt us. It has become a favorite to lean on when we're feeling rejected, neglected, or challenged by someone we love. But, seeing as how only 0.5 to 5 percent of the population meets criteria for NPD, it's unlikely that every single one of our exes or every pushy in-law, demanding boss, and frustrating parent is a narcissist.

I want to emphasize that this is a heavy diagnosis that shouldn't be used lightly. NPD can be very destructive. It leaves its victims walking on eggshells, feeling insecure and confused. But the first victim of NPD is the narcissist themselves; they have probably suffered from some serious emotional wounds as a child and now cannot find a way to tolerate disappointment, engage in healthy relationships, or establish a foundation of self-esteem. Even "successful" narcissists with good jobs and families aren't very happy, no matter how they appear.

These days, presenting as egocentric and unempathetic has become synonymous with being narcissistic. People generally misuse this term when someone they love hurts them or when someone acts in a way that they perceive as selfish, thoughtless, or mean. In its weaponized form, the word *narcissism* doesn't capture the full clinical picture, though. Rather, it's a shortcut to saying, "You do whatever is best for you, and you don't care that you've hurt me." However, if the (perceived) exploitation and (perceived) lack of empathy are the only traits the person is displaying, they're three criteria short of having NPD.

Here are the four mistakes people make when casually diagnosing someone as a narcissist.

1. We Don't Gather Enough Data

A common mistake people make nowadays is to look at one behavior (or perhaps a few, if I'm being generous) and jump to a diagnostic conclusion without looking at a person's full history and patterns in relationships. They focus on *their* individual experience with the person instead of looking at how they act in other relationships and contexts. Remember, NPD shows up starting in early adulthood and is *persistent* and *pervasive*; if someone has NPD, there will be evidence outside of their thoughtless actions with you. Again, narcissists aren't narcissists with only one person.

Further, relationship changes and challenges can make people appear narcissistic. When siblings grow up in different developmental stages, it can make one or both seem self-centered. When children start to individuate from their parents, there will be growing pains. When couples experience hard life transitions, it can make them less empathic or more self-focused. We all have a *touch* of narcissism, which can get bigger at certain points in life, but unless we're acting in ways consistent with NPD criteria across *all* our close relationships, we don't actually have a disorder.

2. We Mistake a Lack of Expressed Empathy with a Lack of Empathy

Generally speaking, people hide their vulnerable feelings when they're in conflict, and it's easy to view someone as selfish and uncaring when they don't tell us their true feelings. Conflicts are upsetting, and we've all developed ways of protecting ourselves, whether it's getting loud to be heard or emotionally withdrawing to prevent a panic attack. Underneath these less-than-ideal responses, though, we feel awful. We feel scared, insecure, inadequate, unimportant, and alone. We hate fighting with our loved ones, and we *really* hate that we've hurt them, especially unknowingly. We're not being defensive because we have a narcissistic belief in our own superiority; we're doing it because we're terrified that the person won't understand us and will see us negatively, so we need to show them our side and explain to them why we aren't to blame. (This isn't effective, but hey, humans aren't perfect.)

To demonstrate this, let me tell you how narcissistic I can look when fighting with Lucas. When I'm at my worst, I am snarky and passive-aggressive. I seem calm and collected, cold and calculating, but on the inside, I'm a wreck. I am *so anxious*. Panicking, in fact. I'm trying to keep track of our conversation because I'm getting overwhelmed and lost, and I want to burst into tears every second, but I'm trying *not* to burst into tears and am fighting to quell the panic, and this self-restraint makes me seem disengaged. Looking at us argue, you wouldn't know how much pain and regret I feel for having hurt him because you'd just see the cool defensiveness. It's important to remember that most of us do care, very deeply in fact, when we've hurt people we love, and the protective responses we display during arguments aren't the full emotional picture. Nowadays, when we fight, I can usually skip the cold part and go straight to my actual feelings, and Lucas gets to interact with the vulnerable part of me instead of the protective part. (What a treat for him!)

Narcissists, on the other hand, actually are uncaring. They don't feel bad for hurting others; they feel justified in doing so and then get annoyed at the other person for being upset by it. Narcissists do have vulnerable feelings beneath their harsh exterior, but those feelings are directed toward themselves, such as inadequacy and self-hatred. They don't have the whole empathy part that feels sadness or hurt at what someone else may be going through.

3. We Confuse an Inflated Ego with Grandiosity

Someone who thinks highly of themselves does not immediately meet the criteria for NPD. There are plenty of people whose confidence borders on (or fully crosses into) conceit or vanity who aren't narcissists. Perhaps their apparent self-love is a mask for feelings of inadequacy, but it's also possible they have an incredible degree of healthy confidence and an unshakable belief in their ability to achieve their dreams. (In truth, most of us strive to be this person—the one who "manifests" their life goals and won't let in a drop of external doubt about their abilities.) But whether it's an inflated ego, vanity, self-absorption, or just unusually healthy confidence, these traits do not make a narcissist. To have NPD, the person must also require external validation and admiration, and to be seen as superior to others. This is the difference between a big ego and grandiosity. Grandiosity goes several steps beyond confidence—it's a near-delusional sense of importance, where someone exaggerates their achievements and expects others to see them as superior.

4. We Mistake Jerks for Narcissists

Some people suck. They're immature, mean, selfish, and unremorseful. Some people don't respect other people in their lives. They lie and they cheat, and they don't care that it hurts others. But they can be all these things and *still* not be a narcissist. There's a lot of room for people to be awful without meeting the criteria for a personality disorder, and that's because (you guessed it!) people are flawed. Some people feel justified in behaving badly, while others just don't know any better yet. Our growth is messy and not linear. In the process of figuring out how to have healthy relationships, some people have a lot of unhealthy ones, and often through their own fault. We learn from our mistakes, and sometimes the mistake is that we repeatedly act in immature and egocentric ways. Your ex might be a jerk who has a lot of self-reflection and self-work to do, but it doesn't mean they have NPD.

I have been a jerk in some relationships. To this day, I deeply regret how I ended a friendship in college. She was a best friend like I'd never had before. We were inseparable, and then she went abroad for a semester, and somehow things changed. I can't even recall why our relationship felt different, but it did. She seemed needier in a way that frustrated me, and I handled it terribly. Our group of roommates didn't include her as much. We acted "cool" and better than her. The apartment became *very* awkward. We weren't friends by the end of college, and I desperately wish I had handled everything better because she's someone I'd love to have as a friend. In this situation, I seemed narcissistic. I wasn't empathic because I was too consumed by my own feelings and justifications. As a result, I threw away a years-long friendship that could have lasted a lifetime, and I regret it. I've thought about it often and grown from it, and I've fought for friendships in a way that I would never have had I not gone through that. The point is, I was not a good person in that relationship, but that didn't mean I had NPD. It just meant I was a jerk.

They're Not Gaslighting You

Because narcissism has become so weaponized, I've had clients fearfully ask me if they have narcissism after being labeled as such by their partner, child, or parent. Some are in tears as they question their ability to interact with others in a healthy manner. Others come with the NPD criteria in hand, ready to review each one to see if they check off five of the nine. *The reality is that anyone who genuinely worries that they are a narcissist, probably isn't.* That level of openness and willingness to self-reflect is not typical of a narcissist. Plus, narcissists don't tend to believe or care that they've hurt others, whereas my clients are deeply distressed by the possibility that they've unknowingly caused others pain.

My clients' concern is fueled by a steady increase in the armchair diagnosis of narcissism. Our expanded awareness of this disorder has created a fascination with it. How many books and shows are written about narcissists? How many articles and reels? As scary and destructive as someone with NPD can be, we're a little bit obsessed with them, which has led us to see narcissists everywhere we turn. Maybe it's self-protective, to educate ourselves so that we don't fall prey, or maybe it's because we're morbidly curious about people who can be so abusive with such little awareness or remorse. While this rising fascination with narcissism has undoubtedly helped some people avoid or escape bad relationships, it has also misled many others to inaccurately see narcissism when it's not there.

This is one of my bigger concerns since I've seen relationships be irreparably damaged or end because the term *narcissism* was weaponized. It's hard to recover when your spouse tells you (and your couples therapist), "Listen, I've figured out why this has been so bad, and it's because you're a narcissist. Good news is, we're in couples therapy now, and I can point out all your narcissistic ways so you can change them." As you can imagine, the other person usually feels shocked, angry, or devastated, or a combination of all three. These sessions don't get any better when I challenge the armchair diagnosis after assessing this

Are They a Narcissist, or Did They Just Hurt Your Feelings?

alleged narcissist and witnessing their genuine empathy and attempts to work on the relationship over time.

It's the same when narcissism is volleyed between children and parents; the accusation puts the accused person in an impossible situation. They can either agree that they're a narcissist and then walk on eggshells for the rest of their relationship to prove that they're not bad, or they can face the reality that their loved one sees them so negatively that they would accuse them of having a serious personality disorder and also won't take responsibility for their side of the problems.

As with gaslighting, I have rarely seen people accurately diagnose narcissism. To put it bluntly, I have never seen a client in a couples therapy session call their partner a narcissist and be right. In fact, the person misusing the label usually tends to be more narcissistic and have more therapy work to do than their partner. (Remember how abusive partners are masters at weaponizing therapy speak to their advantage.) More often, I'm the one telling a client my concerns that their partner or parent or friend may have narcissistic traits, which is why they're finding the relationship so volatile and conflict resolution so one-sided. It's hard for a person involved with a narcissist to accurately identify the disorder because people with NPD are great at making other people think they are the problem. It's an insidious process, and rarely do people realize what's happening until others point it out to them or the narcissist harshly devalues or leaves them.

Now, you might be in a relationship with someone who has NPD, but instead of jumping to "narcissist!" it's helpful to use other adjectives and be more specific about your concerns. Saying that a certain behavior was selfish or that a person seems unremorseful is more exact than calling them a narcissist. After all, from those nine criteria, we know NPD has many problematic characteristics; someone who annoyingly seeks validation or admiration is very different from someone who unashamedly exploits others. By pushing ourselves to be clearer and

123

more targeted in our analyses instead of using the loaded word, we will more accurately navigate hard parts of our relationships or identify if we need to leave them.

So, You've Been Accused of Being a Narcissist

If you chose to read this book, there's a *very* good chance you're not a narcissist. People with NPD don't tend to care about using clinical terms correctly, much less improving their relationships. This is why you might be especially surprised if someone says you're a narcissist. Don't panic—here's what to do.

Ask Them to Explain

As you know, the word *narcissist* is both descriptive and vague. You need more information. What did you do or say that makes them think you meet the criteria for a serious clinical disorder? Was it one action, or have they noticed a pattern in your behavior that's concerning them? Perhaps most critically, do they think you lack empathy for them? Ask calm, clarifying questions so you know exactly what's happened to prompt this statement.

Validate Their Feelings

Even though you're probably hurt or outraged that they called you a narcissist, start off by validating their hurt and fear. Someone who weaponizes that word is probably afraid that they're going to keep getting hurt by the person they love, and they're using "narcissist" to get your attention. Mission accomplished—they now have your attention. For example, you could say, "I see why you felt hurt and alone when I told you I couldn't have the conversation about our holiday plans earlier today. I know it's important to you, and I understand how it must have felt like I was shutting you down or telling you it wasn't a priority."

This step is of critical importance because, as you'll recall, narcissists lack empathy. In validating their feelings, you are showing them that you do care about how they feel, demonstrating an understanding of their perspective and emotions. One of the best things you can do to counter an inaccurate accusatory diagnosis is to act in ways that show how that diagnosis doesn't fit your behavior.

Share Your Experience

Now that you've made sure they feel validated and know you care, here's the chance to share a bit more about what was going on for you internally. Try to be honest and vulnerable. Don't just walk them through what you were *thinking*; explain how you were *feeling* during the interaction. Make sure to share any feelings that can help them see you in a more compassionate and nuanced way. To continue with our holiday example, you could say, "When you brought up holiday plans, I immediately got anxious. I don't want to disappoint either of our families, but I know we'll inevitably have to since we're splitting them between both sides. I hate imagining either of our parents sad, and I had a knee-jerk reaction to table the conversation until I had time to work through those feelings a bit."

Apologize if Necessary

Maybe you did mess up a little bit—not to the level of narcissism, but enough for someone to feel really hurt and uncertain whether you care about them. If there's any part of how you acted that you want to take responsibility for, now's the time. Maybe you apologize for being thoughtless. Or, with our holiday plans example, you could apologize for not sharing what you were feeling and explain why you asked to put off the conversation. This is an easy thing to take responsibility for: that you didn't share enough about the feelings that fueled your responses and that you gave them the wrong impression by not doing so.

Challenge Their Use of the Word

It's okay, encouraged even, for you to challenge their use of the word *narcissist*. Tell them that you take this word pretty seriously, and if they really think you're a narcissist, you want to have a much bigger conversation, perhaps with a professional who can help explore this. Truth is, if you love them, you wouldn't want them to stay in a relationship with a narcissist, so if they truly think you meet the criteria for NPD, then this needs to be addressed.

If They Continue Calling You a Narcissist, Get More Support

If, despite these steps, the person is unable to see you more compassionately and still fully believes you are a narcissist, then it's time to recruit professional help. This could start with you recommending that they read a book on narcissism so that they can develop an accurate understanding of the disorder, but if they have made up their mind and want to skew everything you do as pathological, a book may just reinforce their belief. Better, find a therapist. You need a qualified third party to step in and make an assessment. Just the fact that you're willing to seek an outside opinion is a good indicator you don't have NPD, but they may need someone to set them straight.

Remember, You Can Distance Yourself or Leave

If this person clings to this diagnosis and weaponizes it whenever you're in a fight, you can consider your options, and one of them includes stepping back in closeness or leaving the relationship. If they truly think you're a narcissist, it will be hard to have a healthy relationship anyway.

They might not be ready to do the actual work of being with you and will instead keep resorting to the quick solution of saying you have NPD and need to make all the changes for the relationship to work.

So, You Think Someone Is a Narcissist

If you read this chapter and thought, *Yikes, that definition sounds a little too familiar,* then there's a chance someone in your life has some narcissistic traits or could even meet the criteria for NPD. Or perhaps other people have told you they're worried you're in a relationship with a narcissist. If you're wondering about this, here's what you should do.

Educate Yourself

Luckily for all of us, there are tons of great resources about narcissism and how it shows up in all kinds of relationships. Start by reading articles written by professionals. Follow experts (not influencers) on social media. By that, I mean therapists with degrees in psychology. Buy some books and do a deep dive. Narcissists can be surprisingly hard to identify, but the more you know, the easier it is. At the same time, be conscious of your consumption. Don't read books intentionally looking for evidence that someone is a narcissist; if you do that, confirmation bias makes it likely that you'll find it even if it's not accurate.

Consider the Evidence

If someone keeps acting in ways that feel consistent with narcissism, take note. Try to get a fuller picture of how they act, not just in your relationship but with others too. Are they only narcissistic during arguments? For example, do you feel like they don't care about your feelings when you're fighting, or do they always seem to lack empathy? Do they need reassurance that you think they're great right after a conflict, or do they need a *constant* influx of admiration from you? Are they trying to live vicariously through you, controlling your decisions to make themselves look good? Context matters here. The point of this exercise isn't to create a scorecard you can throw in their face but, rather, to see an accurate picture of this person and relearn to trust your observations and instincts since being in a relationship with a narcissist can make you second-guess yourself.

Recruit Professional Help

No surprise, it's helpful to get a therapist to support you as you go through this analysis and reflection. If you've been in a relationship with a person who has NPD, I'm guessing it's been pretty tough. You might have been on the receiving end of some abuse tactics, which are making you doubt your perception of reality. A qualified professional can help you assess what's going on and make sure you've got an accurate understanding of this relationship. However, remember that an individual therapist doesn't have the full story; they only have your version of it. They can't (and shouldn't) attempt to officially diagnose your partner or parent or friend with NPD, but they can observe concerning behaviors and patterns and make recommendations from there.

Listen to Your Gut

You might get the feeling that something's not quite right in your relationship with this person. You might be shocked or confused by their reactions and behaviors, or maybe the way they view and talk about themselves and others isn't sitting right with you. Listen to that feeling. Don't rely on the feeling alone—you still want to educate yourself, gather data, and talk to a therapist—but don't ignore your instincts.

Don't Tell Them They're a Narcissist

Tempting as it is to tell the person, "Hey there, I think you may be a narcissist. Let's work on fixing you," it's not going to work. Either the person isn't a narcissist and they'll be hurt and defensive, or they *are* a narcissist and they'll blow up. Calling out a narcissist won't get you good results. Rarely, if ever, will someone with NPD hear and accept that they have NPD. Instead, they'll go into a fit of self-righteous rage and start twisting things around until you think *you're* the narcissist.

Decide If It's Workable

Narcissism, like all disorders, exists on a spectrum. Some people have a milder version of the disorder and, for example, have more capacity for empathy, self-reflection, and change. They won't have a ton of capacity compared to someone who doesn't have NPD, but perhaps they're able and somewhat willing to work on themselves. Knowing that there will likely be a limit to how much work they can do, you can decide if you want to stay with them and work on things.

If it's a romantic partner and you want to try, find a couples therapist, preferably one with a lot of knowledge and experience working with people who have NPD. See if your partner will go to individual therapy and sign a release so that their therapist and your couples therapist can communicate. There's no guarantee, but this will give you the best chance at change.

If It's Unworkable, But You Want to Stay in the Relationship

Many people have family members, partners, or bosses who are narcissistic, and they don't want to end the relationship or can't end it without significant consequences. If you're in this situation, it's time to protect yourself and set expectations. Be cautious with how vulnerable you are with this person. Don't be swayed by their idealization of you so that the fall from the pedestal won't hurt quite as much. Don't try to have a reasonable conversation about your hurt feelings or self-growth—it won't go anywhere. Do accept that a relationship with this person may be flawed and stunted.

If It's Time to Leave, Do So and Do It Carefully

You might realize the person's narcissistic traits and tendencies are too entrenched to change and are causing you too much harm. Or maybe they have a mild case of NPD, but you don't have the capacity or willingness to do the work with them, which is perfectly understandable. If you choose to end the relationship, do it with forethought and intention. People with NPD are easily wounded, and being left will trigger some rage. They won't be able to fathom that you could leave them since they think they are so fantastic, infallible, and desired. Leaving them will bring their low self-esteem to the surface, and their defense mechanism will be to double down with displays of grandiosity, superiority, and anger. They might retaliate to regain a sense of power. I don't mean to scare you; I just want you to anticipate a bad reaction and have a plan in place. For more about this, I strongly encourage you to read more about this disorder by checking out the recommended resources at the end of this book and by working with a therapist.

After It's Over, Focus on Healing

If you've been in a long relationship with a narcissist, some emotional damage has been done. Your self-esteem and identity have probably taken a hit. Focus on healing and rebuilding. Use the term *narcissism* to help understand what you went through, but don't become obsessed with it. It's a way of understanding who the person was and their impact on you so that you can heal and move forward. ■

Chapter 8

Are They Love Bombing You, or Are They Just Being Nice?

———————

Love bombing, like gaslighting, is an abuse tactic intended to gain control over the other person. However, it can be even harder to detect because it is an unhealthy extreme of an otherwise healthy and normal behavior during courtships and post-arguments, which is when people put extra effort and love into establishing the relationship or repairing after a fight. Plus, unlike gaslighting, love bombing feels nice, at least in the beginning. However, love bombing is quite different from normal displays of love and gestures to reconnect, as this chapter will show.

Hugo Is Love Bombing

Gianna couldn't get over how lucky she was to have met Hugo. First of all, he was French, which meant he had an unbelievably sexy accent. He was charismatic and fun but still serious and intense. He was also unusually successful for someone in her peer group. He had founded a start-up right out of college and throughout his twenties and managed to sell the company for quite a hefty sum. This launched him into an accelerated career trajectory compared to herself and her friends, who were still trudging up corporate ladders at their respective jobs.

Gianna was happy and fairly confident in herself, as much as anyone can be at the age of twenty-four. She was passionate about her work, had

They're Not Gaslighting You

a great group of friends, and took at least two wonderful vacations a year. What didn't always bring her great happiness was her love life. Men her age frustrated her. They ghosted, breadcrumbed, cheated, lied, you name it. She felt like none of them put much effort into dating, let alone a relationship, leaving her a bit discouraged and perhaps even jaded.

Then she met Hugo at a music festival. He shamelessly flirted with her, willingly offering to grab the next round of drinks or tacos. He grabbed her hand when they moved from one stage to another and seemed happy for the world to know he was courting her. This behavior didn't stop after that first night either; it only got bigger. Two days after they met, Hugo sent her three dozen long-stemmed red roses; he'd remembered her address from the Uber they shared home that original night. With the roses was a note asking her to meet him for dinner that weekend at a fancy restaurant downtown. He could have just texted her to ask her out; the romantic gesture he'd made instead left Gianna in awe.

When they met for dinner, Hugo insisted on paying. He insisted on paying for everything for the next two months. By the third week, Hugo said Gianna was his soulmate, and he couldn't imagine living without her. He blew off work to pick her up from the office and take her out to beautiful meals. He was always present and reachable when they weren't together too. Gianna never had to worry about when he would text again or when they'd see each other; he texted many times a day, and they always had a date on the books.

While the gifts and expensive meals were wonderful, it was the outpouring of verbal affection that wooed her the most. Hugo's confident use of the word *soulmate* made her feel loved and desired. At night, lying in bed, he'd pour out confessions of how, when he saw Gianna swaying to the music at that festival, he realized he was only half a person. He said that his heart finally felt whole, that he knew she was the only one for him, that they were meant to be together, that nothing could tear them apart. "Let the world try, let our family and friends try to stop us," he said, "but this is a forever love that will persevere through it all."

Are They Love Bombing You, or Are They Just Being Nice?

Gianna was enchanted. Like most people, she had always wanted to hear someone say those words. She felt seen, special, and cherished.

When Hugo said he loved her after four weeks, Gianna believed him and said it back. When Hugo asked her to move into his spacious apartment in the city, Gianna said yes, even though he wanted her to move in within the next month. Now that he'd met the only love of his life, he didn't want to delay his future any longer than he had to. When, a few days later, Gianna told Hugo that her mom was worried she was moving a bit fast, Hugo pulled her in close for a hug. "People won't understand our relationship," he said. "Our love is the stuff they make movies about. People will judge us or try to stop us from being happy, but we won't let them." At the time, Gianna thought this was incredibly romantic. She was willing to ignore the part of her that shared her mom's worry and felt rushed into living together.

Five weeks later, Gianna had finished unpacking her last box. She and Hugo had been living in unimaginable bliss. He showered her with anything and everything she wanted. One night, Gianna came home and told Hugo her friends wanted to have a girls' night that Saturday, so she'd be out with them. Hugo grew still and said, "I thought we were hanging out this Saturday."

"I know, but it's so hard to get all of us together with our crazy schedules. Is it okay if we skip this Saturday?" Gianna answered.

"Sure, I get it. We finally moved in, so now you don't think you need to spend time with me anymore," Hugo answered. "I guess I should have gotten that Chanel bag for someone who does want to go to dinner with me."

Gianna's heart dropped to the floor. "Hugo . . ."

"Kidding, kidding. *Mon Dieu*, Gianna, I'm just kidding. Ditch me on Saturday, it's fine."

But it wasn't fine. Hugo's passive-aggressive response was the beginning of many more to come. When Saturday came, he ignored her all day, leaving rooms she entered and giving one-word answers to her questions. Gianna felt awful all day, guilty and scared that he'd break up with her. When she got back from dinner, his passive-aggression turned into direct anger. He accused her of being with another guy since she didn't answer all his texts (of which there were *many*). Gianna apologized profusely and promised to share her location, check in with him every fifteen minutes the next time she went out without him, and not go out again for a few weeks so they could reconnect. She loved him and wanted to make him feel safe and secure with her, and she had to repair the trust she'd broken by going AWOL.

After the apologies and concessions, Hugo softened. His warmth returned, as did his gifts. As a joke, he got her another Chanel bag with a GPS tracker hanging from the expensive handle. He said it was so he wouldn't lose her to the "big bad city." She laughed at the silliness but left it on and always used that bag just to show him she could be trusted.

When Gianna was invited to a high school friend's small wedding, she wasn't given a plus one. Only married couples were extended that invitation since the hosts were trying to keep costs down. Gianna was scared to tell Hugo, worried he'd think she was trying to exclude him. How can someone not bring their soulmate to a wedding? Instead of talking to him about the awkward situation, she declined the invitation entirely. Hugo found the RSVP response with "Sorry, I am unable to attend," checked off, and told her he was touched she would do that for him. So touched, in fact, that he asked if he could take her shopping for an engagement ring the weekend of the wedding. Gianna was excited, but she had another feeling as well. Anxiety? Pressure? She wasn't sure, and she certainly didn't say anything about it.

Defining Love Bombing

Love bombing is the excessive showering of affection, gifts, proclamations of love, requests for commitment, expressions of shared values and goals, and compliments. Although it may appear charming to have

Are They Love Bombing You, or Are They Just Being Nice?

someone show this level of interest and investment, it's actually a way abusers rush people into commitment and position themselves as an overly significant part of the other person's life. It's marked by constant communication, where the abuser always stays in contact and thus remains top of mind with the object of their attention.

Although we often think of gifts as a necessary component of love bombing, abusive partners can lure someone in without spending a lot of money; over-the-top affection and flattery do the same work as excessive gifts. For example, a love bomber may offer lavish compliments or say whatever they think the other person wants to hear, such as claiming they have the same values or goals (sometimes outright lying in the process). The abuser presents themselves as being generous, selfless, and fully attuned to the other's needs—they can do anything and everything the other person wants and meet all their needs for affection, support, and admiration. Other people will fall short in comparison, so what's the point in spending time with them? But as we'll see, this fuels isolation. By becoming the most important person in the other's life, they can push all other relationships to the side.

Love bombing can happen at any point in a relationship, but it's most often seen at the start. This is when an abusive partner attempts to secure the relationship as something serious, not leaving any room for you to doubt or end the budding relationship. The abuser is skilled at presenting themselves as an ideal partner or friend who is seemingly emotionally available and shares all the same dreams and interests as you. They figure out what you want to hear and say it, sprinkling plenty of compliments along the way. You want to own a house in a neighboring city? Guess what? The love bomber just attended some open houses in that city. Is it true? Absolutely not, but they know you'll be excited to find someone with the same goal and will feel like it's "fate." You can easily identify love bombing when you look at the larger context of a relationship, looking to see if the person is using other abuse tactics to gain power and control. However, at the start of the relationship,

They're Not Gaslighting You

there is no context or additional data yet, making love bombing harder to spot.

Love bombing is also a typical follow-up to fights. As you'll recall from chapter 3, abusive relationships follow a cycle in which tension increases until an abusive incident occurs, which is followed by a period of reconciliation, and finally calm. It's during the period of reconciliation that abusers renew their excessive attentiveness and pampering, from constant compliments to pricey gifts, trying to show their remorse and ensure the person doesn't leave. They are also likely to return to "soulmate" language, using this as an excuse for their behavior. "How could I not be jealous someone was trying to flirt with my soulmate? It's natural to defend something so amazing and special" or "We'll go through hard times, but we're meant to be together. It's written in the stars."

Love bombing is an effective way of reestablishing the "us against the world" mentality and lulling a survivor back into feeling cherished and protected, even though this feeling won't last—because it never does. Love bombing is a temporary display of intense affection meant to solidify the survivor's belief that the abuser is a kind, generous, loving person (their soulmate, no less!). This temporary display of affection occurs in the *idealization phase* of the relationship, but it is cut short when the abuser gets angry. As soon as the person does something that upsets the abuser, such as making other people or obligations a priority, the abuser will feel scorned, and their excessive love will quickly shift into anger. This paves the way for abusers to move into the *devaluation phase*, when they become mean, either through demonstrative displays of anger or icy withholding of communication. They denigrate the victim for their choices and accuse them of not prioritizing the relationship.

From here, there are two options. Either the abuser will return to the idealization phase and reengage with love bombing, or they will enter the *discard phase*, where they end the relationship since it no longer serves them. This can be incredibly shocking and painful to the person who has been convinced of their soulmate status and can't understand why the other person would suddenly leave after such intense talks about their fit and future together.

As we saw with Gianna and Hugo, love bombing comes with an emotional price tag: the forsaking of other relationships and obedience to the abuser's expectations. Hugo used love bombing to keep Gianna close and compliant, and then to repair the relationship after he treated her badly. She slowly stopped seeing other people since it upset Hugo so much—a small price to pay for being with your soulmate, right? However, Hugo continued to use money and flattery to keep her in his orbit until, one day, he decided she had hurt him too many times, and he abruptly ended things. He gave her a week to move out, wouldn't help with any of the expenses, and stopped talking to her—unless, of course, it was to send a horrible text at 11:00 p.m. letting her know he was so much happier with her gone. The love bombing effectively destroyed her life for a period of time until she learned about what happened to her and started to heal.

The Evolution of the Term

The term *love bomb* was invented to explain a recruitment tactic used by the Unification Church of the United States, an offshoot of the Unification Church established by Sun Myung Moon in the late 1950s, which many have called a cult. It became generalized to describe how cults attract new members and was later adopted by the psychological community to describe the similar strategy abusers use for keeping partners close to them. It's not surprising that a term connected to cults has crossover meaning for abusive relationships, as these two share many similarities. Both follow a pattern in which the victim is initially made to feel special and seen, after which they are drawn into the group and indoctrinated, and then finally devalued and ordered to exhibit obedience, isolation, and loyalty. There is little room for freedom of thought or expression once you're in a cult or abusive relationship, and both do an excellent job of convincing you that others will try to make you leave because they don't understand or are jealous of the higher love you've found.

The great part of this term is that it's very easy to understand: an explosion of affection, flattery, and devotion so powerful it obliterates your critical thinking and erases the rest of your life. It overwhelms your senses so all you can see is the person worshipping you. It wipes out everything so that the abuser can come in and set up camp. Interestingly, the term hasn't evolved or been misused quite as often as others, such as gaslighting. It's just become misunderstood. People are misconstruing normal gestures of love or attempts at reconnecting after a fight as love bombing. Again, the key to correctly identifying love bombing is to look at the intention of the person exhibiting the behavior and to examine the behavior within the full context of the relationship.

Oscar *Isn't* Love Bombing

It's been three days since Oscar met Damien, and he is counting the minutes until they have dinner tonight. They met standing in line at a café, both bemoaning how complicated drink orders slow down the process—can't anyone just order hot coffee anymore? They chuckled at their shared frustration and, since neither had any specific place to be, they sat down with their hot coffees to chat.

Oscar was the bold one and asked for Damien's number. It's not often he meets a guy he hits it off with right away; usually, he has to talk himself into a second date. But with Damien, he's hoping there will be one, and many more. After they had coffee, Oscar couldn't help himself and texted Damien a few hours later. He knew he should wait a little longer so he wouldn't seem so desperate, but why play those games when you find someone you really like? Damien answered within ten minutes, so clearly, he agreed about being direct.

Are They Love Bombing You, or Are They Just Being Nice?

They picked an Italian restaurant halfway between both their apartments for dinner. Damien had been there before and loved it. As Oscar walks there, he fiddles with the small gift he purchased for Damien earlier that day. Damien had talked at length about his funny hobby of collecting antique colored glass vases, and Oscar knew a fantastic antique store near his office, so he dropped in and found a small red vase. Oscar doesn't want to come on too strong, but he also wants to show Damien he was listening during their earlier conversation and cares about his hobbies. Oscar feels instant relief when he walks into the restaurant and sees Damien sitting at a table for two with a bouquet of spring flowers lying on the second chair. Damien brought him flowers! They sit down and laugh about how "extra" they're being about this first date, but they feel like they have a real connection and are excited to get to know each other better.

When they have their first big fight four months later, they both worry they'll break up over it. Damien storms out of the room and tells Oscar he needs time to think. Oscar worries when he hears this because, as he has learned, Damien tends to go silent when he's overwhelmed, which leaves Oscar assuming the worst. A day goes by without any communication. Oscar sends a text and tries calling a few times but doesn't hear back. He knows Damien needs time, but Oscar needs to know if their relationship has a future. He loves this man and wants to work through the fight if Damien will. After work the next day, Oscar pops into the antique store again. This time he buys one hundred dollars' worth of colorful vases and a card, on which he writes, "I love the way you order coffee and I love you, Damien. I know our fight was awful, and I'm sorry for overreacting, but I want to figure this out with you. I'll give you space, but I miss you, and I'm ready to talk when you are. Love, Oscar."

But Damien isn't ready to talk yet. He gets the vases and card and puts them in his kitchen. He knows Oscar is probably panicking right now, but he also feels like Oscar is going overboard. Damien doesn't really think they'll break up over this fight. He just needs time to process and collect himself. Oscar's texts, calls, and now his gift, are feeling a bit too pushy to him. After all, Oscar knows that Damien takes longer to recover after a fight. The next day, Damien finds a ridiculous teddy bear and another card from Oscar sitting on this stoop. He texts Oscar, "Stop love bombing me. You know I need time to process after our fights. You can't control my feelings and push me into getting over this."

Oscar is crushed. His attempts at reconnecting have not only fallen flat, but they may also have pushed Damien further away. Oscar's panic rises at this realization. He was trying to remind Damien of his love and that they had something worth fighting for, but Damien felt like Oscar was being abusive. Was calling twice too much? Were the vases too expensive? But Damien literally hasn't spoken to Oscar in days. Doesn't that justify Oscar trying to connect? Or is he being abusive and controlling? Devastated, he stops reaching out, determined to give Damien space. Damien's harsh words achieve their desired effect, and he contacts Oscar two days later to talk and repair. Oscar is too afraid to bring up his concerns about Damien using the phrase *love bombing* since things are just getting back to normal, and he doesn't want to start another argument. But it continues to bother him and makes him much more restrained when showing his affection.

The Weaponization of Love Bombing

As I mentioned earlier, love bombing is the abusive extreme of perfectly normal, even good, relationship behavior. The tricky part about differentiating between healthy and abusive relationships is that they have similar patterns. Abusive relationships, as we know, go through cycles of tension, conflict, reconciliation, and peace. Healthy relationships go through a cycle that's very similar: *harmony, rupture, repair.* Just like in abusive ones, in healthy relationships, there can be periods of increased tension, the ruptures (or fights) can feel pretty awful, and repair can feel uncertain.

Because of these parallels, people mistakenly see normal relationship behaviors as love bombing and weaponize use of the term. This usually occurs for two reasons.

1. We Misread Courtship as Love Bombing

Showing extra affection at the start of a relationship is normal. It's how we show a person that we like them, are interested in getting to know them, and want to pursue a relationship with them. Without expressing our attraction and interest, the relationship wouldn't get off the ground. Early in dating, we need to be more expressive with our feelings and generous with our time, and this is often done through communication, gifts, doting words, and time spent together.

Notice that I said "extra" affection, not "excessive." This is a vague and difficult distinction because one person's extra is another person's excessive. Because of this, it's really hard to know what level of love you're showing the person you're dating, and you risk going overboard in their eyes. For example, a celebrity's newest love interest might buy them a six-figure car early on in dating, but if a person did that for you or me, we'd probably be shocked and a little worried. That's obviously an extreme example, but it gets the point across. Some people have a higher tolerance or expectation for gift giving, and they wouldn't balk at a pricey necklace on the third date, while others see gifts differently and wouldn't feel as comfortable.

Perceptions of romantic gestures also vary depending on who is extending them. By this I mean that if you really like the person being romantic toward you, you'll be thrilled to get daily texts. However, if you're not super keen on the person trying to win your affection, you'll find it annoying or even invasive to get a "have a great day!" text every morning. The same goes with friends. Some people appreciate a lot of contact from a new friend, while others are turned off by it. A behavior from one person is cherished; from another person, it's abhorred. How we view gifts, affection, and communication is subjective, so it's easy to mislabel innocent displays of affection for love bombing.

2. We Confuse Repair with Love Bombing

Fights require reconnection; in therapy, we call this *repair*. Healthy repair includes a renewed energy and focus on the relationship, similar to how we invest at the start of a relationship. Repair can be done through words of affection and commitment, gifts or thoughtful gestures, or time spent together. Healthy repair also includes a recognition of how we contributed to or worsened the argument and an apology when appropriate. Reflecting on what we could have done better and taking responsibility helps the other person feel safe because they see that we don't think it's okay to act a certain way and want to change it. When a conflict pulls people apart and makes them feel less close or secure in the relationship, repair brings them back together and heals some of the wounds, making them feel happier and stronger.

For example, after a big fight, someone might send their friend their favorite cupcakes or make a bigger effort to call. They're trying to reestablish closeness by showing care. In a romantic couple, one partner might send more frequent texts like they did at the start of dating: "Hey you, good morning, can't wait to see you later" and "Good night, babe, sleep well!" Their renewed enthusiasm for texting isn't meant to control or manipulate their partner but, rather, to show they care about and are paying attention to the relationship. However, if the partner receiving these amorous messages is still angry, they might feel the other person is trying to ignore their feelings or make them move on from the argument by "love bombing" them with nice texts.

With repair, we extend gestures of affection and remorse while knowing that they may not be received or magically end the fight.

Are They Love Bombing You, or Are They Just Being Nice?

Ideally, everyone is ready to move forward at the same time, but sometimes one person is still hurt or angry and doesn't want to move on yet. A well-adjusted person will offer repair but not get angry if the other person isn't quite ready. In contrast, an abusive person will blame the other person for keeping the fight going and might even accuse them of trying to keep the upper hand or punish them by "refusing to let it go."

For the record, I love repairing after fighting. I could do it the millisecond after the fight is over; hell, I could do it during the fight. It soothes my anxious soul to reconnect with Lucas, but I also know how important repair is for relationships. After we've processed an argument and de-escalated, I'm all for increased expressions of love and commitment. You can count on me to send a text apologizing for my part in the conflict and reinforcing to him that even though fighting sucks, there's no one I'd rather fight with, and I love building a life with him even when we're having a hard time with each other. I'll also probably do something to show him I'm thinking about him, like sending a cute throwback photo of us when we were dating or making his favorite dinner. It's not love bombing because it's not intended to control him. I'm not trying to erase the fight altogether or convince him to overlook my bad behavior. I'm trying to take responsibility and apologize, then reconnect. Sometimes, though, he's still feeling raw from the argument and isn't ready to jump back to being sweet. It can be hard when I'm feeling eager to reconnect and reestablish our close dynamic, but I give him space and let him come around in his own time. If I were to get furious with him for not accepting my gestures and insist that he "let it go," that would be a different story.

I should also note that Lucas engages in repair too. He'll apologize for his role in fights and return the sentiment of loving our life together. He'll send a sweet photo or, more likely, a funny one. And this is an important component of repair versus love bombing: In healthy relationships, repair is a two-way street. Both people can and should take responsibility for their less-than-desirable behavior and try to reconnect.

Both should say sorry and express a renewed desire to improve communication. Love bombing, in contrast, is where one person grovels and suffocates the other with amped up affection.

However, I should note that repair isn't always even. Rare is the relationship where both parties repair equally and in the same time frame. There's almost always one person who wants to put the fight behind them and reconnect sooner, and that's the person who will initiate repair most often. Being the person to always start repairing can be exhausting and somewhat demoralizing, so it helps when both people do it, even if it's not an even number of times.

I've heard many people confuse repair with love bombing, such as when their partner gives them gifts, particularly if it happens after an argument. There are usually two conditions when this happens. First, the person believes that their partner was to blame for the entire argument and that they themselves did nothing they should own or apologize for. Second, the person isn't over the fight and thinks their partner is attempting to buy their forgiveness. You can see how these two conditions lead to assumptions of love bombing. The person is viewing their partner as the sole bad actor, perhaps even abusive, which led to the fight in the first place. Already vigilant, they see their partner through this negative lens and view their partner's words or tokens of affection as attempts to get back into their good graces—in other words, as manipulation or abuse.

Investing in a new relationship or reconnecting after a conflict are good things. They create and strengthen our attachments. But overloading someone with affection, gifts, and communication in an attempt to eclipse other parts of their life and get them under our thumbs isn't a good relationship behavior, and we should make sure we know the difference.

So, You've Been Accused of Love Bombing

As you try to show your love or make repairs after an argument, your gestures may be painfully misattributed as love bombing. Remember that "excessive" can be subjective, so while your level of affection might be reasonable to you, it might be too much to the other person. But, in fairness to you, also remember that the person may be overly vigilant and seeing love bombing when it's not there. These steps will help you figure out what's going on and what you can do about it.

Self-Reflect

First, ask yourself a tough question: "*Did* I go overboard?" Did you send a lot of texts or go a little over the top with your compliments? Were you so excited to meet someone you liked that you started people-pleasing and saying what they wanted to hear? Were you coming from a place of insecurity and anxiety as you tried to rush a resolution and reestablish closeness? Did you give the other person enough time to process and self-soothe after the argument? Did you give them space if they weren't ready to reconnect, even though you were desperate to be close again? If you were pretty intense or quick about the repair, you can acknowledge that to them: "I see what you're saying. I hate feeling disconnected from you and I moved too fast trying to bring us back together. I'll be aware of this next time and try to pace it better."

Validate Their Perspective

Maybe you self-reflect and decide you really didn't go crazy on showing interest or affection or trying to repair, and you think the other person is being very sensitive about this. That's okay; you don't have to agree with their assessment of your approach. Instead of jumping right into defending yourself, start by validating their experience. Again, this is the best thing any of us can do when we're accused of using an abuse tactic. Being willing to hear and validate someone shows that we care about their experience and aren't trying to control or manipulate their perspective.

With a new person you're seeing, you could say, "I'm really excited to get to know you, but I see how I came on too strong for you." For older relationships, try saying, "I really hear that this felt like too much for you and that you could have used more time before I tried to bring us back to a good place. I also get that my way of doing it didn't work for you, and maybe we need to talk about what ways would feel better for you."

Explain Your Intent

Once you're sure the other person feels heard, you can explain what you were trying to do by showing your affection or engaging in repair. For courtship stages, explain how you're really interested in them and wanted them to know that. For repair, you can share how painful it is to be in conflict and feel disconnected and that you are ready to reconnect with them.

Invite Dialogue

Be curious about how you can express your interest or repair love post-conflict. Clearly, your strategy didn't work for them if they accused you of love bombing. For a new relationship, invite them to share what level of communication or types of exchanges feel okay to them. Maybe you enjoy exchanging daily texts, but maybe they think that's too much right now. For more established relationships, have a calm and open-minded conversation about how you can both feel seen, safe, and loved following an argument.

If This Doesn't Work, Pause the Conversation

Continuing in a conversation where the other person won't listen or back down from their accusation won't be productive. If they genuinely feel you were love bombing them, and your attempts to validate and explore this go nowhere, then suggest you take a break from the conversation so you can both think about this. Give yourself more time to consider their concerns and to solidify your own perspective before restarting the conversation later.

When Nothing Works

As you now know, the tricky thing about challenging an accusation like this is that your attempts can be construed as further evidence of abuse. With the steps outlined above, the person could still say that your validation, empathy, and dialogue are other examples of love bombing since you're playing the part of being nice to fix the issue instead of owning up to your bad behavior. There's not much you can do at this point besides agree to disagree, recommend they do some research on love bombing, and consider if this will be a relationship that works for you.

So, You Think Someone Is Love Bombing You

You may feel that someone has indeed love bombed you at the start of your relationship or following bad arguments. Perhaps you've noticed how their displays of affection follow a pattern of being intense but short-lived. The following steps explain how you assess and limit the impact of real love bombing, but you may want to consider exiting the relationship because love bombing is usually an indication that the relationship won't be a healthy one.

See If They Can Change

First things first: They might not be love bombing you. This person might just be wildly excited to have any kind of relationship with you, and their compliments, gifts, and excessive communication is a sign of their genuine interest in pursuing that relationship. It might be too much for you, though, and make you uncomfortable. If that's the case, talk to them. Let them know you're excited too, but the attention is a lot and you want to slow down the pace. Be kind but firm in turning down gifts or asking to lower the expectation for how often you communicate.

If this friend or potential partner seems sad or embarrassed, that's okay. This might feel like a rejection to them, and they're allowed to process that. If your request sends them into a rage, or they blame or criticize you for asking to ease up, that's not okay. If this is the situation you find yourself in, then keep reading for other recommendations.

Don't Let the Flattery Work

Be wary of overly effusive flattery early on in any relationship. Although compliments are lovely, be careful not to internalize them as how this person truly and consistently views you. An abusive person will put you on a pedestal during the idealization stage of the relationship, which is when love bombing occurs, only to rip you off it when they devalue you. Don't let them convince you that you're the most special, most perfect person alive, or their "soulmate" and "other half." I'm sure you're wonderful, but you also have flaws. Remember that anyone who idealizes you is likely to devalue you later on. You want someone to be infatuated but not obsessed with you. You want to be loved and appreciated but not thrown on a pedestal.

Turn Down the Gifts

Gifts can become weapons only when they're accepted. If you don't take the gifts offered during love bombing, they can't be used against you

Are They Love Bombing You, or Are They Just Being Nice?

when the person switches to devaluing mode. Be mindful not only of how many gifts you receive, but also at what point in the relationship you receive them. They should be commensurate to where you are in the relationship and not used as part of a manipulative apology following an abusive incident. However, also be careful when turning down a gift because this "rejection" can make abusive people furious. If it does, you've got some important information about them and should consider if this is a healthy relationship for you.

Verify Values

It's easy for someone to proclaim they share the same values and dreams as you, but dig a little deeper with this person, especially when you're first getting to know them. Ask them questions about their goals and values in life, then see what they say. Don't always give them your answers first; otherwise, they may parrot whatever you tell them. Abusive people are great at using information, but they can't if you don't give them that information.

Talk to a Therapist

You need to speak with a professional about your relationship. If this person is truly abusive, it's not a relationship you should stay in or try to work on. Trying to address love bombing with this type of person will be ineffective and could prompt them to switch tactics, such as gaslighting you by saying you're crazy to even think their behavior is love bombing. The better strategy is to accurately assess love bombing early in the relationship and leave before you get sucked in too deep.

Look at the Relationship Overall and Distance Yourself or Leave

If you're being love bombed, chances are you're experiencing other forms of abuse as well. I encourage you to take a good look at this relationship.

They're Not Gaslighting You

Is this person using other unhealthy tactics to maintain closeness and control? Are they isolating you? Gaslighting you? Erupting in anger over small issues? Are you walking on eggshells around them? Like all abuse tactics, love bombing is usually an indication the relationship is abusive, or at least on the path to becoming abusive, and you should stop walking down that path as soon as possible. ∎

Chapter 9

Are They a Sociopath, or Do They Just Like You Less Than You Like Them?

———————

The word *sociopath* has become a favorite to use, particularly when describing exes who seem to have weathered the breakup with ease and moved on quickly. What could be more sociopathic than our exes getting over us faster than they should, right? (In case it needs to be said, I'm joking.) Let's define what "sociopath" actually means and identify when and why it's so often misused.

Sid Is a Sociopath

Sid and Kelly were together for three years and married for one. They met in a running club Kelly had belonged to since graduating from college; Sid joined to meet people since he had just moved to that city. From the second their eyes met, Kelly felt adored—he flashed a full, genuine grin at her and immediately walked up to her to talk. Kelly felt special that Sid had picked her to say hello to first, particularly given how handsome he was—it's one of the first things people say when they meet him. He joked with her that even though he'd run fifteen marathons, he wasn't sure he'd be able to keep up with Kelly on the group's three-mile run, given how fit she was. Kelly laughed and teased him back, challenging him to beat her if he could.

Sid was unbelievably charming with her family and friends. They were all immediately impressed by him. By month four of dating, Kelly's mom was urging her to marry Sid. And Kelly felt the same way; Sid was scarily perfect for her. He wanted to run marathons worldwide, just like she did, and it turned out he loved all the same musicians that she did. Sid had plans to buy a penthouse condo downtown to use during the work week and a country house outside the city for weekends. If she was being honest, Kelly really wanted a nice home in the suburbs and didn't like the idea of commuting between places, but Sid insisted it would be best, so she agreed.

Sure, they had their problems. Sid would lie sometimes, usually about weirdly small things. For example, he ordered a movie on her television and when she asked him about it, he said he never ordered it or watched it. Sid had been crashing at her place while she was away for work, and Kelly honestly didn't care that he had ordered a movie; she just wanted to ask him if he liked it since she hadn't seen it yet. But he insisted that it wasn't him and told her to change her password in case it was hacked and even contact the streaming service for a refund. She'd catch him lying to her friends or random people like servers and cab drivers. When she pointed out the lies, he'd ignore her, act like he had no idea what she was talking about or make a joke and move on. Eventually, Kelly just accepted that he fibbed.

When Sid proposed, Kelly said yes, but a tiny part of her felt like it was a mistake. The lying wasn't great, plus she had this gut feeling something was wrong. But all couples have problems to work through, and in so many ways, he was still her dream guy. When the wedding planning started, she learned that Sid wanted it to be a huge event. He said he needed to invite everyone he knew, and it would propel him forward in his career to make the wedding fancy. When Kelly told him her parents didn't feel comfortable paying for such a fancy to-do, he

Are They a Sociopath, or Do They Just Like You Less Than You Like Them?

flew into another rage about how selfish they were and how they were trying to stop her from being happy. He said that Kelly would need to pay for it then because he was saving for their down payment to buy their dream home. Kelly took money out of her retirement account and paid for an extravagant wedding.

Fast forward two years, and Kelly is reeling from learning that Sid was in over $150,000 debt and hadn't worked for eight months. He'd been let go of three jobs in the past three years due to poor performance and a bad attitude, but he'd never revealed this to Kelly. He'd always insisted on separate bank accounts, so Kelly had no idea what his true financial situation was. Sid had taken out a loan to hide his unemployment. He had never even started saving money for the down payment. Kelly had drained her retirement and been funding their entire life and was now also on the hook for this loan.

Things only got worse when Kelly started digging. She found online dating accounts, messages from women asking Sid to come over *again*, and three maxed-out credit cards. She found grandiose headshots he'd paid a fortune for because he apparently planned on pursuing acting. She found bookmarked listings for million-dollar villas in California and names of casting agents. Kelly even investigated Sid's running history and found nothing; he had never run a marathon in his life.

Why had she believed him? She had let him convince her that he was wealthy and ambitious and caring. Kelly had thought *she* was the bad partner for not supporting him enough, for not investing in his insane far-fetched goals. Kelly remembered a time when Sid didn't speak to her for an entire week because she didn't feel entirely comfortable putting $25,000 into his start-up idea. He had acted like she didn't exist until she apologized profusely, agreed it was a brilliant idea, and gave him $10,000. In the divorce process, Sid tried to sue her for alimony. Then he'd ignore her lawyer's repeated efforts to continue with the process, not communicating for weeks and months at a time. Kelly found out Sid got married in another state before their divorce was final. She knew it wasn't legal, and she wasn't sure how he did it, but, seeing him more clearly now, she imagined he had used a fake name.

Kelly's life was in ruins. Her bank accounts were emptied, and she had become distant with so many people in her life. But when she did rebuild her relationships, people told her how they didn't like Sid. At first, he was nice and charming, but he seemed . . . fake. His stories didn't feel genuine, and his apparent emotions always seemed incongruent with how he said he felt. When Kelly's best friend said she thought Sid was a sociopath, Kelly thought she might be right.

Defining Sociopath

Let's start with the basics: The term *sociopath* isn't in the DSM. I discuss it in this book because it's the word we tend to use, but it's not a clinical diagnosis. When we call someone a "sociopath," what we mean is they meet the criteria for antisocial personality disorder (ASPD). Note that although people tend to use the terms *sociopath* and *psychopath* interchangeably, the two disorders have differences and are not synonymous. Misuse of the term *psychopath* certainly causes its own set of issues, but I'll be focusing on sociopath because that's the buzzier word at the moment.

ASPD is classified in the subcategory of *dramatic and erratic* personality disorders in the DSM. To be diagnosed with ASPD, someone needs to have at least three of these seven criteria present since the age of fifteen:

1. **Lawbreaking behaviors:** Repeatedly disobey the law, commit crimes, disregard social norms, and violate rules.

2. **Deceitfulness:** Have no problem lying, cheating, or using any kind of exploitation as a means to a desired end.

Are They a Sociopath, or Do They Just Like You Less Than You Like Them?

3. **Impulsivity:** Act rashly and impulsively without considering the consequences for themselves or others.

4. **Aggression:** Are generally irritable and quick to aggression, often getting into fights or verbal altercations.

5. **Recklessness:** Don't care about maintaining safety, either their own or other people's.

6. **Irresponsibility:** Are irresponsible and negligent, failing to uphold promises or meet obligations such as following through with work demands.

7. **Lack of remorse:** Don't feel bad when they harm others and will rationalize why their actions were justified.

To qualify for a diagnosis of ASPD, the individual must begin exhibiting these characteristics in childhood or early adolescence, which can include setting fires, breaking curfew, hurting animals, and destroying property. In other words, you can see indicators of ASPD early on in someone's life. (Although, as with all personality disorders, you can't officially diagnose someone until they're at least eighteen years old.) In other words, a person doesn't suddenly become a sociopath at twenty-five years old, nor do they become a sociopath in only one relationship. It's also worth noting that a person can't be diagnosed with ASPD if they have another disorder that would explain their behavior, such as bipolar disorder, in which manic episodes can cause impulsivity, inability to conform to norms, irritability, and so on.

Looking at the above criteria, the descriptor *antisocial* really hits the nail on the head. It's a great summation of what's troubling about this disorder. People with ASPD don't adhere to society's rules or care about violating other people's rights. They're living by their own self-serving code of conduct, one that can involve a lot of pain for those that interact with them.

They're Not Gaslighting You

When we think of the classic villain in a true crime story, we're often thinking of someone with ASPD—someone sly, cunning, and calculated. They don't subscribe to the idea of the social good or respecting other people's safety and autonomy. They're only interested in taking what they want, regardless of how it impacts others. People with ASPD are ten steps ahead, plotting how they'll get what they want from people, and willing to do whatever it takes to reach their ends. They'll lie, steal, cheat, kill. You name it, they'll do it.

Sociopaths aren't always violent criminals, though. In fact, *most* aren't. As you'll remember, all these disorders are a spectrum. So, while the vast majority of murderers and serial killers have ASPD, not all people with ASPD are murderers or serial killers. In fact, recent research suggests that there's a high number of people in CEO roles who have sociopathic tendencies. This makes all too much sense—these high-achieving people aren't necessarily breaking laws (although a fair number certainly do)—but they are ruthlessly self-serving as they climb to the top and make money for their shareholders. They aren't held back by guilt or empathy when it comes to hurting others. They'll abide by the rules of society if it behooves them, and much of the time, appearing like a law-abiding citizen who cares about issues like the welfare of others or the environment is a boon to their reputation. But the appearance of caring isn't genuine caring, and they'd abandon the facade the minute it didn't serve them.

I (briefly) worked with one person who met criteria for ASPD. He lied through his teeth and, even when caught, wouldn't give up the story. He often indulged in illegal drugs, spent a lot of his partner's money, cheated on her several times, and would stay out until the morning without telling her where he was, who he was with, or when he'd come home. He tried to smile his way out of every transgression and, when that didn't work, he quickly got mean and resorted to gaslighting, proclaiming his victimhood, and claiming his partner was insecure, jealous, and controlling. He had no regard for the law, for societal rules,

Are They a Sociopath, or Do They Just Like You Less Than You Like Them?

or for normal expectations in healthy relationships, and there was no way to make him change.

Strangely, despite our fascination with sociopaths, we have a really hard time believing it when we see it. Apart from the most egregious examples, like serial killers, it's hard for us to accept that people could flagrantly defy social norms, and it feels like an undeniable part of the human experience to feel empathy and remorse. This is why we keep giving people second and third (and infinite) chances even when they've consistently shown us they don't care about hurting us; it's just too much of a stretch to believe that they actually don't care. So, if you were to interact with someone who has ASPD, you might not see it at first, or even for a while after. Even if someone with ASPD were to shout the evidence in your face—"I keep cheating on you and I don't care it's hurting you! I've stolen from every company I've ever worked for!"— you'd still probably think, *They just admitted to bad behavior—that's a good sign*! But you'd be overly generous. They do realize it's wrong; they just don't care.

I have years of personal stories that showcase the many ways in which people can ignore sociopathic behavior—because, believe it or not, my husband, Lucas, is a professional poker player (and the gambling world is one toward which sociopaths probably gravitate). Since graduating from college, this man has been self-employed playing cash games in casinos. Everyone we tell thinks this is the coolest thing ever, but from what I've seen, it's not the James Bond-esque experience I imagined when he first told me what he did for work (a lot fewer tuxedos, a lot more rumpled sweatshirts).

Anyway, he plays poker with a wide variety of people, some of whom are . . . lacking a moral compass, shall we say? He has so many stories of players who recount their criminal histories without an ounce of remorse. The only reason they avoid breaking the law again (*if* they do) is because jail or prison really sucked, not because they recognize the moral wrongness of their actions.

They're Not Gaslighting You

These people sit together at a table playing poker for hours. They get a lot of data on each other, from how they play the game to how they interact with the other players. But despite all this data, Lucas has a lot of stories of how people *still* refuse to see others for who they are. A common example happens when someone at the table has hit a bad streak and is down a lot of money—not just one day, but for many days or weeks. When they run out of chips, they ask other players for money so they can buy in and keep playing. Now, some of these people have criminal histories that verify how their sociopathic symptoms pre-date the poker room. They've broken laws, hurt others, stolen, violated parole, and when you ask them about it, they have no remorse or conception that they did something wrong. Despite all of this, other players will still lend them money! They know this person has a well-established history of violating societal norms, and they even have recent data of seeing this person borrow money from other players and not pay it back. Nevertheless, when the person tells them, "Don't worry, I have the cash now, I'm paying everyone back tomorrow, you know I'm good for it," *they believe it.*

Two things are happening here. First, people feel awkward saying no to someone. Second, they believe that someone wouldn't violate the social contract of moral behavior by lying to their face. But guess what? Some people don't care about this social contract and are just interested in getting what they want, regardless of how it will impact others.

If you find yourself in any kind of relationship with someone who has ASPD, you're probably not feeling great. You're with someone who will act without remorse, cannot feel empathy or create a deep emotional attachment to others, and is or will probably be abusive. You can't have a healthy relationship with someone like this because they're lacking the capacity and motivation to establish emotional connection or engage in good communication. They might pretend to do so, placating you with fake affection or apologies, but you'll feel that something isn't quite right. That feeling comes from a complete absence of authenticity behind their actions. Remember from the DSM criteria that people with ASPD don't have empathy or know how to foster intimacy. To gain the personal benefits of relationships, they fake their feelings and use deceit or exploitation to create bonds with others.

Cammie *Isn't* a Sociopath

Theo is still reeling from his breakup. This is what shock feels like, right? Absolute panic and yet total numbness at the same time? He's sitting on the floor of his kitchen looking at the empty shelves where half of his dishes used to be. More than half are gone now, since Cammie was the one who bought their kitchen set. When Theo got home earlier today, he walked around their apartment—*I guess it's my apartment now*, he thought—and looked at the destruction. He knew she was moving out today, but he didn't anticipate just how devastating it would feel.

Cammie cheated on him, then left. Theo is having a hard time wrapping his head around that reality. It was only a week ago that he caught her in a lie, and she admitted to sleeping with a project manager from work named Mark. "Actually, it's more than sex, Theo. I really like him and I want to be with him," Cammie had said. She was so calm and collected when she was confronted about her betrayal. Theo was shocked and didn't know what to do. He said, "Okay. I mean, what can I do with that besides say okay?" Cammie nodded and started packing.

Later that night, she came into the bedroom and asked if they could talk. She wanted to explain why it happened. Theo mumbled an agreement, but he could barely hear her as she talked about how disconnected she felt in their relationship and how she had tried to fix things. She said she didn't mean to sleep with Mark, but she didn't think Theo would even care. Theo thought to himself, *Is she actually blaming* me *for sleeping with another guy?* Seeing Theo's blank stare, Cammie eventually stopped trying to explain.

They're Not Gaslighting You

What Theo really can't grasp is that the cheating lasted for so long. It wasn't one night, or a couple of nights, or during a work trip. Cammie had been sleeping with Mark for eight months. She lied to him for eight months. Theo is replaying every conversation with her, trying to figure out what were lies and what was truth.

And then there are all the questions Theo keeps asking himself. How could she have had sex with someone else, then come home to him? Did she feel bad? No, right? Because if she felt bad, why did she keep doing it? Does she not care about him at all? Does she even have feelings? What kind of person cheats for *eight months* and then leaves only when they're caught? Who can keep two relationships going at the same time? Is she a con artist? No, it's worse—she has to be a sociopath. Only a sociopath would do something this objectively wrong without shedding a tear when her partner confronts her.

Meanwhile, Cammie is sobbing as she moves into an empty apartment across town. It's a shabby place, the only thing she could find at the last minute, but she had to get out. Seeing the devastation on Theo's face was soul-shattering, and she had to leave so that he could start to heal. She hoped that talking that night would open a conversation where she could explain and help him understand, but he was so shutdown, so unreachable, that she stopped trying.

Cammie hates herself. She can't believe what she's done to Theo; she might never forgive herself for it. But even though she's spiraled into deep shame, she also understands why she cheated. Theo had stopped caring about her or investing in their life. He was content to watch TV or play video games instead of spending quality time with her, no matter how often she asked if they could go to dinner or see a show. She told him, quite a few times, that she was feeling disconnected and unhappy, but whenever she voiced these feelings, he'd shut down. Every request for time or affection felt like a criticism to him. Cammie asked him to try couples therapy and he said that was for married people who were about to get divorced. Cammie tried to change things, she really did. She felt like she was begging on a daily basis for him to pay attention to her and their relationship, until one day, she gave up, just like she felt Theo had given up. And the day she gave up, she saw Mark in a new way.

Mark paid attention to her. He remembered to ask her how her dentist appointment went because he knew she got anxious about any medical concerns. He brought her coffee in the morning, and he didn't balk when she said she wanted to go kayaking. The more Mark cared and paid attention, the more it stood out how little effort Theo put in. Maybe he took her for granted, or maybe he just didn't like her as much anymore; Cammie honestly didn't know.

The moment she kissed Mark should have been the end of things with Theo. So why did she stay so long? That's the thing she can't figure out. Maybe, Cammie wonders, she was worried on some level that Mark, as attentive and fun as he was, wasn't interested in a serious relationship with her. She saw it as a fling, a way to finally get some of her needs met while she waited for Theo to change. She's ashamed she let it go on for so long. Cammie had wanted to tell Theo that, but she was also so, so angry at him. Angry that he didn't listen to her pleas, angry that he stopped paying attention to their crumbling relationship, and angry that he got to feel self-righteously wronged by her infidelity when she had been feeling wronged and neglected for months.

As Cammie sobs in her apartment, where the wallpaper is peeling off at the corners, she finds herself wishing she could hug Theo and hear him say, "You messed up but it's okay. I finally get what you were trying to tell me. You need me to show up for you and for us, and I will. We'll get through this."

The Weaponization of Sociopathy

Sociopath is a fun word to use when we're mad at someone. First of all, it rolls of the tongue in a very satisfying way. Saying someone has antisocial personality disorder is a mouthful that doesn't pack the same punch. The word *sociopath*, by contrast, packs so much meaning into a few syllables. It communicates that the person we're referring to is awful (the worst of humanity!), that they hurt us and didn't care, and that everyone should hate them as a result. It's all-encompassing in its pathologizing—so relieving, so *easy*, to see someone who hurts us as a less-evolved human.

However, an armchair diagnosis of sociopathy overlooks a few important factors, as you'll see here.

1. We Mistake Non-Pathological Bad Behavior for Sociopathy

We call someone a sociopath when they act cruelly, appear emotionally unaffected by our pain, or seem unremorseful. I'll note that "act cruelly" covers a lot of ground—anything from ghosting (disappearing from a relationship without saying anything), breadcrumbing (leading someone on through small acts of interest), cheating (self-explanatory), yelling, stonewalling, and more. But, as you now know from chapter 7, people can be jerks without having a personality disorder. People can also be young or immature (or old and immature!) and act in unhealthy ways because they haven't figured out how to act better yet. They might be cruel but feel remorse. They might feel justified in how they treated you but still have empathy for how it hurt you. They might be exploiting you but simply not know any better.

Humans are a complicated species. Despite our amazing cognitive capacities and our innate desire to be good (well, most of us anyway), we often cause harm. People act in ways that can damage their relationships, both intentionally and unknowingly, but that doesn't make them sociopaths. In fact, anyone in a close and meaningful relationship will end up hurting the other person and will also end up getting hurt at some point because close relationships inevitably involve a degree of pain, be it disappointment, sadness, anger, or frustration. Even when we're doing our best, we hurt each other. We can't equate normal missteps and hurt with sociopathy.

2. We Want Our Exes to Be Sociopaths

People *love* to call their exes sociopaths, just like they love calling them narcissists. I don't know if weaponizing one is worse than the other. To me, calling someone a sociopath is extreme. You're calling them out as a human who has an underdeveloped (or nonexistent) capacity to be a law-abiding, respectful, moral member of society. And in doing so, you're saying they were the entire problem in your relationship. Unless you were with a person who displayed a variety of extreme behaviors that qualify as ASPD, that conclusion isn't fair, accurate, or serving you. Again, you're missing out on the opportunity to reflect on your part in the problem, examine how you could have been more effective in the relationship, and identify how you can change for the better in your next relationship. If you label your ex a sociopath and call it a day, you're cutting yourself short.

The colloquial use of the word *sociopath* is shorthand for uncaring. Take the Olivia Rodrigo song "good 4 u"—when she calls her ex "a damn sociopath" based on his finding a new relationship within a few weeks of breaking up, we understand that this simply means he isn't as distraught about the breakup as she is. But maybe it's not because he's uncaring; maybe it wasn't a good relationship for him. Or, perhaps, he did some growing during and after their relationship and was ready for a new, healthier relationship with someone else. That's the goal, after all: to learn from each relationship and try to do and be better in the next one. Calling an ex a sociopath might make you feel better ("It was all their fault, not mine! And I'm better off without them!"), but it's not true, and you owe it to yourself to acknowledge that.

3. We Ignore the Actual Criteria

We always seem to forget to consider whether the sociopath in question is displaying any problematic traits *besides* hurting us. Are they breaking laws? Do they exploit other people in their life? Have they shown empathy or regret at other times? Have they provoked physical altercations with others? Does this history of problematic behavior go back a long time, as in, since they were a kid or young adult? Remember, someone with ASPD doesn't display their traits in only one relationship or context; it's pervasive and persistent.

Let the record show that I have never seen someone use the term *sociopath* correctly in their relationship. Instead, people in a relationship with a true sociopath have a hard time seeing it because of the very traits that make that person sociopathic: They lie, manipulate, exploit, dominate the narrative, gaslight, play the victim when it suits them, and twist reality around. People in a relationship with someone who has ASPD don't know up from down, are riddled with self-doubt, question their perception of reality, and feel at fault for everything going wrong in the relationship. Like those with narcissistic partners, they usually need someone else to point out how unhealthy and abusive the other person is.

Does this mean no one can accurately spot a sociopath? No, of course not. Plenty of people have correctly identified a person in their life as being sociopathic or, the better way of saying it, having traits consistent with ASPD. When they do spot it, they probably don't call that person a sociopath to their face and try to change them because they know it won't work. People with ASPD have very little capacity to change, and even less desire to do so. The most a therapist can do is help teach some empathy and get them to agree to abide by society's rules, but it will take effort on the person with ASPD's part. It's a lifelong condition with no "cure," just management. So again, while you might enjoy calling someone a sociopath to make yourself feel better, you need

Are They a Sociopath, or Do They Just Like You Less Than You Like Them?

to remember that the word has a very heavy meaning. If you genuinely think you're dealing with someone who has ASPD, then this is a relationship you should think about exiting.

So, You've Been Accused of Being a Sociopath

It's likely that someone, probably an ex, hasn't called you a sociopath to your face, but maybe they told mutual friends or posted a thinly veiled accusation on social media. It's also possible someone in your life has charged you with being a sociopath, and if that happens, we're going to look at what you should do. You'll notice it's an almost identical playbook for what to do if you've been accused of being a narcissist; since ASPD and NPD are in the same personality disorder category, it makes sense your response would also be similar.

Ask Them to Explain

I'm guessing that by calling you a sociopath, the person wants to communicate that they think you don't care about them and are being selfish, but you need to know what happened that prompted this accusation. Try to present as curious and not outraged when you ask them to explain. (Although it would be understandable to be outraged, it won't help you figure out what happened.) Ask them to explain more clearly what you did or said that makes them think you're a sociopath.

Validate Their Feelings

I know it's hard to do when you've been accused of defying society's ethics and laws, but this person is clearly hurt, and they could use some validation. Recall from chapter 4 that validation doesn't mean you agree with what they're saying, it just means you understand it. Validating people's feelings helps them feel heard and calms their activated nervous system, which will then allow them to be more receptive to hearing your perspective and feelings.

Just like with NPD, people with ASPD lack empathy. By validating their emotions, you're demonstrating your ability to genuinely care about their feelings.

Share Your Side

The person accusing you probably thinks you were being selfish and coldhearted without any concerns for their feelings. This probably isn't true. Once you see that they feel a little better from your validation, share your side of the story. Explain how you were feeling and how this led to your actions in that moment. Offer your understanding of how this hurt them and express that you care that it hurt them. The point is to show them that you're a human with feelings and empathy, not a sociopath who's okay with stomping all over people.

Apologize if Necessary

I have to put this in here because, if someone went so far as to use the word *sociopath*, there's a chance you made a mistake, maybe even a big one. There's also a chance this person is weaponizing this term to control you, which is admittedly a much bigger problem. But assuming they called you a sociopath as a way of grabbing your attention and making sure you saw how hurt they were, consider if an apology is needed. If you could have done something better, then say so. It doesn't hurt to own your mistakes and admit you can grow; just don't take all the blame here.

Challenge Their Use of the Word

If this interaction is going well so far, now is the time to bring up the problem with using the word *sociopath* to describe what you did: It's not describing what you did, but *who you are* in a global way. Explain why their use of this word was hurtful and unfair, and express your concern about jumping to diagnosing serious personality disorders when one of you makes a mistake. Ask that they not pathologize you, no matter how hurt they are in the moment, and stick to sharing their feelings instead of making armchair diagnoses.

If They Won't Drop the Term, Get Help and Assess the Relationship

I'm having a hard time imagining that this person could still be convinced you're a sociopath after you do the aforementioned things, but it's possible that they've decided you're truly lacking in empathy and morality. If the other person sees you in such a rigidly negative light, you should also consider if this is a relationship you want to be in. Remember that abusive people can claim diagnoses and weaponize therapy terms as a way of gaining power and control; if that's what's happening, you need to be careful. You don't want to be in any relationship with someone who uses diagnoses to shame, inspire doubt, and control you. Plus, it's strange for them to truly believe you're a sociopath but not significantly distance themselves or end the relationship altogether. That alone should raise some questions for you about whether this is a relationship you want to be in.

So, You Think Someone Is a Sociopath

Some of you may be wondering if someone you know is a sociopath. After reading the criteria, perhaps some puzzle pieces are falling into place. Maybe you're seeing someone in a new context and dots are connecting, like how their history of quiet illegal conduct, volatile relationships, lack of remorse, and selfish, self-aggrandizing goals have made them a difficult and emotionally dangerous person to be in a relationship with. If you think you're dealing with a sociopath, here's what to do. Again, since ASPD and NPD share qualities, you'll notice the recommendations are almost identical.

Educate Yourself

As with narcissism, the best first step is to learn all about ASPD. Although the extreme criteria required for this diagnosis would make it seem easy to spot someone with this disorder, it can be challenging, particularly if they only meet the minimum three criteria and if they're skilled at concealing their lack of empathy. Read articles and books about what it's like to be in a relationship with someone who has ASPD, and see if the information resonates.

Gather the Evidence

If you know someone with ASPD, you should be able to see a pattern in their lack of empathy and unremorseful exploitation of those around them. Start taking note of instances of this possible pattern—notice when they lie, take advantage, deceive, and don't care. And don't focus solely on your relationship; look at how they interact with and treat other people in their life too.

Trust Your Gut

If you have an instinct about someone, listen to it. If their actions don't feel right, notice that feeling and reflect on it. If they seem disingenuous and make you uneasy, pay attention to that. I've sat in a room with a sociopath once and let me tell you, you feel yourself being pulled into their narrative, but alarm bells are going off in your head because you're being manipulated. I told my consultation group that it felt emotionally

Are They a Sociopath, or Do They Just Like You Less Than You Like Them?

unsafe in that room; if this is how you feel around this person, trust yourself. Remember to educate yourself and get other support too, but don't ignore that gut instinct.

Recruit Professional Help

If you're in any kind of relationship with someone who has ASPD, you need support. Even after educating yourself and documenting evidence, it'll be hard to trust yourself in this assessment, and having a qualified third party will help. Plus, people with ASPD tend to hurt those around them, and you may need someone to help you rebuild your self-esteem, set boundaries, or leave. Just as with NPD, a therapist can't diagnose this person with ASPD through secondhand information, but they can provide a reality check and feedback on the problematic behaviors and patterns they're observing.

Don't Tell Them They're a Sociopath

If you've determined with some confidence that this person has ASPD, part of you may want to shout it in their face. "I know you're a sociopath!" That instinct would be understandable, but doing so would not be effective. A sociopath wouldn't care, and it wouldn't change their behavior or feelings toward you. Plus, it could make them angry. An angry person with ASPD could lash out without any concern for your safety, so it could be dangerous to confront them.

Consider When and How to Leave

Unlike with narcissism, which can be workable with some people who have milder cases and more insight, staying with someone who has ASPD isn't recommended. People with this disorder can't have healthy relationships because they're lacking the emotional skills and motivation for it. When you read the criteria for ASPD, you see a person who is

They're Not Gaslighting You

self-focused to a fault, unremorseful, exploitative, and dangerous. Make a safe exit plan with the support of family, friends, a partner, or a therapist.

After It's Over, Focus on Healing

Once you're out, it's time to heal. Continue educating yourself about how it can affect people to be in a relationship with someone who has ASPD. Rebuild your self-esteem and self-trust. Invest in other parts of your life, parts that probably fell by the wayside when you were focused on trying to understand and fix this relationship. Explore possible areas of growth for other relationships, such as setting stronger boundaries or listening to your intuition. ■

Chapter 10

Are They Bipolar, or Did Their Mood Just Change?

Bipolar disorder is probably one of the first diagnoses to be weaponized, if not *the* first. People have been aware of bipolar disorder for a long time, far before people knew very much about personality disorders. Bipolar disorder is also commonly missed and misdiagnosed, making it a term that professionals and laypeople alike misunderstand. As you read about the details of this disorder and its variations, you'll see why.

Fiona Has Bipolar Disorder

Fiona can remember distinct periods of time in her life when she's been depressed. It's always been a part of her, for as long as she can remember. She just . . . stops caring. She hates her life in every way. She wants to stay in bed all day and pretend the world doesn't exist. She doesn't want to talk to anyone and gets very irritated when people try to reach out or help. Fiona can't help snapping when people are nice. Then she feels bad about snapping, which adds to her self-loathing.

Fiona's thankful she doesn't always feel depressed. She's also diligent about reconnecting with people once she feels better. This has been especially important since she started dating Aiden. He's a truly wonderful guy and she still can't believe he likes her, because while Aiden is all easygoing and even-keeled, Fiona feels like a hurricane. She is energetic and driven and, for lack of a better word, intense.

They're Not Gaslighting You

Meanwhile, Aiden is relaxed about basically everything, including Fiona's intensity. That is, until recently.

Fiona recently quit her "soul-sucking corporate job" and is on week two of her "funemployment." The past few days, however, have really *really* not been fun. After so many years of working, Fiona was excited to take time off to explore her hobbies and relax, but this time off hasn't been what she'd hoped for. It turns out that the structure provided by her work was important for her. Fiona did okay in the first week, trying to be productive around the house. But she couldn't seem to use her time efficiently and by now, any attempt at a routine is gone. Instead, she's been staying up until 4:00 a.m. writing a novel. She sleeps a few hours, then gets up when Aiden wakes up around 8:00 a.m. She's "cranky," as Aiden gently puts it, but a more accurate way to say it is that Fiona has been irritable and mean. Everything Aiden does seems to annoy her and she can't wait for him to leave for work so she can be alone.

But one night when Aiden comes home, he finds Fiona ready to explode with excitement. She's made some real progress on her novel, and she can't wait to tell Aiden every detail. This is the work she's really meant to do with her life and, if she's honest, Fiona genuinely thinks this novel is going to be a *New York Times* Best Seller. It has everything a great novel needs to be a massive success. This could define her! This could change her whole life's trajectory! And here's Aiden, living his boring life, not realizing she's about to experience this level of success. As soon as he walks in the door, Fiona is talking a mile a minute.

"Aiden! Hi, how are you, all that good stuff. I'm sorry but I can't wait to tell you about the novel. I had an epiphany today that the main character is *me* but she's me in the future once I've figured out the things that have gone wrong and fixed all of them. So, I'm writing my auto-biography but of me not right now, but in like five years, so a future autobiography? Is that what it's called? But anyway, Book Me doesn't see the signs until someone basically tells her to put her phone down and look around once in a while, you know? It's just like walking through

172

Are They Bipolar, or Did Their Mood Just Change?

the city and bumping into people because you're not really there, you're in your head, you're missing out on life, and Book Me does that!" Fiona says rapidly.

"Hey, can you slow down a bit?" Aiden is trying to listen while putting away his coat. "I'm having a hard time tracking all this. The book version of you is you in the future, I understand that part. But—"

Fiona interjects, "No, no, no. Okay, so I didn't explain it right. Book Me isn't really me in the future; it's me in the future in the *book*. But not real me; Book Me. Like a *nom de plume* but a written character. Okay? And that's why it's been so easy for me to write!" Fiona rushes on, gesticulating with excitement as she talks.

"I'm really not following any of this," Aiden confesses. "Maybe it'd be easier if I read some of the book. Can I read a chapter or something?" He's getting worried about Fiona. She's not making a ton of sense.

"How are you not getting this? Are you not listening to me right now? It's exactly what I've been telling you—*it's me in the book in the future. Book* Me, not *me* me." Her eyes narrow. "And guess what? You're not in the book. So that means we break up and it's probably because you doubt my ability to be a novelist, just like you doubt everything I do, and I'm sick of you questioning me and undermining me, just like everyone else, just another person saying I should slow down when I'm close to doing something *big*, just another naysayer and roadblock or barrier, those things the runners jump over in the Olympics, one of those, but one that gets knocked over when the runner *does* make it over. That's why I changed my laptop password to an *eighteen-letter code*, so no one deletes my novel or takes my idea to sell it themselves because everyone is only looking out for themselves and I'm looking out for *my*self. This book will be my *War and Peace*, my *Moby Dick*! You'll be crying into your sad little breakfast cereal some day when you see my name on the *New York Times* Best Seller list and I won't be sad for you at all!" Fiona finishes, out of breath and red in the face.

They're Not Gaslighting You

"What are you *talking* about?!" Aiden asks, half shouting and half pleading. "I asked if I could read a chapter because you are not making any sense right now! Now you're saying this book is going to be a best seller? And I'm a hurdle in the Olympics? I don't even understand what it's about! Why are you acting like this?"

"Oh my god, forget it!" Fiona throws up her hands. "I need to finish making dinner—just forget it." Aiden follows her into the kitchen and sees that there are chopped vegetables covering every surface—a bowl of chopped carrots on top of the toaster oven, a cutting board with chopped tomatoes balanced on the side of the sink, and trays of chopped peppers and onions on the counter. The kitchen is a mess.

"What's happening right now? Why did you cut up so many vegetables?" Aiden asks incredulously.

"I'm *cooking*! I'm doing what the chef said to do—you chop everything up one day and then cook it the other days. But I realized that's stupid; I can chop it *and* cook it the same day and we can have it all right away and I'll start with a lasagna and pasta and then make enchiladas or tacos and then use the rest for the stir fry, even though I know you don't like the stir fry but *I* like the . . . wait, stop talking!" Fiona suddenly shouts. "Get me my laptop! Grab it right now! I have an idea but if I don't write it down, I'll forget it!" Pushing Aiden aside to get to her laptop more quickly, she hurriedly opens it and pounds on the keys to wake it up, desperate to write down her idea.

Aiden quietly walks up behind her and looks over her shoulder at the Word document open on the screen. As Fiona bangs on the keyboard to record her thought, he reads what's already there and his stomach drops. The sentences are all incoherent ramblings. Nothing she has written makes sense. She says the same thing over and over in different ways; it's repetitive and impossible to follow. This novel is just like her ramblings from a moment ago.

Quietly, Aiden walks into the other room and calls his parents. He has no clue what to do, but he knows Fiona needs help.

Are They Bipolar, or Did Their Mood Just Change?

Defining Bipolar Disorder

In previous editions of the DSM, bipolar disorder was listed as a mood disorder and was classified in the same section as all the depressive disorders. However, the newest DSM identifies more than one form of bipolar disorder and gives these disorders their own category. The version of bipolar disorder that we tend to think of (and weaponize) is usually bipolar I, but there's also bipolar II as well as cyclothymia. As you read through the various criteria for the three disorders, you'll see why it can be so hard to accurately diagnose and so easy to weaponize.

1. **Bipolar I disorder:** To be diagnosed with bipolar I disorder, a person must have had at least one manic episode. That's right; no depressive episode necessary. Although it's typical for people with bipolar I to experience both depression and mania, it's not always the case. This makes it very important to define a manic episode:

   Manic episode: A period of abnormally elevated energy or mood lasting at least one week (or any duration if the person requires hospitalization). These elevations in energy or mood can present as euphoria, irritability, agitation, or anger. During this period of time, the person must also exhibit at least three of these symptoms: increased energy or activity, inflated self-esteem, decreased need for sleep, increased goal-directed activity, rapid speech, racing thoughts, distractibility, and risky behavior. Mania can sometimes involve psychotic symptoms as well, like delusions (having false, fixed beliefs not based on reality) and hallucinations (seeing or hearing things that are not there).

2. **Bipolar II disorder:** To meet criteria for this diagnosis, a person must experience at least one major depressive episode and at least one *hypomanic* episode—but not a full manic episode. This is notably different from bipolar I, where a depressive episode

They're Not Gaslighting You

isn't required, and a person experiences hypomania instead of mania.

Hypomanic episode: The criteria for a hypomanic episode are similar to those of a manic episode but are less severe and do not cause significant impairment. Plus, there are no psychotic features. The elevated mood must last at least four days (as opposed to the week required for a manic episode).

Major depressive episode: To meet criteria, a person must exhibit at least five of these symptoms for at least two weeks: depressed mood, loss of interest or pleasure, changes in appetite or weight, sleep disturbances, restlessness or sluggishness, fatigue, feelings of worthlessness or guilt, difficulty concentrating, and thoughts of death or suicide.

3. **Cyclothymic disorder:** The least extreme or impairing of this category, a person can be diagnosed with cyclothymia when they've had numerous periods of hypomanic symptoms as well as numerous periods of depressive symptoms that do not meet the criteria for a major depressive episode, over a period of at least two years. In addition, symptoms must be present at least half the time and a person shouldn't be symptom-free for more than two months at a time. Needless to say, diagnosing this disorder requires some very careful mood tracking.

As you can see, all these variations of bipolar disorder involve different presentations of elevated mood episodes. I once heard someone describe these disorders as an energy distribution issue; people have too much energy (manic or hypomanic), too little energy (depressive), or vacillate between the two.

Manic episodes are more intense and extreme than people realize. It's an incredibly elevated state where people lack good judgment and decision-making abilities, feel pressured to talk and act, and engage in

Are They Bipolar, or Did Their Mood Just Change?

very risky behaviors. When people with mania also exhibit psychotic symptoms, they might have extreme delusions such as thinking they can fly, but they don't always have this component. When someone is manic, they don't seem like themselves; they're irritable, harried, incomprehensible, and irrational. You can *feel* their elevated energy levels. Bipolar I disorder is often diagnosed when a person ends up hospitalized during a manic episode.

Hypomania is much harder to spot. It includes a similarly elevated mood and all the accompanying symptoms, but it's less severe. In a hypomanic state, someone might speak rapidly and be hyperfocused on an idea or topic, but colleagues or friends might not notice the difference. A person would still be able to go to work and function relatively normally, even though they're experiencing a real disruption in their sleep, arousal level, mood, and cognition. They may be able to internally notice the shift, and someone who sees a lot of them such as a parent or a partner can probably tell too, but it's not the dramatic shift of mania.

Some people think hypomania sounds great, and indeed, the increased energy, focus, and confidence it brings can be very productive and positive. Unfortunately, hypomania can come with extreme irritability that makes people easily annoyed and harsh. There's also no guarantee that the increased energy will get channeled effectively. When in a hypomanic state, some people end up pouring resources into an unnecessary project or splitting their attention between so many things that nothing is accomplished.

Additionally, in a manic or hypomanic state, people have a decreased desire for sleep. Even in an extreme manic episode, however, people still need *some* sleep. They just struggle to fall or stay asleep and get fewer hours than necessary. However, their body still needs the usual amount of sleep to be regulated, which is why people diagnosed with bipolar disorder need to be diligent about their sleep schedules.

Then, of course, there's the depressed component for bipolar II disorder and cyclothymia (and often bipolar I disorder). During a major depressive episode, a person feels sad, apathetic, hopeless, irritable, and sometimes suicidal. They struggle with basic daily tasks like brushing teeth or showering. Because these mood episodes and symptoms are easy to miss or attribute to something else, bipolar II and cyclothymia can take a very long time to diagnose. Many people talk about being misdiagnosed for years before finally getting an accurate diagnosis and treatment plan. Bipolar II is commonly mistaken for major depressive disorder, borderline personality disorder, ADHD, schizophrenia, and even posttraumatic stress disorder. To make it even more confusing, many of these disorders often co-occur and have overlapping symptoms. Someone with bipolar II and ADHD might, for example, wonder if their way of jumping from task to task is due to their inattention or hypomania. Many times, they won't get a clear answer.

Bipolar I is much easier to diagnose since mania is hard to miss. As you'll recall from the DSM criteria, a diagnosis of bipolar I requires just one manic episode; no need to get a history and find a depressive episode. Interestingly, this means a person could never have another manic episode again but still technically have bipolar I. It also means someone could have hypomanic episodes in the future, but never experience mania again, and still qualify for the bipolar I diagnosis. However, in this scenario, it would probably make more sense to diagnose them with bipolar II since hypomania appears much more prominent in their mood shifts. But this example shows how assigning disorders requires some subjectivity in clinical judgment.

We won't dive too deep into this, but it's worth noting that there are additional types within these diagnoses. For example, you can have *rapid cycling bipolar disorder*, when you experience four or more mood episodes (mania, hypomania, or depression) within a year. Some people experience rapid cycling for a period of time in their lives, whereas others consistently have more frequent mood episodes than others with the disorder. There's also *bipolar disorder with mixed features*, which is when

Are They Bipolar, or Did Their Mood Just Change?

someone experiences a mixed episode of depression and mania or hypomania at the same time or very close to the same time.

Not to make it more complicated, but there's also *bipolar disorder with seasonal pattern*, where the seasons can impact mood episodes. This is actually quite common. (As an interesting side note, did you know that spring is a terrible time for mental health? People are more likely to have manic episodes or die by suicide in spring than at any other time of year. Just another reminder that we're animals who are impacted by the world around us, including the amount of sunlight we're exposed to.)

You'll notice that minute-to-minute mood shifts are not part of the diagnosis for bipolar disorders. People who are bipolar experience mood *episodes*, which last days or weeks and are distinctly different from their mood baseline. However, the presence of mixed features makes it easier to weaponize this term. When a person is feeling both depressed and elated, it can be incredibly confusing and concerning. Apply this extreme affect to how they feel about the relationship, and it's not hard to see how we could call our partner bipolar when they dump us right after a romantic vacation, for example.

Bipolar disorder can make maintaining relationships very hard. This is particularly true pre-diagnosis, when a person is experiencing distinct mood episodes without understanding what's happening or how to manage it. It's not uncommon for people experiencing a mood episode to make harsh global statements about others that don't reflect how they truly feel. For example, a parent with bipolar disorder might fly into a rage over something small that, just a week earlier, they wouldn't have even noticed. A partner could feel overwhelmed with euphoria and want to elope, or they could be buzzing with irritability and claim they've always been unhappy in the relationship and want to leave.

When the mood episode is over, however, people could feel and act very differently. There's also a high comorbidity with substance use, as people with bipolar disorder often attempt to "even out" their moods through alcohol or drugs; this impacts relationships as well.

Many children of parents who have bipolar disorder talk about the emotional unpredictability in the house, overuse of drugs or alcohol, and the feeling that there were distinctly different versions of their parents depending on their moods.

However, there are great treatment plans for managing symptoms. The standard of care is medication (mood stabilizers like lithium or lamotrigine) and therapy. Tracking moods, identifying triggers, monitoring and prioritizing sleep, spotting early warning signs of a mood shift, managing stress, and increasing coping skills are all a part of good mood management. It's also helpful to have loved ones be involved, as they can help notice a change in mood, remind someone to take their meds, and so forth. For a great book about how to navigate bipolar disorder in a relationship, check out the resources section.

Stas *Doesn't* Have Bipolar Disorder

Stas loves his wife, Emmy. He loves their son, Cam, too. But he doesn't love his life. He knows his life looks perfect on paper and people think he's the luckiest man alive, but Stas isn't happy. He actually didn't want to have children, but he felt pressured into it by his wife, and so here they are.

Even though he does deeply love his son, being a father wasn't something he wanted. Stas hates waking up early with Cam to do a loud and messy breakfast, and he really hates driving everywhere for school and playdates and activities. He misses going out for leisurely dinners without hurrying home to pay the babysitter. He misses time with his friends, a clean house, a *quiet* house, and traveling. Stas also hates what having a kid has done to his marriage. The first year was full of fighting, the second year was a quiet truce, and now they're just so . . . distant. They haven't had sex in over a year. They make no effort to have date nights. They live parallel lives, with the only shared track being their son.

Are They Bipolar, or Did Their Mood Just Change?

Despite this, Stas is a great father and husband. He does everything he's supposed to, and even does it with a good attitude; he wasn't raised to be a pouter or a victim. But he's becoming unhappier by the day, and Emmy can tell. She notices that he is having a harder time getting up every morning and staying up way too late watching TV, and even though he's physically present when he needs to be, Emmy can tell he's emotionally far away. So, one day, she brings it up.

"You seem unhappy recently. Is everything okay? Something happening at work?" Emmy asks.

"I'm tired of everything," Stas replies unenthusiastically.

"Me too! So tired. Let's try to get to bed early tonight," Emmy answers, trying to be helpful.

They don't talk about it more. Stas wishes that Emmy would ask him why he is tired, but she doesn't. He feels alone in his suffering and believes that Emmy just wants to make it all go away with a quick suggestion like getting more sleep. Stas stews in this feeling for a week—how alone he is, how unheard, how unhappy—before walking into the kitchen one evening while Emmy is prepping dinner.

"Emmy, I'm so sorry that this is going to be a surprise to you, but I'm not happy in our life. I think I want to leave," Stas says.

"What?" Emmy asks in shock.

"I've been unhappy for a long time; I think you know that. I just don't see how I can keep living this life and not be unhappy every day. I need to make a drastic change," he replies.

"Stas, I asked you last week if you were okay, and you said you were just tired. Where the hell is this coming from?" Emmy asks, blindsided and angry.

"Like I said, I've been feeling this way for a while. I know this isn't fair to you and I'm so sorry, but I feel trapped. I feel like if I don't do something, I'll slowly suffocate. I feel like I'm drowning on land," he says.

"So, you jump right to leaving me? What about talking to me about it first? Or trying couples therapy? Or *something*! This isn't like you.

They're Not Gaslighting You

You've been depressed. I really do think you have depression, and suddenly you're saying you want to leave? You literally told me two weeks ago how you can't imagine your life without Cam, and now you're saying you've been unhappy for *years*? That's crazy, Stas!" Emmy exclaims.

"I know I said that, and I meant it—he's the best part of my life! But I'm still not happy. I feel like a monster saying this, but I didn't really want kids, you know that. I *do* love Cam, but I don't like the way my life has changed since having him. I don't know what else will fix it besides leaving," Stas says, crying.

"You're having a mental breakdown right now. You're clearly depressed, and you don't mean what you're saying. You've got to be bipolar because you're not in your right mind. This is crazy. We just booked a vacation to your favorite hotel. You were so excited to go! *You* signed Cam up for soccer so you could take him every Saturday! How can you go from making plans with our family to wanting to *leave* our family?!" Emmy shouts.

The conversation continues like this. Stas tries to explain how he was doing his best to invest in their life, to see if he could make it one he'd be happy in, but he's realized it's not possible. Emmy keeps throwing out examples of how present and engaged he's been, how happy he's seemed, and trying to convince him his desire to leave is a result of a psychological breakdown.

Stas understands her point. He has worked hard to appear like a great father and husband to his family and to the world. He has kept his inner suffering a secret, hoping he could change how he felt. Stas can't really answer the "Why now?" question that Emmy keeps asking. He's hit a breaking point he didn't know existed. It's not fair to her—after all, he could have volunteered to share more—but to him, that exchange showed how distant their relationship has become and how much he needs a change.

Stas moves out, and Emmy calls his mother, saying he has abandoned the family. Emmy insists that Stas must be bipolar. One day, he's

Are They Bipolar, or Did Their Mood Just Change?

booking a vacation, the next, he's "suffocating" and has to leave. She's read about people who have these sudden manic breaks and start talking nonsense and making huge, impulsive decisions. Stas will realize what he's done once he's in his right mind and come back.

The Weaponization of Bipolar Disorder

The word *bipolar* has been thrown around as an insult or accusation for quite some time. It's almost always referring to an extreme emotion or mood shift, and it's also almost always used incorrectly. The misuse of this word is quite similar to how people weaponize borderline personality disorder (which you'll learn about in chapter 12), in that someone exhibiting a strong negative emotion is labeled as pathological. But weaponizing this term is problematic because it increases stigma for those who have bipolar disorder and cuts off any possibility of an open conversation.

Here are the top four mistakes we typically make when we misuse the term *bipolar*.

1. We Assume Strong or Sudden Feelings Are Pathological

We all have strong feelings sometimes, and while it might be hard for those around us, it's not a clinical issue. Some people show their feelings in an outward, demonstrative way, where the whole world knows, while others keep their feelings hidden. Having big feelings is not in itself pathological. Think about kids! Kids have huge feelings about every little thing, and their feelings change second to second, but we don't diagnose them as all being bipolar. Instead, we teach them how to manage their feelings and regulate their bodies.

Telling your loved one that their strong feelings must mean they have a disorder is almost guaranteed to minimize their experience and make them feel unheard and unsafe with you. It's the next level of saying "calm down" when someone is upset. Has saying that ever worked to help someone calm down? No, it hasn't, because even if someone were overreacting and their feelings were arguably out of proportion to the situation, being told to calm down would only make them feel invalidated and compel them to prove why their reaction makes sense, which inevitably leads them to amplify their reaction.

Big feelings are soothed by validation, understanding, and curiosity. In contrast, big feelings are fueled by accusations, judgments, and name-calling. Calling someone bipolar when they're upset cuts off any potential for a vulnerable, honest conversation about what's going on and makes them feel judged, even shamed, for having their feelings. This is no way to connect with someone and navigate their emotions together.

2. We Assume Mood Changes Are Pathological

Just as all humans sometimes have strong feelings, all humans have mood changes. That's something we clinicians talk about in therapy quite a lot—no matter what your mood is right now, it will eventually change. We can't say when it will shift, but sure enough, it'll happen. Sometimes these shifts in mood can be quite dramatic—you go to bed happy, and you wake up depressed. This can be due to a situational factor, like getting an angry email from your boss first thing in the morning, but sometimes it's an inexplicable change that you can't figure out the trigger for.

Someone you love might be very affectionate toward you one day and then be incredibly irritated with you the next, but that doesn't mean they have bipolar disorder. Maybe they had a bad night's sleep and are generally irritable, and you're collateral damage. Maybe they're fed up with being the only person who makes doctor's appointments for your kids, and for whatever reason, their built-up frustration explodes on that day. Your dad could be loving most of the time but get

Are They Bipolar, or Did Their Mood Just Change?

uncharacteristically icy with you because he disapproves of your decision to go skydiving (but he doesn't want to tell you, so you have no idea why he's being rude). People usually have reasons for being upset with people they love; even if those reasons feel unfair to you, it's worth exploring.

Having quick or frequent mood changes does not equal bipolar disorder. As you'll recall, a diagnosis of bipolar disorder requires a manic or hypomanic episode. That's very different from someone whose feelings about a person or relationship happen to change. Because guess what? Our feelings about these things *do* change! There have been times when I've thought, *I don't know if I can be married to Lucas forever.* Those times have been when we're deep in conflict and can't seem to find our way back out. No joke, two days later, when we're out of the dark times (as I call them), I think to myself, *There's literally no other person I'd want to spend my life with except Lucas.* Those are indeed two polar opposite ways to think about my spouse. Nevertheless, I do not have bipolar disorder. I am simply a person whose feelings change depending on external circumstances, and those shifts can seem sudden or dramatic at times.

Conflating mood changes with bipolar disorder involves a misunderstanding of elevated mood states; we can wrongly think that anxious energy or even attentional issues are hypomania. I, too, have periods when I "frenzy," as Lucas and I jokingly refer to it, when I get in a zone of frantic productivity and clean and organize a part of our house with sudden and unexpected vigor. This short burst of focused energy doesn't last long, and it's definitely not my normal state of operating, but it's not a hypomanic episode. I don't have any other symptoms besides more energy, and it doesn't last the four days (or seven, for mania) required for a clinical diagnosis. I am slightly more irritable during these bursts, particularly if Lucas slows me down. These moments would be prime opportunities for him to accuse me of being bipolar. After all, twenty-four hours earlier, I was probably proclaiming how it's perfectly acceptable to have a messy house when you have young kids, and now

I'm threatening to throw away every toy I can find (especially the loud ones). But this armchair diagnosis would be inaccurate, and it would also make me feel criticized and deflated. It also wouldn't help Lucas express what he's really feeling, which is confusion about my change of mind and some stress about my frenzied state.

3. We Assume the Conflict Makes No Sense

In my experience, the most common situation in which bipolar disorder is weaponized is during a fight or after a breakup. People will claim that the argument or breakup happened because the other person was bipolar and suddenly blew up or exited the relationship as a result. They can't reconcile how a person could have been happy (enough) in a relationship with them, only to suddenly get upset about something or end things on what they consider insufficient grounds. If you don't get why your friend isn't talking to you over something as small as not wishing them happy birthday on social media, or confused as to why your parent is freaking out about getting the house organized for Thanksgiving, or upset that your ex left you when you thought things were great, you can just point to bipolar disorder and make sense of it all.

I get it, I really do. If you think I haven't mentally diagnosed an ex as part of the "I don't care that it's over!" phase of a breakup, then you're wrong. (Sorry, Noah—you've had a lot of diagnoses over the eight years we dated.) Doing this in moderation can, in fact, help us heal by allowing us to dampen our loving feelings so that the loss isn't as painful. When we have an explanation that makes more sense and helps us view our partner as less desirable, we can convince ourselves that we're better off without them. Personally, I feel okay with people using this coping mechanism for a little while. But eventually, we have to let go of the imagined diagnosis so we can examine the relationship's ending more critically and gain insights that we can carry forward into our next relationship (this applies to other relationships too, such as friendships). If we stay at the "They must have been bipolar" stage, we miss an important opportunity for self-reflection and growth.

4. We Simply Don't Understand the Other Person

Bipolar is a great catch-all term when we have no clue why someone is feeling or acting in a certain way. Unreasonably mad at us? Bipolar. Giddy about something silly? Bipolar. Suddenly irritable and throwing away the kids' toys? Bipolar. Throwing a fit because our spouse-to-be won't invite all our book club friends to our wedding? Totally bipolar. The term is used to reflect our confusion about what triggered someone's reaction.

However, when we use a diagnosis to explain something that confuses us, we miss a huge opportunity to understand our loved ones. Instead of assuming someone's grouchy mood is because they have a disorder, we should be curious. Why are they so grumpy? Did something happen at work, or did we upset them somehow? Or is it just an inexplicable mood shift that even they can't explain? Can we give them some space to feel what they're feeling, whether for a reason or out of nowhere, and be accepting?

It's also worth pointing out that we don't always need to know why someone's mood changes. We don't have the same mood forever, no humans do, and giving people in our lives the space to have shifting emotional states is a necessary part of being in a relationship. Not every part of our emotional experience needs to be analyzed and understood. Sometimes it's enough to say, "Huh, they're feeling pretty tense today. I'll be kind since I can tell they're not feeling great and if they want to talk, I'll be here for it."

Bipolar disorders involve significant shifts in mood and accompanying symptoms. They're much more than someone changing their mind or feeling a way that we don't understand. When we weaponize bipolar disorder, we're invalidating our loved one's emotions and dismissing their needs. Moreover, if someone we love does have undiagnosed bipolar disorder, weaponizing the term during a fight will make them less likely to actually consider our concerns and seek help.

So, You've Been Accused of Having Bipolar Disorder

You may have experienced a loved one labeling you as bipolar because you felt or acted a certain way that they felt was extreme or nonsensical. The way they say it will matter a lot, of course. Tone changes everything, and since I don't know whether they communicated this to you with blame or with genuine concern, I'll give you a general game plan for the best way you can respond.

Take a Breath

You need to be in a calm place where you are responding to the other person with intention instead of reacting impulsively. Take a few deep breaths or walk away for a longer break if needed. If you blow up at them, it will only fuel their conclusion that your moods are out of control and you have a disorder.

Check In with Yourself

Do a quick assessment of your mood. Are you in a depressed state? Unusually joyful and energetic? Has your mood changed suddenly without apparent triggers? Are you feeling a little out of control with your speech or actions, or noticing that others can't follow what you're saying? Have other people mentioned this to you before? Is there a family history of bipolar disorder? You're asking yourself these questions to start understanding why someone might be confused or concerned about your mood and if there's other evidence that you might have this disorder. If you see their point, it's a good time to get evaluated by a mental health professional.

Ask Them to Clarify

I can have you self-reflect all day, but you'll also need to hear from the person about why they used that word. Ask them to explain what they saw in your mood or behavior that made them say you were bipolar. Is it because you're fighting and they don't understand how you feel? Or do they have actual concerns about your mood's stability? Basically, you're trying to figure out if they weaponized the term or if they have legitimate concerns you need to address.

Explain as Needed

If the person is merely confused about your mood shift or current emotional state, try to explain it. You can share what triggers or other contributing factors explain why you're feeling or acting a certain way. Providing this information may help them understand where you're coming from.

Address the Weaponization

If it turns out the other person weaponized the word *bipolar*, it's worth having a conversation about how this made you feel and why you don't think it's a productive way to work through concerns or issues. Explain how their jumping to a diagnosis makes it hard to have a vulnerable and productive conversation, and ask if you can both commit to avoiding weaponized therapy speak.

If They're Genuinely Concerned, Make a Plan

If the person is still genuinely concerned that you have bipolar disorder, hear them out. Maybe they've seen patterns in your mood that suggest something more is going on. Maybe it's a parent or a friend who's noticed a trend of worsening symptoms over the years and is finally speaking up. If you think they may have a point, it's worth getting a clinical evaluation from a qualified therapist. Either you do meet the criteria for bipolar disorder and can start a treatment plan, or you don't, and now you both have that knowledge.

If They're Weaponizing It, Consider Your Options

Sometimes, persistent weaponization of therapy terms is an abuse tactic. Even if it's not this extreme, the continued use of a clinical term is problematic. If someone keeps calling you bipolar despite your requests that they not, you need to consider possible next steps. That could include having another, more serious, conversation about this issue, setting some new boundaries, or ending the relationship altogether.

So, You Think Someone Has Bipolar Disorder

If you read the clinical criteria for bipolar disorder and thought someone you know might have it, then here's what to do.

Be Calm and Kind When You Tell Them

Don't bring up your concerns during a fight. Bring it up during a time of peace in your relationship. To have the best chance of being heard, find a calm moment and be compassionate with how you explain the symptoms you've noticed. Gently point out where their behavior has seemed extreme or has interfered with their life.

Acknowledge That You Don't Know

It will help if you acknowledge, right from the start, that you don't actually know if they have bipolar disorder. You're not an expert, and even if you are, you're not able to diagnose someone you know. By saying that this is just your thought based on observations and not a conclusion you're making with any clinical confidence, you remove yourself from a judgmental position in this conversation. Instead, be this person's teammate, expressing concern and a desire for them to consider what you're saying.

Ask for Consideration and Exploration

You don't need the other person to refute or accept the diagnosis in this conversation. What you're asking is that they start to become more aware of and reflect on their mood states and possibly consider a professional evaluation. This might be the first time someone's bringing this up to them and, if they do have bipolar disorder, it can be scary to consider this possibility.

Set Realistic Expectations

It's unlikely that the person will see your point and immediately seek an evaluation or therapy. This is especially true if they are in a manic or hypomanic mood state, where their ability to self-assess is impaired. Plus, if their elevated mood state involves euphoria, they'll be feeling great, so they won't understand the problem. This might be a conversation you have many times before they agree to seek help.

Prepare for the Two Possible Outcomes of an Evaluation

The person you're worried about might be surprisingly receptive to your concerns and seek an evaluation. One of two things will happen. First, the evaluation could determine they don't have bipolar disorder. If this happens, you'll then have to address whatever behaviors and mood shifts led you to this conclusion in a new way. Second, they could get diagnosed with bipolar disorder. Then your job will be to support them as they navigate the complicated health care system to get therapy, medication, and any additional help they might need.

Remember It's Okay to Leave

We all feel guilty leaving a relationship because the other person is struggling with a mental health issue, but at the end of the day, we have to do what's best for us. Some people can weather the mood shifts and accompanying symptoms of bipolar disorder; some people can't. If you're in a relationship with someone who refuses to get help or if their mood episodes are too difficult for you to tolerate even with help, it's okay to leave. ◼

Chapter 11

Did They Violate Your Boundaries, or Did They Just Not Know How You Felt?

Boundaries are important pillars of communication and respect, but they aren't the be-all and end-all line in the sand we may think they are. As you'll learn, some boundaries are universal and uncrossable, but the majority vary from person to person and, as a result, need to be expressed and, at times, negotiated. Claiming a boundary violation is a quick and easy way to control someone's behavior, and that's why it's important to clarify what this phrase means and how to healthily navigate boundaries in a relationship.

Holly Violated a Boundary

Morris and Holly have been together for just under a year. Their biggest issue has been dealing with Morris's family. Or to be more accurate, their biggest issue is *Holly's* trouble dealing with Morris's family. Morris always thought he had a pretty solid relationship with his parents. They support him emotionally and help him out with money when he needs it, which Holly thinks is a sign they're trying to control him. Sure, they make little comments here and there about what they wish he'd consider (namely, law school—it's *always* law school for them), but they accept

They're Not Gaslighting You

his choices. Holly says she's protective of him and that's why she bristles every time law school is mentioned. She even suggests his parents are abusive because they want to control him, but when Morris gets upset, Holly murmurs, "Fine, fine, just think about it."

This is what Morris fell in love with: Holly's fiery spirit. She's confident and brave and doesn't care what people think of her. But the flip side of this is that Holly can steamroll people. She has strong opinions and an unfailing moral compass; some might even call her self-righteous to the point of destruction. Morris has heard people say that about her, and he gets it. But Morris has talked to Holly about her attitude toward his father several times. He gets Holly's frustration, but he really wants them to have a good relationship. Plus, it's *his* father and thus *his* annoying conversation to deal with.

Morris has told Holly in no uncertain terms how he doesn't feel comfortable with her interjecting on his behalf. He's explained that this is his relationship to manage, and although he appreciates her support, he needs Holly to be supportive behind the scenes. Morris has also explained that this is a matter of autonomy to him. He needs to know Holly will give him the space to independently deal with times when his parents annoy him about law school. Morris had an ex-girlfriend who liked to manage his relationships to a point that felt really controlling, and he's still healing from that.

Holly says she understands why this is important to Morris and that she'll back off, even though she acknowledges it will be hard for her. Morris believes her but, knowing Holly can let her emotions take over, he worries it might happen again. Unfortunately, he is proven right one weekend while they are at Morris's family home in Vermont. Like clockwork, Morris's father drops a not-so-subtle comment about how law school applications are down this year, and people are finding it easier to get in. Morris internally rolls his eyes and is about to respond, but Holly beats him to it. She raises her voice and lays into Morris's dad.

Did They Violate Your Boundaries, or Did They Just Not Know How You Felt?

"Oh my god, enough of this. We're sick of hearing you talk about law school whenever we see you. He doesn't want to go to law school, okay? This is so narcissistic, trying to make him do something you want. I'm sorry, but I can't listen to you do this one more time!"

Morris is mortified and furious. He can't believe Holly has done what he explicitly asked her not to do and, even worse, that she has spoken for him. Now, his dad probably thinks he's as angry as Holly, but he isn't. Sure, it annoys him to get reminders about the future his parents wanted for him, but he certainly isn't angry about it. His dad looks so wounded, like he is on the verge of tears. "I didn't realize it was that upsetting," he murmurs before leaving the room.

Morris turns to Holly in disbelief. "How could you do that? I told you not to interfere with this. I told you he would inevitably bring up law school but that I wanted to handle it *my* way with him since he's *my* dad. Why did you blow up at him when I asked you not to get involved?"

"I know it's easy for you to be a pushover, but *I* don't like seeing people get walked all over," Holly answers without remorse. "He finally gets how annoying it is, and I bet he'll stop bringing it up, so you're welcome."

Morris decides he has to end things with Holly. Maybe if she had apologized for overstepping and then tried to repair things with his dad, he could imagine staying together, but instead, Holly doubled down on her outburst and remained cold to both his parents for the rest of the day. They leave that evening, not staying the night like they originally planned. Morris has asked Holly several times to respect this boundary and she either doesn't care or can't do it, and that is all the information he needs to end the relationship.

Defining Boundaries and Boundary Violations

Just as sovereign countries are bounded by designated borders between them, relationship boundaries are the social limits that distinguish acceptable behaviors from behaviors that intrude on our autonomy. Boundaries designate the line between safe, totally fine behaviors and behaviors that make us feel unsafe or infringe on our personal rights.

A boundary violation occurs when someone crosses that line by acting in a way that makes us feel as though our sense of personal control has been taken away. There are some boundaries we all agree are important and should be uncrossable—I call these *universal boundaries*. Violating universal boundaries, especially when done repeatedly without remorse or regard for the impact it has on the other person, amounts to abuse. Moreover, just as there are different types of abuse, which you'll recall from chapter 3, there are corresponding types of universal boundaries. The main ones are emotional, physical, sexual, and financial boundaries (and more, but we won't be able to cover everything). There can be some crossover between these boundaries, as you can imagine. For example, violating a person's physical boundary will also likely cross an emotional one too. There's no need to be very specific on which type of boundary is crossed when it happens; it's enough to know that there are different categories, and one significant boundary violation might lead to a slew of others.

Did They Violate Your Boundaries, or Did They Just Not Know How You Felt?

Universal Boundaries

Emotional	Physical	Sexual	Financial
Degrading or humiliating someone	Hitting, punching, slapping, or choking someone	Forcing nonconsensual sexual acts	Demanding someone give up control over their money or outright stealing it
Gaslighting someone and making them doubt their own reality	Restraining someone, preventing them from leaving a room	Requiring a sexual act as a show of commitment or as an apology	Limiting access to shared funds without reasonable cause
Controlling who someone can talk to or be friends with	Threatening someone or another living being in the home (e.g., pets, children)	Engaging in unwanted sexual touching despite being told to stop	Withholding money as punishment or in retaliation
Mocking what someone says, especially when done publicly	Throwing items as a threat or to harm another	Refusing to use birth control despite being asked to do so	Giving an "allowance" or budget as a way of controlling another

They're Not Gaslighting You

With universal boundaries, there's no room for leeway or nuance. If one of these boundaries is crossed, particularly repeatedly and without remorse, it constitutes abuse. That's why this accusation carries so much weight; telling someone they've "crossed your boundaries" can insinuate they've committed an abusive act.

Outside of these universal, uncrossable boundaries, there are also *individual boundaries.* Rather than applying to all people, these boundaries are specific to the person and defined by their own preferences and needs. As such, they are flexible, fluid over time, and full of nuance. If they are crossed, it can be uncomfortable, but it isn't necessarily abuse.

Since individual boundaries are much less rigid and permanent than universal boundaries, they can vary depending on the relationship or situation. For example, you might hold a firm boundary for privacy with coworkers but find this boundary less essential with close friends or partners. Likewise, you might be fine with your spouse kissing your neck at home, but you wouldn't want them to do it at a school event for your kids. These boundaries may also change over time in a specific relationship as people become closer, encounter new difficulties or hurts, mature, or grow apart. This is because what individuals need to feel safe across types of relationships and within relationships is not static; as a person or relationship changes, their boundaries tend to shift as well. Finally, individual boundaries can be discussed, negotiated, and sometimes adjusted. You might have a boundary to only speak to your mother once a month because you have a tough relationship with her, but if she is really sick and she asks to talk more frequently, maybe you'll call a little more often.

It's vital to understand that you need to directly express your individual boundaries, or else people will discover them only after they have been crossed. Identifying these boundaries might feel vulnerable, and explicitly stating them can be uncomfortable, but people are not mind readers. Without making your individual boundaries known, you leave

Did They Violate Your Boundaries, or Did They Just Not Know How You Felt?

the door open to having them "discovered" after someone inadvertently violates them.

It's also important to note that a boundary is not the same as a preference. We all have things we'd like to happen (or not happen), but a preference isn't automatically a boundary. A boundary is a line drawn to ensure safety and autonomy, whereas a preference is something that would make you feel happy but is not integral to your sense of relational security or independence. For example, some people think it's perfectly fine to talk less often with their partner when one of them is traveling. They might enjoy the quiet or time to themselves. But another person might get angry and anxious if they don't hear from their partner who's away and would rather talk more frequently. Neither person is right or wrong; they just have different preferences.

As you'll read a little later in this chapter, knowing whether someone has violated a universal or individual boundary will guide how you respond.

Lily *Didn't* Violate a Boundary

Ada and Lily are best friends within a larger group of friends who all met at college and have stayed close post-graduation. The group is fun and supportive, and they also happen to inter-date one another quite frequently. That last factor can make their group dynamic even more fun (and it helps a lot with vacation planning—fewer rooms are needed when everyone is coupled up!), but it can also make things hard when a breakup happens. This is what happened when Britt, another friend in the group, ended things with Ada a week ago.

Britt and Ada were chaotic from the start. The collision of their strong personalities created a lot of drama, and their relatively short relationship was jam-packed with hurt. Ada feels especially sensitive about it; she thinks Britt was cruel in how she ended things, not least in doing it over the phone instead of in person. While Ada accepts that

They're Not Gaslighting You

Britt can't just magically disappear from her life, given the many friends they have in common, it would make her life a lot easier if Britt moved across the world right about now.

Instead of disappearing or moving, however, Britt is having a birthday party and invites their whole friend group, Ada included. Ada thinks this was a jab, even though all her friends say it was intended to be kind and inclusive. Ada asks another member of their friend group, Lily, to go out for lunch so she can talk through the party situation.

"I just don't understand how it could have been about being nice. You dump someone, then invite them to celebrate you? Like, no thanks! I feel like she's trying to steal the whole friend group in the breakup, which is really unfair because *she* is the one who ended things," Ada says.

"I hear you, babe, I really do. I think it's just tough. The birthday party was already scheduled, and I don't think she wants you to feel hurt or excluded if you're the only one not invited, you know?" Lily offers.

"I guess. I don't know. Whatever—I'm over it." Ada takes a deep breath. "Anyway, what do you want to do that night? Burn some sage to get her essence out of my apartment so I can move on from this?"

The joke hangs in the air between them for a moment.

"Well . . . I was actually going to go to her birthday," Lily says gently. "I told her yes before you guys broke up. I think you should come too, even just for a bit. It might help put things behind you."

"You're not serious right now," says Ada.

"Yeah, I am. Everyone's going, and you should too!" Lily replies.

"Wow. I can't believe you'd go to her party after how she treated me. She was so dismissive and made me so insecure, then *dumped me*, and you're going to go celebrate that person?" Ada snaps.

"Babe, I know she did some really not okay things, but I think it was just a very complicated relationship. You know I love you, and I get your side, but I don't want to be put in the middle. You're my bestie, but you're both my friends, and I was thinking this could be a chance to move forward," Lily tentatively says.

Did They Violate Your Boundaries, or Did They Just Not Know How You Felt?

"Honestly, I think it's really disrespectful of you to go. You're choosing her side if you do—you get that, right? It's such a boundary violation. I'd never expect a friend to act like that. I'd just feel like I couldn't trust you again, knowing that you didn't care about my boundary with something this important," Ada responds.

Lily is at a loss. She knows Ada is hurt by the breakup, but she doesn't want to make this rift in the friend group even worse by choosing sides. She thinks Ada did some things wrong in the relationship too but doesn't want to say that right now. Hearing that Ada considers this a boundary violation makes Lily feel very anxious. She can't go to the party now since Ada will see it as a breach of trust in their friendship. But that's not fair, is it? Then Ada would be policing who Lily can be friends with. She wishes Ada could be upset and disappointed about people staying friends with Britt but also understand that her breakup doesn't mean the end of the entire friend group and that asking people to take sides isn't fair.

The Weaponization of Boundary Violations

As you've learned, claiming that a boundary violation has occurred (when it hasn't) is problematic. At best, it can lead the other person to feel uncomfortable or upset. At worst, it can be way for abusers to control another person. As discussed in chapter 3, actual abusers have caught on to this tactic, setting overly broad limits on another person (e.g., "It's my boundary that you do not talk to people of the opposite sex") and making it seem as though that person is unreasonable or disrespectful if they don't rigorously hold themselves to those limits. One way to spot this form of weaponization is the unhealthy way abusive people enforce their "boundaries." While a well-adjusted person might start a dialogue about how to negotiate an individual boundary in a way that honors both partners' needs, an abusive person will never consider if their boundary can be shifted or why it might be damaging or significantly limiting to the other person. Instead, they will accuse, blame, and manipulate their partner as their way of keeping that person within their controlling limits.

As you can see, when abusers weaponize boundary violations, they do so for the purpose of gaining power and control. However, when well-intentioned people incorrectly claim that a boundary violation has occurred, they are generally making one of four errors.

1. We Think Our Boundaries Should Be Obvious to Others

We all have different expectations and things that make us uncomfortable. More often than we'd like, we only recognize a boundary we have *after* someone has crossed it. For example, imagine that you've recently taken a dating relationship to "exclusive status." You and your new partner agree you don't want to be jealous or possessive of each other. However, the next time you're out together, you notice that your partner feels free to innocently flirt with others, and it bothers you—a lot, in fact. To you, it feels like just a step short of full-on cheating. You could claim a boundary violation and accuse them of cheating, but would that be fair? After all, your partner is still learning the limits of the relationship, which means learning how your lines are different from another person's. How can they know this bothers you unless you explicitly tell them, "Hey, I don't think flirting is okay once we're exclusive"? The answer, of course, is by accidentally crossing the boundary and realizing that it upset you.

The point is that boundary violations are an inevitable part of the process of developing a relationship with someone. When someone you're close to unknowingly does something that crosses a line, it isn't helpful to accuse them of violating your boundaries. They're still

Did They Violate Your Boundaries, or Did They Just Not Know How You Felt?

learning your individual boundaries and will continue to throughout your entire relationship, as you will for them.

Many individual boundaries are lines in the sand, as opposed to concrete. They move or even disappear depending on a person's self-esteem, life experiences, maturity level, and relationship security. When I was a teenager, I had a strict "no friends with exes" policy for myself and my boyfriends. I hated when my high school boyfriend, Noah (prom breakup guy, if you recall), stayed in contact with Aaliyah, a girl he'd flirted with and who clearly liked him. Even after being together for a year, I really didn't want them talking or hanging out. Today, though, not only is my husband, Lucas, still friends with his ex-girlfriend, but *I'm* friends with her too. She's absolutely lovely and I can't imagine considering it a boundary violation for Lucas to have her in his life. I might as well share that I was also more rigid with friendships in the past. I had unreasonably high expectations and would feel mortally wounded when friends didn't measure up to them; finding out a friend was being nice to someone I didn't get along with would feel like a personal affront. If that happened now, though, I wouldn't think twice because I'm more secure in myself and thus in my relationships.

On the other hand, perhaps you're someone who used to be a lot more trusting and open in relationships, only to be burned by a partner who cheated or a friend who took advantage of you. For example, maybe on a fun night out you let a close coworker record the two of you drunkenly singing karaoke but, after finding out they showed the video to your boss, you decide not to socialize as casually with workplace friends. As a result, your boundaries may become a lot more constricted, at least for a while, where things that didn't bother you in the past now feel like acts of betrayal or cruelty.

The point is that as we go through life, our boundaries shift. As you can see, this is part of what makes it difficult for people to anticipate or assess boundary violations. If you expect and demand that the people

They're Not Gaslighting You

close to you honor your specific boundaries on certain topics, but you're not telling them what the boundaries are or when and how they've changed, you're setting your loved ones up for failure.

2. We Confuse Universal and Individual Boundaries

We know that there are important limits in all relationships that, when crossed, equal abuse. Again, these are universal boundaries that our society follows to protect people's safety and autonomy. However, many people confuse these boundaries with the kind that are person-specific. They think that a colleague calling after work hours ("You're manipulating me into working unpaid hours"), a friend ordering food on their phone without asking ("You're taking my property"), or their partner grabbing them from behind for a sexy snuggle when they're not in the mood ("You're infringing on my bodily autonomy"), are instances of universal boundary violations when, in reality, they're individual boundary violations *specific to them*. The examples above *aren't* universal boundaries. For example, I don't care if someone contacts me in the evening (I just won't answer), my friends can use my phone whenever they want (if I unlock my phone for them, that is), and if Lucas pulled me close when I wasn't in the mood, I'd just tell him that.

And again, people unknowingly cross each other's individual boundaries all the time. It's simply inevitable. If it feels like a boundary violation when someone uses your DoorDash account without first asking permission, that's valid, but it's essential to let them know that's how it feels before you accuse them of violating your boundary. Remember that individual boundaries only become known after they're communicated or crossed, so having a violation is an opportunity to discuss what lines are important to you. Blowing up at them before doing so will create an unnecessary and unproductive rift.

Did They Violate Your Boundaries, or Did They Just Not Know How You Felt?

3. We Mistake Preferences for Boundaries

Boundaries protect our needs for safety and security. Preferences promote feelings of happiness, pleasure, or calm. When someone crosses a boundary, it compromises our physical or mental health. When someone disregards a preference, we may feel annoyed, but it doesn't pose a risk to our well-being. For example, I'd prefer it if Lucas closed all the cabinet doors in the kitchen, but besides a bumped elbow, I'm not at risk for serious physical or emotional harm if he doesn't comply with it. In contrast, I have an emotional need for him to respect my privacy. If I ever found him going through my phone without my consent, it would compromise the trust in our relationship. I'd hope that my two closest friends would invite me if they were planning a fantastic night out, but it's not a boundary issue if they don't include me every time. I'd love it if my mom only said complimentary things about my tattoos, but it's not crossing my boundary if she has more critical feedback. You get the idea.

When we feel unheard by and unimportant to the people we love, our preferences tend to morph into boundaries. This is our way of seeking security in our relationships by asking people to respect and value our desires, but it's also a good way to find more opportunities for hurt and disappointment. Having too many preferences expressed as boundaries can make you rigid and controlling in relationships. People shouldn't have to comply with your requests all the time, just as you shouldn't have to comply with theirs.

4. We Make Others Responsible for Upholding Our Boundaries

Boundaries are maintained and enforced by the person who sets them. (This is especially true when it comes to individual boundaries.) In an ideal world, people we're close to would maintain our boundaries as rigorously as we do, but that won't always happen. If you tell your

They're Not Gaslighting You

parent not to raise their voice at you because it makes you feel unsafe and anxious, and then they raise their voice during your next fight, it's up to *you* to uphold your boundaries. That might mean reminding them of your need for quieter dialogue, or it might mean telling them you're leaving the room (and the conversation) until you can talk about it together calmly. It's not realistic or helpful to tell your parent that *they* have to leave the room because they got loud. It's your boundary, so you need to uphold it.

If you're with someone who keeps committing the same boundary violation over and over again, despite repeated requests to respect them, you need to decide how you'll enforce it. There is always the option of leaving the relationship. Removing yourself from the situation is the ultimate way of enforcing a boundary. Understandably, this is often not something we want to do, but if conversations and explanations don't lead to change, then ending the relationship might be the best course of action. It's important to remember this option because it reminds you that you are never without agency. Leaving might be a choice you won't want to make, but you *do* have that choice.

That's the big takeaway about boundaries: People might cross them unintentionally or intentionally, once or repeatedly, but either way, it's up to you to communicate and enforce your own boundaries. At the same time, not all boundaries are the same in terms of importance. Some literally keep you safe from harm, while others are closer to preferences. You shouldn't treat all boundaries equally. It's up to you to decide how strictly to uphold them, and when, and with whom.

Did They Violate Your Boundaries, or Did They Just Not Know How You Felt?

So, You've Been Accused of Violating a Boundary

If you're in a close relationship, chances are you're going to violate the other person's boundaries at some point. This is especially likely if the person has not told you what boundaries are important to them. However, you might also be unjustly accused of violating a boundary, perhaps a boundary you didn't know about or a preference masquerading as a boundary, and you'll need to know what to do.

Be Curious

You can't address the situation until you know what the person thinks and feels about what happened. Before you jump into defending yourself or calling them out, take a moment to better understand. Ask them what their boundary was and how they felt about it being crossed.

If It Was a Boundary Violation, Time to Repair

If you discover you unintentionally violated their boundary, you have some repair to do. Acknowledge and validate their feelings. Explain to them that you understand how your actions hurt them and that you recognize the need to be more careful in the future. If it's a boundary you fully embrace, then voice that. But, if it's a boundary that you think may be difficult for you to always respect, then talk about it. See if it's a flexible boundary with some room for negotiation.

If It Wasn't a Boundary Violation, Time to Talk

This is a tougher scenario. Perhaps what they're claiming as a boundary is actually a preference, or maybe you feel they're raking you over the coals over a small mistake. You can still validate their strong feelings (remember from chapter 4 that this is almost always a helpful thing to do), but this situation also warrants a larger conversation about how mistakes are discussed and repaired between you two. You have the right to point out concerns that using the word *boundary* is getting in the way of a helpful conversation about your respective needs, discuss what will make you feel safe and secure together, and determine how to heal when those needs aren't met.

If This Doesn't Work, Pause the Conversation

If the person is too upset to talk calmly, it's wise to pause the conversation. Tell them you want to talk about this issue productively, and in order to do that, you'll need some time before you can keep talking. Tell them you'll deeply consider what they've said and ask them to do the same for you. Reinforce that you want to better understand their needs in the relationship, but you also want to ensure you can navigate times like this one.

Get Some Outside Help

Some boundaries can be hard to negotiate, even in healthy relationships. If you're stuck in that situation, try therapy. It might help to have a professional third party support you both as you figure out how to respect each other's needs without feeling controlled, sacrificing things you don't want to, or getting resentful. That can be family therapy, couples therapy, or individual therapy. It doesn't matter what type of relationship you're in—I've worked with siblings who wanted to have a stronger relationship, and I've even heard of friends going to therapy for help navigating problems like these.

When Nothing Works

There's a chance the other person is committed to weaponizing this term, and nothing you do or say will sway them. If they hold fast to the accusation that you violated their boundary and nothing will make it right but a complete admission of wrongdoing and a vow to never do it

Did They Violate Your Boundaries, or Did They Just Not Know How You Felt?

again, you need to weigh your options. You can give them the admission and vow, but you may be assuming unnecessary blame and agreeing to a boundary that you find unreasonable. You can try to keep talking and working through the misalignment, perhaps with some outside help. If this is a recurring problem, you can consider downgrading the closeness of the relationship or leaving it altogether. It's no one's favorite option to leave, but remember that exiting an unhealthy relationship is the ultimate boundary you can set.

So, You Think Someone Violated a Boundary

Someone might have knowingly violated one of your boundaries, and perhaps this isn't the first time. Once you've checked with yourself that it's truly a boundary and not a preference, it's time to address the issue. Remember, people *do* cross boundaries sometimes, and it doesn't automatically mean they're awful or abusive and you need to end the relationship. Here's what you should do next time it happens.

State the Boundary

First things first, the other person needs to know the boundary they violated. You can't assume they know unless it's one of those universal boundaries we looked at earlier in the chapter. (And if they violated one of *those* boundaries, you should consider if you're in an abusive relationship that needs to end.) You need to ensure they're aware of your boundary before addressing that they crossed it. This can be done with kindness and firmness, and it needs to be detailed. Don't just say, "You crossed my boundary." This isn't enough information, and it's a conversation killer. Instead, try, "Hey, I'm sure you didn't realize this, but I don't like when people use my phone without asking, even if it's just to take a picture. It got stolen two months ago and now I'm jumpy about it. It would help me if you asked anytime you wanted to borrow it."

Enforce the Boundary

If you've already been clear about your boundaries and the person continues violating them, you need to enforce them. You can't only rely on others to respect your boundaries; you have to maintain them yourself. How you enforce your boundary depends on what it is, but if, for example, you have a limit about how mean arguments get, you could explain that the fight has gotten too harsh (that they're swearing, mocking you, and so on) and you need to stop talking until you've both calmed down.

Continue Enforcing It

There's no guarantee the person will respect the first enforcement. Sometimes people forget the boundary or, with the example above, a really anxious person might keep trying to engage you in conversation even though you've said you need to stop. This is when you maintain the line you've drawn. Maybe you just keep restating why you need a break from the conversation until you've both cooled down. Maybe you leave the room. Do what you need to in order to enforce your boundary.

Talk About It Later

Setting a boundary in the heat of the moment—as it's been violated—is important to do, but you may have more success helping the other person understand why it's important if you talk about it post-fight. Wait until things have cooled down and then ask them to talk. Explain why the boundary is important, and you can even acknowledge why respecting it might be understandably hard if they feel differently about the issue.

Did They Violate Your Boundaries, or Did They Just Not Know How You Felt?

For example, you could say, "When you start swearing and raising your voice, I feel really overwhelmed. My parents were quiet fighters, so I'm not used to that decibel increase! I stop being able to hear you and I won't be able to have a productive conversation anymore. I know you grew up in a household where people got loud and it feels okay for you, but it makes me panicky. If we get that heated again, I'll need to take a break from talking until we've both calmed down a little."

Talk to a Therapist and Keep Track

You might need to assess how acute these violations are if they continue. Is someone is crossing your explicitly stated boundaries with no concern for how it makes you feel? Are they willing to talk about why this is a problem for you? Is it happening repeatedly or frequently? A therapist can help you assess the situation and make recommendations such as, for example, whether you might have success if you continue working on it or whether the relationship isn't worth saving.

For Romantic Relationships, Try Couples Therapy

I'm a couples therapist, so obviously I'm going to recommend you consider couples therapy. I've worked with a lot of couples who have struggled with boundary violations, particularly during arguments. It can really help to have a professional third party step in and set some ground rules for engagement and explain why respecting boundaries is critical for a healthy relationship. Even if it's the exact same thing you've already said to your partner, it has a different impact coming from a therapist. When I set clear, evidence-based rules of engagement for the couples I work with, often it's things they've already said to each other, but it just lands differently from me. Most people who are violating boundaries aren't doing so with malicious intent; they're either emotionally escalated and thus have less control, or they're unaware their behavior is crossing a boundary in the first place.

If Nothing Changes, Consider Distancing Yourself or Leaving the Relationship

Unfortunately, leaving the relationship has to be a consideration if you're with someone who refuses to accept your boundaries. If, after conversations about why these boundaries are important to you, they don't see or respect them, there's very little you can do. You can't force a person to change; you can only respond to their actions. You can also consider subtly distancing yourself. For example, if the person violating your boundaries is a family member or friend, you can pull back on how close you are with them. There's a chance you can find a great, albeit less close, relationship with this person by giving them fewer opportunities to hurt you. ∎

Chapter 12

Are They Borderline, or Do They Just Have Strong Feelings?

Along with the rise of accusations of narcissism has come the overuse of the term *borderline*. This personality disorder has become a favorite armchair diagnosis for anyone who exhibits intense feelings in their relationships. However, assuming extreme emotions equals borderline personality overlooks the many facets of this disorder that extend beyond strong feelings.

Joel Has Borderline Personality Disorder

Hannah is tired of this. It's another day and another problem with her boyfriend, Joel. She used to love how vibrant and passionate he was, how communicative and deep, but now she's just exhausted by it. His sensitivity to the world around him, once a trait she admired because it opened her eyes up to things she hadn't seen before, feels solely focused on her and their relationship now. Hannah knows that Joel has had a hard time in relationships in the past, but she thought his self-awareness about this would mean things would be different.

This time, Joel is upset about a short text Hannah sent him in response to a long message he sent her about their communication, and her brevity sent him over the edge. He was trying to explain how their last exchange was hurtful, and he included detailed examples so she

They're Not Gaslighting You

wouldn't misunderstand him. Somehow, his lengthy explanation led her to become frustrated. She responded to his message—which Hannah will refer to as a "novel" when she tells her friends about it—with "I hear what you're saying but we need to talk about how much we dissect every interaction we have. I'm at work right now, I can't get into this, so let's talk about it tonight."

Joel immediately becomes angry at her response. How dismissive, how cold! She didn't appreciate the great lengths he went to in order to craft a very clear, calm message to her. He's trying to communicate his feelings and improve their relationship, and she just writes it off. His anger then turns to panic. Does "talk tonight" actually mean "break up"? Hannah has been increasingly distant with him; maybe she's over this relationship.

Joel becomes consumed with an all-encompassing anxiety. He can't get his mind off the idea of breaking up. He wants to text her again but knows that might anger her even more. He wants to call her, but she won't answer at work. Hell, that makes him want to call her fifteen times until she picks up. But Joel knows all of this will upset her, so instead, he does something he knows will calm him down. He grabs the scissors he keeps in his desk and goes to the bathroom. Joel cuts his thigh with the scissors, being careful to not go too deep. The thought crosses his mind that maybe he should just end it all, but there's still hope he can convince Hannah not to leave.

Later that night, when Hannah walks in the door, she sees a desperate Joel waiting for her. He tries to temper his panic as he goes up to her and starts explaining his text—why he sent it, why it was so long, and how he won't do it again. He quickly pivots from this to suggesting that they need to start communicating more so that they don't misunderstand each other like this. He suggests a daily check-in where they can go over their feelings about the relationship and make requests.

Hannah is overwhelmed by Joel's intensity. He's clearly anxious to fix the current tension, but his suggestion of a daily check-in isn't

Are They Borderline, or Do They Just Have Strong Feelings?

a solution she can accept. They don't have time for it (and she doesn't have the energy).

"I wanted to talk about the text because this keeps happening a lot, and I'm actually worried the check-ins will be the same thing. It feels like you have a lot of issues with me and want to dive really, really deep into every conversation we have. I just want to have more fun and be less evaluative of our time together. I'm feeling really exhausted by how often we analyze our relationship; it's just very intense for me," Hannah explains.

Once again, Joel feels dismissed. Not only is she not putting in the same effort as he is, but she's also criticizing him for putting in effort. He replies, "Wow, okay. Relationships require communication to work and I'm just trying to help us do that better. If you don't appreciate my efforts to do that, then I guess I'll find someone who does. Because it's work, Hannah. Do you know that? It takes emotional work to keep bringing up problems and trying to solve them! But I guess you're not mature enough to do that work!" Joel's getting louder and more upset, tears welling up in his eyes.

"Joel, I'm not unwilling to do the work of a relationship. But do you see what I'm saying? We have more intense conversations about us than any other couple I know. We have to pick apart everything we say, and it feels, I don't know, like an emotional roller coaster, more than it has to be," Hannah says.

"Okay, then I'm just too intense! I can't help that I really care about you and would do anything to make this work! Do you even know how awful I felt today after getting your short message back to all that I'd written? I literally thought I should just kill myself if this is how our relationship is going to be!" Joel yells.

Hannah is sad to hear this, but not surprised. Their conversations often end up here, with Joel talking about suicide. It's not that she isn't worried, but Hannah has empathy fatigue. Even a conversation about having less intense conversations is intense.

"If you feel that unhappy in this relationship, then I think we shouldn't be together. I don't want to make you feel that awful, Joel. But I also need things to become easier," Hannah answers.

At this comment, Joel pivots. He doesn't really want to end things. So, he starts promising they'll have more fun and less intensity. He begs her not to leave him, saying that he knows he can be a lot but it's because he feels so deeply for her. For the rest of the evening and the entire next day, Joel seems repentant. He's more doting and less demanding. But a week later, they're having the same fight, ending with Joel storming out of the apartment to get drunk at a local bar. He'll stumble home, falling on the sidewalk and breaking a finger on the way, which will make Hannah concerned and kick her into caretaking mode. The pattern keeps on going, with Hannah becoming increasingly exhausted by their dynamic and Joel becoming increasingly panicked about abandonment as he senses Hannah's fatigue.

Defining Borderline Personality Disorder

The word *borderline* represents our initial understanding of this personality disorder: It was intended to represent someone who is on the line between neurosis and psychosis. If we look at the DSM criteria for borderline personality disorder, or BPD, we'll see a pattern of emotion dysregulation, chaotic relationships, unstable self-image, and marked impulsivity. As with other personality disorders, these symptoms begin in early adulthood. To be diagnosed with BPD, a person needs to exhibit five of the following nine criteria:

1. **Desperate attempts to avoid abandonment, whether real or imagined:** Go to extreme lengths to prevent someone from leaving, such as pleading with them, threatening them, calling

Are They Borderline, or Do They Just Have Strong Feelings?

them repeatedly, physically preventing them from leaving, or stalking them.

2. **Stormy, intense, and chaotic relationships:** Have relationships that tend to be characterized by extremes of idealization and devaluation in which the person with BPD idolizes someone one moment and then vilifies them the next. Because they struggle to see others in a consistent and nuanced way, their relationships go through tumultuous ups and downs, where they desire intense closeness one minute and then reject the person the next.

3. **Unstable sense of self:** Have a persistent and notable unstable self-image or sense of self. This can manifest as sudden changes in goals, values, career plans, and other significant aspects of identity, and is often seen in fluctuating self-esteem.

4. **Self-damaging impulsivity:** Engage in coping behaviors that pose risks to their health or well-being, such as spending sprees, substance abuse, reckless driving, binge eating, or unsafe sex.

5. **Recurrent suicidality:** Engage in repeated self-harm behaviors, such as cutting or hitting themselves, along with suicidal gestures, threats, or actual attempts.

6. **Extreme mood swings:** Exhibit significant mood shifts that last from a few hours to a few days. This can include intense episodic dysphoria, irritability, or anxiety—usually in response to interpersonal stressors (e.g., a fight with a loved one, perceived sense of abandonment).

7. **A persistent sense of emptiness:** Feel a deep sense of inner emptiness and may try to fill this void with substances, food, or relationships, yet nothing seems to provide lasting satisfaction.

They're Not Gaslighting You

8. **Anger problems:** Have difficulty controlling or expressing anger in a healthy way. They have a bad temper, are prone to constant rage, are quick to fly off the handle, or engage in physical fights.

9. **Paranoia or dissociation:** Are suspicious about other people's motives (paranoia) or feel disconnected from themselves (dissociation). These symptoms usually arise during periods of extreme distress—for example, in response to real or imagined abandonment—and when other attempts at coping have failed to alleviate their distress.

Recall from chapter 2 that a personality disorder diagnosis requires patterns of behavior to be pervasive and stable across settings and contexts, and symptoms must interfere with their work, home, and social lives. We also don't diagnose someone under the age of eighteen with a personality disorder. As a professor of mine in graduate school said, if we could diagnose teenagers with personality disorders, they'd all have one. It's a fraught time with heightened emotions and poor interpersonal choices, which is why we hold off until they're technically adults and have had a chance to work through the tumultuous times.

It's worth noting that although BPD is currently categorized as a personality disorder, there is a growing conversation about whether this diagnosis should be moved into the trauma disorders section. Most people with BPD report a trauma history, and many of the symptoms can be seen as understandable responses to trauma. If someone has been abused, been neglected, or felt unsafe, of course they would have strong emotions in response to possible abandonment. If someone hasn't felt loved or validated in formative relationships, of course they would struggle with a consistent identity and feel a sense of emptiness. The symptoms make sense when viewed through a trauma lens. Recall from chapter 2 that the DSM is a constant work in progress, and it's possible

Are They Borderline, or Do They Just Have Strong Feelings?

we'll one day see BPD move into the trauma disorders category. If that were to happen, imagine how differently we might view it, how much less we'd weaponize or stigmatize it. It shows you the power of the DSM and these categories we've created.

Perhaps the key thing to understand about people with BPD is that they are terrified of being abandoned. The idea of being left by someone they care about induces pure panic. Many have been neglected or abandoned as children and, knowing the visceral pain of having a caregiver let them down, they desperately want to avoid any similar pain in their subsequent relationships. However, this fear of abandonment leads to a whole host of issues, such as hypervigilance to possible signs someone might leave them, which causes them to misinterpret others' words or actions and react very strongly to even neutral gestures from others. Unfortunately, their fear of abandonment leads them to act in ways that push people away, resulting in the very thing they've been trying to avoid.

If I had to pick one word to describe people with BPD, it would be *unstable*. Their identities are unstable, as they struggle to pin down who they are and what they want. Their relationships are unstable, as they swing from intensely wanting closeness to a sudden devaluing of others when their fears of abandonment get triggered. And their behaviors are unstable, as they use maladaptive ways of coping with intense affect that cause more harm in the end. For someone with BPD, nothing feels secure, and the same is true for someone in a relationship with them, be it a child, spouse, close friend, or parent.

If I had to pick another word to describe borderline, I'd choose *intense* because that's the experience of this disorder, whether you have it or you know someone who has it. The feelings are intense, and the behaviors are intense. Even small issues can feel like life or death, and offhand comments can turn into hours-long conversations as the person with BPD tends to read into everything as they search for signs of someone wanting to leave them. There is a constant push and pull, making everyone feel on edge. People with BPD require an intense degree of reassurance and emotional support to assuage their fear of abandonment, but no amount is enough to make the fear disappear. This often causes those around them to feel exhausted and want some distance, which triggers more fears of abandonment and leads to higher demands for closeness and reassurance. You can see how this cycle can be self-sustaining and emotionally draining for everyone involved.

Indeed, people with BPD also tend to have more intense feelings than others, which is why they often resort to extreme coping strategies like self-harm and reckless behavior. Although these behaviors cause more problems and can be life-threatening, they are reliable ways to numb or distract people with BPD from their overwhelming feelings. People close to those with BPD are often afraid of setting them off because they know it could lead to impulsive and dangerous behaviors. They feel they must walk on eggshells to avoid triggering the person with BPD, but unfortunately, this itself can be a trigger. The person with BPD can tell others are being cautious or avoiding them and will become fearful that they're too demanding or difficult to be around and that people will leave them.

As mentioned earlier, people who have borderline typically have a trauma history. Early trauma can significantly impact a person's ability to know themselves, develop trusting and stable relationships, and cope effectively with feelings. These painful experiences usually make it hard for them to believe that people are consistent and reliable and that relationships can recover from conflict. Their traumatic experiences also explain the fear of abandonment that drives much of their interpersonal behavior. They live in fear of people leaving them, so they are in a constant push and pull, trying to keep people as close as possible but then, when the worry of abandonment crops up, pushing people away so that they're the ones leaving, not the ones getting left.

Even though people with BPD are often the creators of their own problems, they truly suffer. Unlike sociopaths, who don't feel empathy

Are They Borderline, or Do They Just Have Strong Feelings?

when they hurt others, people with BPD are desperate for emotionally close and meaningful relationships and care deeply when a relationship goes south. While it can be incredibly difficult to be in a relationship with someone with this disorder because of their emotional volatility and intensity, it's also easy to empathize with them when you step back and consider how much they're struggling. They're explosive and manipulative when they sense abandonment because they don't know any other way of handling the situation or their overwhelming feelings. Unfortunately, the very way they act pushes people away, making "abandonment" that much more likely. It's a cruel irony they're stuck in, and we can have empathy for how hard that must be, even as we disapprove of their behavior.

It's important to point out that there are many people working tirelessly to combat the feelings and behaviors associated with their disorder. People with BPD can (and usually really want to) engage in therapy to help them navigate relationships and life with greater ease and success. They don't want to feel empty and unstable. They want to address the desperation to keep people close that unfortunately pushes people away, which then causes them to use even more counterproductive behaviors to maintain closeness. They're working hard to learn new coping skills and tolerate distress.

Even with that being said, we also need to acknowledge that people with BPD can be abusive. Their desperate attempts to keep a relationship can lead to explosive outbursts, and when someone needs space or tries to leave, the person with BPD can become even more volatile. For example, they might say cruel things—belittling, denigrating, or blaming the other person—or even resort to physical violence to prevent the person from leaving. Their vigilance and intensity make others feel scrutinized and afraid, worried they'll say one wrong thing that will lead to a barrage of accusations and emotionally intense conversations. As you can imagine from this description, it can be hard to be in a close relationship with this type of person.

They're Not Gaslighting You

Layla *Doesn't* Have Borderline Personality Disorder

Angus and Layla are fighting again. Angus is really tired of Layla's constant unhappiness with him. She was the cool girl at first—self-assured, relaxed, not worried about the future—and he loved it, but now she seems so needy and critical. Angus wants to go back to when Layla was more independent. Back then, she was so confident and fun. She was something he wanted to chase and catch. But, having now caught her, he sees there's another side to her. Layla is demanding and emotionally volatile. She's suffocating him. Why can't she just let him live? Her obsessive need to know where he is or who he's with is driving him insane.

Layla is in tears again. Things with Angus have gone south so quickly, and she can't figure out why. Their relationship started out so great, everything was easy and fun, but it feels like a switch was flipped and now Angus is just . . . mean. She's crying because he bailed on dinner with her friends and, when she confronted him, he got furious with her. Layla was confused and upset. Angus was the one who didn't even text her to say he wouldn't be there; he just didn't show up! She looked like an idiot, checking her phone obsessively and looking at the restaurant door to see if he'd walk in. She was worried something bad happened to him. But no, he just decided he didn't feel like going, and he also apparently didn't feel like telling her.

"So what, I can't skip something with your friends if I'm tired? We see them all the time, Layla! This is so controlling. My time and my choices aren't yours to dictate!" Angus says angrily.

"That's not what I'm saying! Can you really not see why this wasn't okay? You didn't even tell me you were bailing. I was worried you'd gotten hurt or something! I totally understand if you were too tired and didn't want to come, but you didn't answer any of my texts or my call. You can't just change your plans and not tell me!" Layla answers.

Are They Borderline, or Do They Just Have Strong Feelings?

"Actually, Layla, I *can* do that. I don't have to answer to you or to anyone else. This is *my* life. If I feel tired from working a TEN-HOUR DAY and don't feel like hanging out with your annoying friends, then I'm not going to. I don't care how much you cry or if you act angry at me about it—you can't manipulate me," Angus says, his anger turning cold.

"What? I'm not trying to manipulate you! I just want you to tell me if your plans change. That isn't a crazy request!" Layla says, as her slow tears become sobs. *Is* she crazy? She's really not trying to be controlling, but she felt so scared and stupid at dinner with her friends.

"Enough with the crying! You always do this. You freak out over small things and then you cry to make me feel bad and apologize. But guess what, it's not happening this time. Are you borderline or something? You overreact to everything that happens and I'm not comforting you this time," Angus says.

Angus leaves and Layla sobs even harder. Her emotions do feel out of control; maybe Angus is right. She keeps getting upset and when they talk about why, she ends up feeling stupid. *Is* she controlling? Borderline? Is she so afraid of Angus leaving that she's overreacting to minor infractions?

Later, Layla will apologize profusely. She'll send a long apology text and, when Angus doesn't answer in a day, she'll ask to come over so she can apologize in person. Angus will say even her apologizing is a little too much. He'll accept her tearful apology, but he'll stay distant for a few more days, making Layla earn his warmth again.

Layla doesn't have BPD. She's reacting normally to a hurtful situation. Angus, on the other hand, does have a personality disorder. (Can you guess which one?) Ironically, he's the manipulative one, turning her feelings into problems and weaponizing a diagnosis to make Layla feel as though her reactions are disproportionate to the situation. He also uses terms of abuse like *controlling* and *manipulative* to shift the blame onto Layla when he's the one who behaved badly and has done so many times in the past. The narrative Angus is creating—that Layla is the abusive one in their relationship—will slowly chip away at her self-trust.

The Weaponization of Borderline Personality Disorder

The vast majority of the time, when the term *borderline* is weaponized, it's against a woman. We tend to associate emotional volatility with women, as unfair and untrue as this is. Rarely have I seen a female client diagnose their male partner with BPD. Instead, they'll call him a narcissist or sociopath. But it's worth noting that the true prevalence of BPD is likely about the same for both genders—despite being disproportionately diagnosed among women—which shows how much the term has been commandeered as a gendered insult or judgment.

Since BPD is a disorder characterized by extreme feelings and behaviors, it's easy for us to pick one example of someone acting consistently with the diagnosis and extrapolate a conclusion. However, BPD is more complicated than one instance of heightened affect.

Nevertheless, there are three main ways people misuse and weaponize BPD.

1. We Don't Look at the Bigger Relationship Picture

We forget that people with BPD experience interpersonal struggles in all their close relationships, not just with us. It's rare for someone with BPD to have a push-and-pull relationship with their romantic partner but not with their family members or dearest friends. Any close relationship triggers the fears of abandonment and leads to a lot of intense affect. And I can't underscore the degree of intensity enough; people with BPD feel emotions more intensely than other people do. The emotions are overwhelming and all-consuming. That's why they use extreme ways of coping, such as self-harm or dangerous, impulsive actions.

When we call someone borderline, we've usually skipped the (necessary) step of assessing their relationships with others; we're just looking at how their feelings toward us seem overblown and drawing a conclusion from that. We forget to consider whether their other close relationships with family members, partners, and good friends are similarly volatile.

2. We Assume Self-Harm Means a Borderline Diagnosis

People also misuse the term *borderline* when they label anyone who self-harms as having BPD. Most people who have BPD self-harm, but not everyone who self-harms has BPD. Hurting oneself as a coping strategy is an unfortunately common occurrence, and people with all sorts of disorders use this method to make themselves numb or, on the other hand, feel something other than numbness. There's also the harsh insinuation that self-harm, particularly when it's by someone who has BPD, is only intended to manipulate. While self-harm might promise the secondary gain of making others be more careful with or not leave them, that's usually not someone's primary goal when they hurt themselves. Their self-harm or threats of suicide are a way of both alleviating and communicating their distress; framing it as solely manipulative is inaccurate.

3. We Think Intense or Seemingly Irrational Feelings Are Borderline

When we see someone react strongly to what we perceive as a small offense (or not an offense at all), we think their overreaction is pathological. Getting that upset feels overblown and manipulative, like a way of controlling us and the relationship in general. But people can have strong reactions for reasons that we don't initially see or understand without it necessarily meaning they have a personality disorder.

For example, people who have an anxious attachment style may seem needy or emotionally intense with their romantic partners when they feel the relationship isn't secure, but they don't have the other symptoms of BPD. While they may engage in intense conversations and refuse to let up until the issue feels resolved, they don't necessarily engage in reckless or self-harm behavior, nor do they experience identity instability. They may not have a sense of emptiness, uncontrollable anger, or passing paranoia. Their fear of the relationship ending is real and painful, but it's not the same degree of intensity and panic as the fear of abandonment that comes with BPD. These other symptoms matter a great deal because everyone can sometimes seem emotionally dysregulated, needy, and angry in their relationships.

Like it or not, we all have feelings, and sometimes they can be intense. This doesn't mean we all have BPD. Although it's certainly tempting to label anyone who has strong feelings or reactions as borderline, this isn't accurate, nor is it helpful. And it's overlooking the important truth that BPD is a rather complicated diagnosis with many facets. Throwing out the accusation of borderline is also a convenient way to not take responsibility for how we might have hurt the person. If we don't understand why our actions led to the hurt, or we think the other person's reaction is overblown, it can certainly be tempting to pathologize them. But people have strong reactions for all sorts of reasons without meeting criteria for a personality disorder.

Here's another big reason why we shouldn't throw this term around: Besides the fact that it's often inaccurate, it also stigmatizes BPD. People who are borderline have usually suffered a great deal as children and continue to suffer a great deal as adults. They're in extreme emotional pain and wish more than anything that they could stabilize their sense of self and relationships with others. People with BPD don't self-harm solely for attention; they do it because they're desperate.

Are They Borderline, or Do They Just Have Strong Feelings?

They're not reckless and impulsive for fun; they act this way because they don't know what else to do with their intense feelings. The stigma attached to this diagnosis only adds to the self-hatred and shame that people with BPD already have, making it harder for them to have self-compassion or seek help.

We don't have to excuse the inappropriate or harmful behaviors of someone who is borderline, but we don't need to vilify them for it either. Their ineffective and frustrating ways of engaging with others often stem from significant trauma, something we can all have more compassion for. And, unlike narcissism or sociopathy, people with BPD are typically motivated to improve their relationships with others and are usually more receptive (and responsive) to therapy. This doesn't mean all people with BPD are willing to do this self-work, and it also doesn't mean we need to stay in a close relationship with someone who is borderline, but it does mean we can view them more gently while we set our boundaries.

Finally, as seen in the vignette with Layla and Angus, weaponizing BPD is an unfortunately effective way of controlling another person. By painting someone as overly and irrationally emotional, we can convince them that their feelings are invalid and that their perceptions are untrustworthy. Abusers know how to use certain words to flip the fault onto their partners, convincing them of an alternate reality where they are always to blame even when they thought they had a legitimate reason to be upset. We need to be careful when and how we use the term *borderline* to ensure we're not letting it become an accusation that empowers us to invalidate and control others.

So, You've Been Accused of Having Borderline Personality Disorder

If your relationship has been struggling and you've been having big emotional reactions, perhaps someone has said you're borderline. Maybe they said it in anger, or maybe they said it with sincere concern and care. Either way, here's what to do if it happens to you.

Take a Deep Breath

It always stings to be accused of having a psychological disorder, especially when it's said during a fight or out of anger. Get to a place of relative calm before addressing anything.

Ask Them to Clarify

Now, ask the person to explain why they used this term with you. Were they frustrated with your reaction and wanted you to calm down? Do they feel you're always pushing them away only to pull them close again? Do they have concerns (predating the argument) about you having BPD, or were they just throwing the word out there to express how upset they were with you? As with bipolar disorder, you're trying to figure out if they weaponized the term or if they have legitimate concerns you need to address.

Consider Their Point

It won't take long to do a quick consideration of what they're saying. Ask yourself a few questions: Has anyone else in your life wondered if you had BPD? Do you have a trauma history that makes it hard to be close to people you love? Do you feel your relationships have been volatile, intense, or short-lived? Do you struggle with low self-esteem, overwhelming feelings that are hard to cope with, risky behaviors that could be self-destructive, self-harm or suicidal thoughts, or an internal emptiness that you can't seem to fill? Answering yes to these questions means you might want to consider an evaluation.

If They Might Have a Point, Seek an Evaluation

If, upon further reflection, you do see a pattern in your relationships that seems consistent with BPD, then seek professional help. Get an evaluation to see if you do meet criteria. If you have this disorder, there are good treatment options you can pursue. Don't be hard on yourself or spiral into a place of shame; it's not your fault you developed this disorder and, now that you know, you can start taking steps to address it so your relationships are more stable and satisfying.

Explain Your Feelings

If you get what the person's saying but think their accusation is incorrect, then try explaining why you don't feel you meet criteria for BPD and, if you feel comfortable doing so, talk about your feelings. Explain why you reacted strongly and what painful fears or vulnerabilities were stirred up. Help them see why you acted a certain way so that they see it's not pathological but, rather, understandable. I should note that you should only do this in a good relationship; if you have any concerns that you're in an abusive situation, skip this step.

Address the Weaponization

You might conclude that the person weaponized BPD and was using it as a way of placing all the blame on you. If that happens, address it outright. Explain that if they have real concerns about your mental health, they should approach that conversation with more care and consideration, and if they're using a diagnosis to judge and blame you, they should stop. Explain how weaponized therapy terms cut off dialogue and understanding, and ask them to avoid doing it in the future.

If They Keep Weaponizing It, Consider Your Options

If you've done the aforementioned steps and they continue to throw the term in your face during conflict, you should weigh your options. You can ignore it, keep addressing the weaponization and try to get them to stop, ask them to go to individual therapy to work on themselves, ask them to seek couples therapy with you to work on things (if it's your partner), create more distance in the relationship, or end the relationship altogether.

So, You Think Someone Has Borderline Personality Disorder

There's a chance you read this chapter and realized the description feels very similar to someone in your life. Maybe you're now wondering if they do, in fact, meet criteria for BPD. If this is you, keep reading for my recommendations.

Self-Reflect and Don't Immediately Diagnose

Even if my description sounded *exactly* like someone you know, refrain from armchair diagnosing just yet. Before you consider if this disorder makes sense for this person, start with some open curiosity. Also, ask yourself what it would mean if they had BPD. Would you relish the relief that you can pin the relationship's problems on them? Or would you feel grateful to have a path forward for addressing the recurring problems you two have faced?

Educate Yourself

This chapter alone isn't enough to decide anything. Read articles and books about BPD and how it might look in various relationships.

Are They Borderline, or Do They Just Have Strong Feelings?

If you've followed the first piece of advice, you'll be open to being convinced that the person doesn't have BPD as much as being convinced that they do.

Look at Their Relationship History

Remember that people with personality disorders don't exhibit symptoms in just one relationship or context. Reflect on what you know about this person's relationship history. Do they often have volatile and short-lived relationships? Do they seem to have a constant fear of being left that prompts them to engage in extreme behaviors? Do they self-harm, act impulsively or recklessly, get very irritated or angry, or seem to lack a stable sense of themselves? Are they like this with past romantic partners, family members, and close friends? You won't arrive at a definitive conclusion, but it's important to look at the bigger picture and not just the hard moments you have with this person.

Talk to a Professional

It's always helpful to have a professional perspective on this. Talk to a therapist about the possibility of this person having BPD. Explain why you want to know if they meet criteria (for example, so you can encourage them to get into therapy or better understand how to navigate the emotional highs and lows of your relationship). Remember, you won't get a secondhand diagnosis out of your therapist, but they can give you clinical insights that inform what you do next.

Decide What You Want to Do

You need to figure out what it means for you if the person in question has BPD. For some people, it feels reassuring to know what's causing their loved one distress and that they can get a treatment plan for it. For others, a diagnosis of BPD means they'd want to leave the relationship. If it's a foundational person in your life, like a parent, and you don't want to consider cutting off communication, maybe just the knowledge will clarify their behavior and help you weather the hard moments more easily. If it's a someone less critical, like a friend, maybe you'll want to gently put a little more space into the relationship so that you don't get overwhelmed by the intensity of their feelings and needs. Think about how important this person is in your life, if you want to maintain a relationship with them, and if you do, what types of boundaries you'll need to make that relationship work.

If You Want to Stay, Talk to Them

This is where you *could* bring your concerns to the person. Be gentle and compassionate as you communicate; even if you're coming from a place of wanting to help explain their experience, it can be hard for someone to hear something like this. Explain that you think this diagnosis might provide a path forward for navigating some recurring problems you've encountered. Provide comfort and reassurance, but also be clear that you need them to consider what you're saying and take some steps to work on themselves even if they (or their therapist) agree the diagnosis doesn't fit.

I emphasized "could" at the start because you don't have to do this. It might make sense to do with a partner or close friend, but less so with a parent or other family member. There are times when sharing diagnostic concerns and asking someone to seek help is a good idea, and there are times when it will only lead to increased unproductive conflict. You'll need to decide which situation it is for you.

If You Want to Leave, You Can Leave

Whether or not you reach a conclusion about a disorder, perhaps this person's intense feelings or self-destructive behaviors are too much for you. Even without an official diagnosis, this is a good enough reason to end a relationship. If you want to end things, then end them. Do

Are They Borderline, or Do They Just Have Strong Feelings?

so compassionately, but stick to your decision. The person might be in extreme distress because of your choice to leave, but that isn't a reason to stay. To the extent that you can and want to, try to help them gather their resources and supports. But at the end of the day, none of us should stay in a relationship we don't want to be in. ■

Chapter 13

Toxic, Triggered, and Trauma Bonded

There are so many weaponized terms to cover, and I couldn't fit all of them into this book, at least not to their full extent. But there are a few terms that deserve honorable mention, and although they won't get their own full chapter, they'll get a shoutout in this one.

Are They Toxic, or Are They Just Not the Right Person for You?

Oh, toxic. Ironically, this word might be the most toxic of all. *Toxic* has become a popular term that means "bad, but like, *really* bad," and it covers a lot of territory. Toxic means abusive, but it also means unhealed. Toxic refers to a psychopath but also to a person who hasn't learned how to regulate their feelings. Toxic is every red flag, bad behavior, narcissist, unaware teenager, borderline in-law, boundaryless friend, and ineffective communicator.

Do you see the problem with this word? It's too vague of a term for us to use with any efficacy. It's used as an umbrella term for basically everything that's bad in a relationship, without clarifying *how* bad, what *kind* of bad, and if it's situational and temporary or persistent and pervasive. It's an easy word to volley when you're hurt or desperate for an explanation, but it does nothing to help you understand what's actually going on and, more importantly, what to do about it.

They're Not Gaslighting You

Saying you think your partner is abusive because you've noticed a pattern of behavior in how they attempt to control and disempower you tells me a lot. Saying someone in your life is toxic, on the other hand, doesn't tell me anything about them. *Toxic* could be referring to a behavior or to the person's personality and, again, it's too vague to tell me anything. Has this person done toxic things (for example, by stonewalling you twice), or are they toxic in general (for example, by criticizing and judging everyone in their life)? And if we're talking about a behavior, was it toxic because it hurt you or because it's objectively wrong? Your sister's refusal to answer your phone call might feel toxic because it's withholding and painful, but it's not categorically a toxic or abusive thing for her to do.

Then there's the idea of toxic relationships which, again, means too much but says too little. Is it an abusive relationship? Then say *abusive*, because that has a very clear meaning and I'll immediately know how to help you. Does the relationship have recurring conflicts and poor communication? Then say that, because again, I know how to help if you're in that type of situation. Is it a relationship with an emotionally immature person who has no desire or ability to self-reflect and take responsibility for their part in the problem? Then say *that*, and you can use *toxic* moving forward and I'll know what we're talking about. "Toxic" means anything and everything; if it's the only adjective you use, I won't have any clue what's going on besides that you are unhappy.

The biggest problem I see with the use of *toxic* is when it's used as a reason to end a relationship without giving the other person a chance to understand or address the problem. If you don't want to stay with that person, then great—problem solved. But too often people say, "You're toxic!" and run away instead of taking on the harder work of talking to the other person about what's not working. Resorting to this catch-all term also absolves people from having to reflect on their role, if any, in the unhealthy relationship dynamic.

236

One last thing: Just as with red flags, we all exhibit some toxic behaviors at times. I don't know anyone who has lived a toxic-free existence. Sometimes we go through tough phases where our communication and coping skills are down, and we'll act more toxically than we might normally; this doesn't make us a toxic person. Indeed, many romantic relationships go through toxic episodes, if you will (should we make "toxic episode" a thing?), where people aren't communicating well, are escalating conflicts, and are generally behaving badly. We need to normalize a certain level of temporary or situational toxicity while also specifying what we mean by saying "toxic." This is the only way we can determine whether the relationship needs help or needs ending.

Are You Triggered, or Did They Just Say Something You Didn't Like?

Triggered is a word that has evolved far past its clinical definition. In fact, I've used it in this book over twenty times in its more colloquial sense. The word derives from a gun trigger, which releases a bullet that, in all likelihood, causes pain or damage. Similarly, an emotional trigger refers to something—an action, words, a certain tone—that sets off a reaction that causes pain or damage, to ourselves and sometimes to other people.

In its clinical usage, a trigger refers to a cue that leads to a trauma response. But let me back up, because *trauma* is itself a heavy, often misunderstood word. Its original meaning referenced what we now call "big T" trauma: life-threatening events such as going to war or surviving a car crash. Nowadays, we also talk about "little t" trauma: events that cause significant distress but aren't truly life-threatening, like being bullied in school or having an emotionally inconsistent parent. Trauma indicates an adverse experience that triggers (there's the word again!)

our fight-or-flight response, overwhelms our coping resources, and can have lasting emotional and physiological impacts.

Trigger was originally intended to mean something that leads to a trauma response, such as panic, anger, dissociation, and so forth. When soldiers return from war, they are often triggered by loud noises, such as fireworks, that sound to them like gunshots or explosions. The noise sets off a physiological and psychological response. In this intended context, being triggered is a significant experience.

But these days, the word *trigger* has become generalized to mean anything that leads to a negative reaction, from discomfort to full-on panic. In this use, trigger isn't referring to a trauma response but, rather, any adverse emotional experience. The problem is that when this term is weaponized, it demands that people treat our reaction as if it were the same degree of severity as a trauma response. We want others to immediately discontinue the alleged trigger and never do it again.

The thing is, the people we're close to will inevitably trigger us (this time I'm using trigger in its newer, less clinical form). It's one of the many hard parts of being in a relationship. When a parent or partner is unhappy with us, it can sometimes feel "triggering," but we can't exactly ask them to never be unhappy with us. (Trust me, I've tried, but Lucas insists on having the full range of human emotions; it's a super toxic trait of his.) What really matters is that we learn how to cope with other people's negative emotions. While it would be nice to stop people from evoking negative emotions in us, it's not a realistic goal, at least not in a healthy relationship.

That being said, it is okay to ask people to be mindful of or refrain from certain behaviors if they are particularly upsetting to you. For example, maybe you grew up in an angry household where parents yelled a lot, and as soon as the decibel level goes up in a conversation with your partner, you get too anxious to listen. It's perfectly all right to explain why this is upsetting to you and how it would be helpful if your partner could keep their voice quiet, even when they're upset. Now, they

Toxic, Triggered, and Trauma Bonded

may not always be able to self-regulate enough to consistently comply with this request, and that's okay too. If they trigger your anxiety by speaking loudly, that's not inherently abusive, or a red flag, or whatever label you might use.

Since *triggered* had a different meaning before it became used clinically, I'm willing to accept its new usage, as long as we realize that calling something a trigger doesn't require someone to stop and never do it again. It's helpful to identify our triggers so we can work on them, alone and in our relationships, but our loved ones will inevitably trigger negative feelings, and it's up to us to manage them. Avoiding relationships with anyone who triggers hard feelings will mean a very lonely existence.

Are You Trauma Bonded, or Did You Just Go Through a Hard Time Together?

I snuck this term in here because although it's not being weaponized, it has rapidly become misunderstood and thus misused, and I think it's important to understand its actual meaning. People inaccurately believe that *trauma bond* refers to the incredible closeness we feel with someone after going through a hard time with them. But, in fact, a trauma bond is the connection that survivors feel with their abuser. Although we'd expect survivors of any kind of abuse to hate their abuser, we often see victims become attached and even protective of their abuser because of the traumatic experiences they went through.

You might be more familiar with Stockholm Syndrome, a term developed to describe a type of trauma bond that occurs in short-term hostage situations, where the victim begins feeling empathy for their captors. The development of this term is a fascinating story. In the 1970s, robbers invaded a Swedish bank, but the robbery attempt didn't go as planned, and they ended up holding four employees hostage in a vault for six days. During this time, the victims formed close emotional bonds with their captors. After being rescued, they defended the people holding them hostage and worried about their well-being. Some victims stayed in touch with their captors after being freed and one even helped pay for a robber's lawyer's fees.

Trauma bonds are what keep victims in a relationship with their abusers. They make people feel empathy toward their abusers, or indebted to them, prompting them to defend the abusers even as they continue to be taken advantage of and harmed. We see this in hostage situations, as with Stockholm Syndrome, but also in abusive relationships, where abusers convince others to feel lucky to be with them. They cast themselves as being good people who put up with all the other person's faults and flaws. Abusers twist reality until other people think they are fortunate to be with someone so patient and tolerant, who loves them despite their many missteps and character flaws. This mix of empathy, gratitude, and dependence is what defines a trauma bond.

It upsets me when people say they're "trauma bonded" with someone simply because they went through a hard time together. We need to have words for explaining the counterintuitive and damaging relationship that can occur between abuser and survivor. We're making a confusing and destructive phenomenon even more confusing by taking away its label. The meaning of words and phrases *do* change over time, but since trauma bonding is an important concept for understanding why people get stuck in abusive relationships, its true definition needs to be upheld.

If you went through a difficult time with someone and feel closer to them as a result, you're probably experiencing an intensified *social bond* with them. That sort of bond is the goal behind a group's initiation rituals, such as the hazing activities that frats employ. Having to rely on people around you to get through something hard makes you feel closer to them. This is just garden-variety relationship building, though; it's not trauma bonding. To use another common example, soldiers aren't

Toxic, Triggered, and Trauma Bonded

trauma bonded after going to war together; they're socially bonded, albeit in an unusually deep way. A captured soldier who defends his captors? That person is, in fact, trauma bonded.

I'll admit, I may be on the losing end of this battle. The mistaken use of trauma bonding is so prolific now, I'm not sure it can be undone. Everyone is saying that they're trauma bonded with friends after going through a hardship or trauma bonded with coworkers from being in a toxic workplace. And listen, I get it. I understand that language evolves. But we should all acknowledge that by redefining trauma bond to mean social bond, we're taking away a term used to explain a troubling dynamic in abusive situations. At this point, maybe it makes more sense to develop a whole new term instead of attempting to reclaim trauma bonded. Stockholm Situationship? Captor Collusion? I'll keep working on it. ■

Chapter 14

Being a Human in a Relationship Is Hard, So Here's Some Advice

All right, now you know everything about weaponized therapy speak. But the question remains: What if you have legitimate concerns that something pathological is going on in your relationship?

For the individual issues discussed in this book, I've provided a brief guide at the end of each chapter that explains how to address these issues with someone else. The resources section at the end of the book has even more information that can help educate and guide you in specific relationship challenges.

But here, in this final chapter, I want to talk about the bigger picture of how you can handle difficulties in your relationships, including what to do if you think you're in an abusive relationship, how to manage the role of social media content in influencing your opinions, and what "working on your relationship" means.

First, take a deep breath as you acknowledge that relationships are hard. I'm a couples therapist who helps people improve their relationships every single day, and even I get frustrated and anxious by challenges in my relationships. None of us get to have a happy relationship without hard times and hard work. It's normal and okay to sometimes struggle with the person you're close to or love. When the struggle happens, don't despair. Within the struggle are opportunities to invest in the relationship and grow, individually and together. And if this specific relationship doesn't make it, you'll still have grown on a personal level, and that's very valuable.

Figure Out If You're in an Abusive Relationship

You know all about this from chapter 3, but I want to reiterate how difficult it can be to determine whether someone is abusive or whether they're behaving badly. There can be a fine line between the two. Many times, we can't efficiently or accurately make this assessment on our own because the abuse has made us doubt our perceptions of reality and feel like we're the problem. If you have any suspicions of being in an abusive relationship, I encourage you to get help. Go to trustworthy friends and family, or find a therapist, and *talk*. Tell someone you trust about what's going on and see what they say. If people are shocked and truly worried about you, that's a pretty good indicator you're stuck in something unhealthy.

If you feel like you can't tell people the bad parts of your relationship because it will betray the other person or make them angry, I'd encourage you to think about that too. It's always okay to confide in people if you're struggling in your relationship and need some extra help. I don't go bad-mouthing Lucas to my friends all the time (outside of him leaving ten thousand water glasses around the house, which *is* pathological, and I'll stand by that), but I also don't hesitate to talk to my friends when we're in a rough patch. I get their take on his behavior as well as mine, and they give me recommendations for how to navigate the conflict. My friends give amazing, balanced advice; as it happens, they're also therapists. The point is, I can trust that they would certainly tell me if Lucas or I crossed significant lines.

I can't emphasize enough the value of finding a good therapist (outside of a friend group, that is). Granted, I'm biased on this point because

Being a Human in a Relationship Is Hard, So Here's Some Advice

I am a therapist and I think therapy is amazing. But bias aside, it's true that to figure out if your relationship is problematic but fixable versus abusive and unsalvageable, you need an objective third party who has no emotional investment beyond wanting to help you. A therapist can't go so far as to diagnose the other person, but they can observe concerning patterns in behavior and negative impacts the person's having on you.

And, at the end of the day, therapy will be a space for you to figure out what *you* are going to do about it. Don't spend fifty minutes talking to your therapist about how and why your parent should change. Your parent isn't there to hear any of this, and they aren't going to change just because you and your therapist agreed they should. Instead, spend that time exploring what you want to do to improve your relationship and your life. Maybe that involves encouraging your parent to grow too, but it starts with you. After all, they won't change their behavior if you don't feel empowered enough to ask them.

If you realize your relationship is abusive, it's time to leave. Truly abusive situations can't be changed, especially if someone is lacking in empathy, motivation to grow, or the self-regulation skills necessary for it. It's not worth your safety, both physical and emotional, to change an abuser, especially when it probably won't work. If you realize you're in a relationship with someone who is seeking power and control by using the tactics described in this book, or perhaps meets the criteria for one of the disorders we've examined, it's time to leave. I encourage you to seek support from friends, partners, family, therapists, and organizations like the National Domestic Violence Hotline. Prioritize your health and happiness above this relationship. There are plenty of healthy people out there for you to be with, and this person just isn't one of them.

Of course, leaving isn't as easy as saying, "Okay, bye then!" Leaving is the most dangerous time in an abusive relationship because the perpetrator will be angry and retaliatory. Particularly if physical violence has been a part of your relationship, you need a good safety plan. I don't mean to scare you, but I want you to seek support and make a good plan for how you'll extricate yourself. There's lots more information on this in the resources section and, again, the Domestic Violence Hotline will be a wealth of knowledge and support.

If you're in an abusive relationship you don't think you can get out of, like with a parent, I acknowledge you're in a tough spot. However, you do have some choices. You can start putting some strict boundaries in place. Don't spend too much time with the person, don't stay over at their place, limit how vulnerable you are with them, and don't engage in their provocations or arguments. You can protect yourself by trying to have a very limited relationship with them, and you can also cut off communication. Some people find that their parent or other family member is just too harmful, and they can't maintain any relationship with them. Some people do this for a period of time; some people do it forever. The resources section has some books that might help you navigate this situation and make a decision about what to do.

If You're *Not* in an Abusive Relationship, It's Time to Do the Work

If you determine your relationship is in a tough spot but not abusive, now's the time for some hard relational work. A good cocktail for working on your relationship is *specificity, vulnerability, and commitment.*

First, be specific with your complaints instead of using words like *toxic* or *red flag.* Explain the action or pattern you're noticing, and don't make it a global attack on their character. (That never goes well.)

Next, explain in vulnerable, personal terms how the issues you've described impact you. Use "I statements" as you share why their action hurt you. By saying, "I felt alone and embarrassed," instead of "You're so inconsiderate, you always forget to call," you'll be focusing on sharing *your* feelings instead of blaming. Painful feelings are easy to empathize with, while blame is easy to feel defensive against.

Being a Human in a Relationship Is Hard, So Here's Some Advice

Finally, commit to addressing the issue. It never hurts to start by reminding the person that you love them (if you do, that is) before sharing why you want to chart a better path forward. You might say something like "I think we have a great relationship and if we can figure out this recurring issue with how we communicate, I think we'll be even better."

This is a nice segue into my second plug for therapy. If you're in a relatively healthy romantic relationship with some problems you want to fix, *try couples therapy*. Most of us need help to identify and address issues in our relationship, and a great couples therapist can help.

What should you look for in a couples therapist?

First of all, find a licensed mental health professional, one that holds some sort of psychology degree and an accompanying license. This lets you know they've met requirements to practice and are held to ethical standards.

Second, look for someone with specific training in couples therapy. I can't emphasize this one enough since a lot of therapists throw "couples therapy" on their website but they haven't had any experience working with couples. When you're talking to potential therapists, they should be able to tell you what trainings they've completed, any certifications they hold, and how they approach couples work (i.e., what clinical orientation they use).

When looking for a clinician to help your relationship, consider the type of therapy they offer.

- *Gottman-trained therapists* will do a lengthy assessment, provide assignments, and give you a lot of research-based information for best relational practices.

- *Emotionally focused therapists* will identify your attachment wounds and needs, and help you connect and understand one another in an experiential and powerful way.

They're Not Gaslighting You

- *Relational life therapy* providers will be kind but direct as they help you see how your childhood informs your current relational coping strategies, balance the power in your relationship, and hold everyone accountable as they work on improving.

There are other options beyond the ones I've mentioned, and it's worth doing some research ahead of time to see what could work best for your relationship. The most important thing is picking a therapist who is highly trained in their given modality.

Finally, pick a therapist you like. Research shows, again and again, that the best predictor of a good outcome in therapy is "goodness of fit" and a strong alliance—in other words, that the client and therapist like each other and work well together. Find someone you trust, who puts you at ease, someone you can imagine being very vulnerable with.

Don't Get Stuck at the Information-Gathering Stage

Be careful about what information you consume and believe, especially if you find it online, and especially when it comes to diagnoses and clinical terms. Social media has a lot of content, and while some of it may be accurate and apply to you, a lot of it probably doesn't. Remember that the algorithm wants to show you videos you like, so it gives you things related to what you've already seen, making confirmation bias almost a guaranteed outcome. (Haven't we all watched one raccoon video only to be flooded with reels of little raccoons washing their food, hugging dogs, and just generally being adorable? One video is all it takes, people, and then your algorithm is inundated with raccoon videos for the foreseeable future. Just imagine what watching one reel about a borderline parent can do—and how that can change your perception of what "borderline" means.) If you found something online that resonates with you, then take it to a professional. For example, if you think you might have bipolar disorder, go get an assessment; if you think your partner might be a narcissist, reach out to a licensed therapist.

Watching a thousand reels won't help you or your relationship—you'll only end up convincing yourself of something that may or may not be true. Consuming information is only step one to change, and too many of us get caught in this stage without progressing to the next one. Remember, information helps you decide what to do. There's no point in realizing someone has OCD if you aren't going to take action.

If you are still in information-gathering mode, go to reputable resources. If it's social media, watch licensed mental health professionals discuss disorders and relationships. If you're searching online, go to well-established websites that cite their sources and give you scientifically based information. Avoid looking to influencers as your only source of information. No matter how compelling they may be, they are not experts.

Support the Person in Getting Help

Remember that diagnosing someone with a disorder is supposed to be a positive thing that leads to increased understanding and a helpful treatment plan (or an exit strategy, if it's a dangerous situation). It's not supposed to be an insult. If you *do* think someone you're close to has a clinical disorder and needs help, approach that conversation with kindness. Remember that, as much as they've hurt or frustrated you, they might be really struggling. You need them to hear and consider your concerns; for that to happen, *you* need to be calm and gentle but persistent. Ultimatums aren't helpful ("Get help immediately or this friendship is over!"), but it is okay to tell the person that this issue feels like it's damaging the relationship to the point where you're now doubting if you can stay in it. Emphasizing the seriousness of the issue is acceptable; making threats isn't.

Now, here's some tough news: The process of securing help may also be challenging. Finding a great therapist who meets the person's specific needs can be time-consuming and frustrating. If the person is receptive to it, help them search for a provider and set up some initial consultations. Be supportive as they navigate the very complex system of health care. Provide encouragement, a sympathetic ear, and help as needed.

Also, bear in mind that even once they get a great treatment team in place, things won't immediately get better. I know that's hard to hear because you've probably been waiting for quite some time to see improvements. However, treating any of the disorders in this book isn't an overnight fix. It takes a long time to find the right therapist, make progress in therapy, and (if medication is needed) find the right type and dosage. Remind yourself of these timeless therapy truths during this process: *Things might get worse before they get better* and *Progress isn't linear.*

I want to reiterate, though, that you don't have to stay in any relationship, or stay as close as you once were. Even if the person has sought help, you don't have to stick by their side or be a constant support. If you're exhausted and unhappy, and don't want to wait for change, it's okay to take some space or leave. Just because you accurately identified a problem and helped them start their journey doesn't mean you need to stay with them.

Focus on Your Part of the Work

Now, I'm going to tell you some even tougher news: The other person in your relationship might have really messed up—who knows, they might even be the worst—but unless they're truly abusive, *you are part of the problem.* I know it's hard to see it that way because you probably feel like you're trying to do everything right to fix or save the relationship. I don't know you, but I believe you're trying your hardest at that. But the thing is, it's always easier to identify what others are doing wrong instead of

Being a Human in a Relationship Is Hard, So Here's Some Advice

what we ourselves are doing wrong. However, only in abusive situations does a relationship go south because of just one person. So, it's possible that you've engaged in some really unhealthy behaviors that have caused or exacerbated problems in your relationship. If that's the case, *it's okay*. Recognizing your errors and choosing self-improvement is more than okay—it's amazing. It's when you refuse to acknowledge or work on your shortcomings that you end up creating more problems.

I hope this tough news is empowering for you because it means that you can start making positive changes even if the other person isn't ready to do the same. *You* can stop fights from escalating, set healthier boundaries for the relationship, and communicate more effectively, even if the other person keeps getting it wrong. Change begets change. You're a part of the relationship system, and changing one part of the system will inevitably change the rest of it. I'm not saying it will be fun or easy, but it will happen. The change might be that you do all your self-growth work, and the other person refuses to do their part, in which case you'll have a decision to make: Stay and hope they eventually do change, or leave. Regardless of the relationship's outcome, you'll have grown as a person and will be better in future relationships, and that's the real win.

Remember, Humans Are Never Done Growing

Making a relationship work requires you and your loved ones to self-reflect, take responsibility, and change. This process won't just happen once; it's a constant cycle you'll go through repeatedly over the course of the relationship. You'll both need to look at yourselves, own what you've done wrong or could do better, and work to improve. Nobody is ever finished learning and growing, not individually and certainly not in a relationship. But that's what can be so great about being in a relationship: It's a never-ending opportunity to become a better person.

They're Not Gaslighting You

And when you mess up (because trust me, you will), be kind to yourself. As I keep saying, humans are wonderfully imperfect. Even when we know what to do, sometimes we just don't or can't do it. Maybe you know not to throw sarcastic barbs into arguments with your spouse but sometimes you're so angry that you do it anyway. That's okay. Acknowledge it and apologize, then move on. It's a "red flag," of course, but we all have red flags. Remember your loved one is also imperfect, just like you, and give them the same grace to make mistakes.

Even being a literal expert in romantic relationships doesn't spare me from having to continue self-reflecting and improving. I keep thinking I've done all the learning and growing I can do, and then, lo and behold, I realize there's more. As my marriage evolves, so must I. Growth is a lifelong process, and you should celebrate that! How boring to be stagnant. How disappointing to never discover new strengths and skills. Don't be dismayed by this fact; embrace it. Your relationship will challenge you in ways you can't imagine yet. When it happens, rise to that challenge. Take a hard look at yourself and do the work. Build relationships with others who are willing to do the same.

That brings up another good point: How do you choose people to have relationships with? In this world of messy humans, how do you know who will be a good person for you to be with? My answer: Choose someone who wants to keep doing the work with you. There is no perfect person or partner for you, no magical human that won't ever hurt, irritate, enrage, or overwhelm you. Being in close relationships inevitably leads to big, scary feelings at times, so pick someone who wants to get through the dark times with you. Remember that when people are behaving badly in a desperate attempt to connect—not control—they'll be able to look at themselves, recognize the bad behavior, and change. Pick someone who has the willingness to self-reflect and grow, even if it's hard. Someone who will hang in there, even during your worst fights, and ultimately say, "Listen, this is awful, and I

Being a Human in a Relationship Is Hard, So Here's Some Advice

don't want to keep arguing like this, but I love you and I want to figure this out with you."

If you take anything from this book, I hope it's this: Being a human is hard and we're all trying our best to walk through the world. We have wounds and scars and bad habits. We rely on ineffective but protective coping mechanisms. We push others away when we're hurt or scared. We fail at being good parents, good siblings, good friends. And to top it all off, sometimes we're unaware of these things. Our modern obsession with optimization is a good thing taken too far—we're striving for a level of perfection that we simply can't embody, at least not consistently. Everyone has different perspectives and self-protective responses. Everyone has red flags, big feelings, and inexplicable mood changes. Everyone behaves badly sometimes. But even then, odds are they're not gaslighting you. ∎

Chapter 15

It's Time to Lower Your Weapons

I see the fallout of weaponized therapy speak with my clients more and more every day. They come into session asking if they truly are a narcissist, claiming their partner is gaslighting them in every conversation, or insisting their parent is borderline. I've been treating individuals and couples for over a decade now, and each year the reliance on clinical labels has increased. I have married couples yelling in a session about red flags they wish they hadn't ignored when they were dating, how their partner triggers them and is abusive for not considering their feelings, or that the other person is just plain toxic.

To an extent, I think this is normal. When we're confused or frightened, we attempt to organize and explain the world, and thanks to our expanded familiarity with the concepts of mental health, we are now equipped with highly specific terms that seem to offer an understanding of what's happening in our relationship.

But as I've discussed throughout this book, we need to save these words for truly aberrant experiences. Misusing these terms causes them to be watered down, in ways that hurt both the people who don't warrant such terms and the people who do.

- **Weaponized therapy speak prevents survivors from getting the help they need.** Even as these words are increasingly diluted, somehow their intended meaning stays as potent as ever. This creates a world where everyone is psychologically troubled, where clinically significant issues and abusive behaviors are pervasive. However, these experiences are rarer than they seem, and when they do occur, they can be incredibly damaging. There *are* malicious narcissists who do incredible damage in their relationships, and we need the term *narcissist* to represent that person instead of someone who acted selfishly a few times. People who have suffered because of being in relationships with clinical narcissists know the difference. People who have been truly gaslit or love bombed, who have been devastated by dating a sociopath, who have struggled to navigate life with someone who has severe OCD or BPD, know the difference. These people deserve to have it known that what they lived through was not the same as typical relationship struggles.

- **Weaponized therapy speak lets real abusers off the hook.** When someone's behavior really does warrant a clinical diagnosis, a diluted label doesn't carry the same weight. After all, if everyone's a narcissist, then nobody is, right? This provides the perfect opening for real narcissists to scoff at the suggestion that their behavior is problematic. Even worse, it empowers abusers of all types to turn these accusations on their victims. After all, who is more likely to see a difference of opinion as gaslighting than someone who requires constant, unequivocal agreement to feel secure? Between their lack of conscience and their instinct for manipulation, no one is better at weaponizing helpful terminology than an abuser.

- **Weaponized therapy speak increases stigma.** Some of the clinical diagnoses I covered are incredibly challenging disorders that people struggle to manage. Their symptoms are distressing to them and to those around them, and if they could, they would happily choose to wave the magic therapy wand and wake up disorder-free. When we use these diagnoses as insults, we add more stigma to people who suffer from them.

It's easy to jump on the bandwagon of hating on sociopaths and narcissists. These people, after all, can do incredible damage and don't care about the destruction they leave in their wake. But people with other disorders, those who have fully intact capacities for empathy and a desire to have healthy relationships, deserve more compassion and understanding from us. Yes, their symptoms can be destructive too, but many people with mental health issues are also trying to identify and treat these symptoms so that they stop interfering with their lives.

Relationships Are Hard Enough Without Weaponizing Words

Human beings are animals that have been both blessed and cursed with a wide range of emotions and the capacity to think (and overthink) about everything in our lives—of course we're going to be messy sometimes. Even when we know better, it doesn't mean we'll do better. If our past hurts and deepest wounds get activated, if emotions or stress send us into fight-or-flight mode, we're not going to act as our most rational selves. People are emotional, irrational, imperfect creatures, who sometimes *feel* so badly that they then *behave* badly. We need to give each other some grace while also working to do better next time. If we constantly pathologize people in our lives, we will miss out on the chance to build something amazing.

Admittedly, allowing for imperfections makes us very vulnerable to each other. As I've discussed, using weaponized therapy speak is a way of shielding ourselves from vulnerability. When we say, "I was embarrassed when you didn't listen to me at the party because I felt like everyone saw you ignore me," we are opening an emotional wound—to the person

They're Not Gaslighting You

who caused it, no less! It makes us feel much stronger and safer to say, "You're such a narcissist. You never pay attention to me because you're only focused on yourself."

But while it feels safer, this latter response doesn't invite the other person to be empathetic or understanding, to foster dialogue or submit to growth. When we choose vulnerability, we are inviting our loved ones to lay down their defenses as well and join us in healing the wound *together*.

Let's Choose Curiosity and Embrace Human Imperfection

Let me tell you my biggest fear: It's that people will read this book and start weaponizing the term *weaponized therapy speak*. It would be too painfully ironic. When a loved one accuses you of a diagnosis or abusive behavior, I don't want your response to be "Hey, that's weaponized therapy speak and you're awful for doing that!" and then go into the many reasons why it's bad to use weaponized therapy speak. I might agree with your conclusion and arguments, of course, but weaponizing someone's weaponization would just be continuing the cycle.

I've had the part hilarious, part terrifying experience of having my own words weaponized by couples outside of session. More than one couple has come in and said that their partner angrily threw my words into their face during a conflict. Something akin to "You're being defensive, and Dr. Morley said not to do that!" And, in a certain gentle tone with good intention, this could work. But usually, it's someone accusatorily pointing out this mistake in a way to get the upper hand in the argument, and that's obviously less healthy or productive. Plus, the other person could then weaponize something *else* I've probably said during session (like not focusing on blame during conflict), leading to a possible never-ending back-and-forth about who is disobeying my recommendations the most egregiously.

It's Time to Lower Your Weapons

I really want to break this cycle. I want people to stop trying to one-up each other in their diagnostic prowess and relational analysis. I want people to recognize and wonder about patterns and behaviors without immediately deciding on a disorder or sounding the alarm of abuse. I want us all to leave more room for people to be incredibly imperfect and to see their hurtful behavior compassionately—not as attempts to control us, but as misguided attempts to get their needs met. I want us to remember in those moments that people who make mistakes in their desperation to connect with us are people who can have insight and can change. In my ideal world, we'd loosen our grip on labels and focus more on empowering ourselves to take action in our relationships, to either improve them or leave them depending on the circumstances.

Let's keep being compassionate toward ourselves for leaning on therapy terms too. It's human nature to want to understand through categorizations and labels. It's why we all love a good label maker; having the flour container say "flour" on it just feels so much *better*. The world is chaotic, and humans even more so. We can't always embrace nuance and curiosity. Sometimes we just need a label to explain groups of people or behaviors. There's nothing wrong with our brains' need to do this. What's important is to be cautious using these terms when attempting to understand our loved ones. These people are important enough to deserve our nuance and curiosity. They shouldn't be assigned quick, reductive labels; they should be given space to be good and bad and everything in between without immediately qualifying for a clinical disorder.

This is a controversial idea, I'll admit, but I don't know that therapy terms need to leave the therapy room much of the time. I've never had to explicitly say to Lucas, "This is my boundary, and you need to respect it." I just uphold the specific boundary with him. The words are helpful for describing and understanding, for informing our decisions and actions, but they don't need to be used in the moment, and they definitely need more context when they *are* used. A word alone is not

They're Not Gaslighting You

enough to capture our experience or that of the other person; we need to address the patterns and acknowledge the hurt feelings rather than saying a buzzword and hoping that leads to change.

We're all imperfect. Yes, all of us. Even you. Even me. (*Definitely* me, as I'm sure you'd agree after my many disclosures.) And everyone else living on this planet too. Instead of pathologizing imperfection, let's embrace it in ourselves and others. Let's make room for people to be emotional and sometimes irrational, to make repeated mistakes as they're learning and growing, to behave badly in a relationship but recognize their errors and try again. Let's accept the unavoidable truth that humans are messy and then watch how the quality of our relationships flourishes in response.

And Lucas, if you're reading this, I'm sorry about the lids thing. I'm even more sorry that I know I'll keep doing it. Nobody said marriage was easy, but as with all meaningful relationships, it's worth the hard work. ∎

Resources

Adult Children of Emotionally Immature Parents: How to Heal from Distant, Rejecting, or Self-Involved Parents by Lindsay C. Gibson

Divorcing and Healing from a Narcissist: Emotional and Narcissistic Abuse Recovery. Co-parenting After an Emotionally Destructive Marriage and Splitting up with a Toxic Ex by Theresa J. Covert

Fight Right: How Successful Couples Turn Conflict into Connection by Julie Schwartz Gottman and John Gottman

Gaslighting: The Narcissist's Favorite Tool of Manipulation by Theresa J. Covert

Is It Supposed To Be This Hard? Telling the Difference Between Emotional Abuse and the Hard Work of Relationship by Mary Pat Haffey

It's Not You: Identifying and Healing from Narcissistic People by Ramani Durvasula

Love Bombing: The Fine Line Between Devotion and Deception by Sara Sylvestri

Loving Someone with Bipolar Disorder: Understanding and Helping Your Partner by Julie A. Fast and John D. Preston

Loving Someone with OCD: Help For You and Your Family by Karen J. Landsman, Kathleen M. Rupertus, and Cherry Pedrick

The New Rules of Marriage: What You Need to Know to Make Love Work by Terrence Real

Psychopath Free: Recovering from Emotionally Abusive Relationships with Narcissists, Sociopaths, and Other Toxic People by Jackson MacKenzie

Recovery from Narcissistic Abuse, Gaslighting, Codependency and Complex PTSD by Linda Hill

Red Flags, Green Flags: Modern Psychology for Everyday Drama by Ali Fenwick

Secure Love: Create a Relationship That Lasts a Lifetime by Julie Mennano

The Seven Principles for Making Marriage Work: A Practical Guide from the Country's Foremost Expert (Rev. ed.) by John M. Gottman and Nan Silver

Should I Stay or Should I Go? Surviving a Relationship with a Narcissist by Ramani Durvasula

Stop Walking on Eggshells: Taking Your Life Back When Someone You Care About Has Borderline Personality Disorder by Paul T. Mason and Randi Kreger

Us: Getting Past You and Me to Build a More Loving Relationship by Terrence Real

When Loving Him Is Hurting You: Hope and Help for Women Dealing with Narcissism and Emotional Abuse by David Hawkins

When Someone You Love Is Bipolar: Help and Support for You and Your Partner by Cynthia G. Last

Bibliography

Abdulghani, H. M., Marwa, K., Alghamdi, N. A., Almasoud, R. N., Faraj, A. T., Alshuraimi, A. F., Mohamed, K. M., Alnafisah, O. S., Ahmad, T., Ahmed, M. Z., & Khalil, M. S. (2023). Prevalence of the medical student syndrome among health professions students and its effects on their academic performance. *Medicine, 102*(43), Article e35594. https://doi.org/10.1097/MD.0000000000035594

Abramson, K. (2024). *On gaslighting.* Princeton University Press.

American Psychiatric Association. (1952). *Diagnostic and statistical manual of mental disorders.*

American Psychiatric Association. (1968). *Diagnostic and statistical manual of mental disorders* (2nd ed.).

American Psychiatric Association. (1974). *Diagnostic and statistical manual of mental disorders* (2nd ed., seventh printing).

American Psychiatric Association. (1980). *Diagnostic and statistical manual of mental disorders* (3rd ed.).

American Psychiatric Association. (1987). *Diagnostic and statistical manual of mental disorders* (3rd ed., text rev.).

American Psychiatric Association. (1994). *Diagnostic and statistical manual of mental disorders* (4th ed.).

American Psychiatric Association. (2000). *Diagnostic and statistical manual of mental disorders* (4th ed., text rev.).

American Psychiatric Association. (2013). *Diagnostic and statistical manual of mental disorders* (5th ed.).

American Psychiatric Association. (2022). *Diagnostic and statistical manual of mental disorders* (5th ed., text rev.).

Bielecki, J. E., & Gupta, V. (2022). *Cyclothymic disorder.* In *StatPearls.* Retrieved October 2, 2024, from https://www.ncbi.nlm.nih.gov/books/NBK557877

Bolton, D. (2013). Overdiagnosis problems in the DSM-IV and the new DSM-5: Can they be resolved by the distress-impairment criterion? *The Canadian Journal of Psychiatry / La Revue Canadienne de Psychiatrie, 58*(11), 612–617. https://doi.org/10.1177/07067437130580110

Bozzatello, P., Rocca, P., Baldassarri, L., Bosia, M., & Bellino, S. (2021). The role of trauma in early onset borderline personality disorder: A biopsychosocial perspective. *Frontiers in Psychiatry, 12,* Article 721361. https://doi.org/10.3389/fpsyt.2021.721361

Casassa, K., Knight, L., & Mengo, C. (2022). Trauma bonding perspectives from service providers and survivors of sex trafficking: A scoping review. *Trauma, Violence, & Abuse, 23*(3), 969–984. https://doi.org/10.1177/1524838020985542

They're Not Gaslighting You

Cho, C.-H., & Lee, H.-J. (2018). Why do mania and suicide occur most often in the spring? *Psychiatry Investigation, 15*(3), 232–234. https://doi.org/10.30773/pi.2017.12.20

Deo, M. S., & Lymburner, J. A. (2011). Personality traits and psychological health concerns: The search for psychology student syndrome. *Teaching of Psychology, 38*(3), 155–157. https://doi.org/10.1177/009862831141178

Dutton, D. G., & Painter, S. (1993). Emotional attachments in abusive relationships: A test of traumatic bonding theory. *Violence and Victims, 8*(2), 105–120. https://doi.org /10.1891/0886-6708.8.2.105

Engel, B. (2002). *The emotionally abusive relationship: How to stop being abused and how to stop abusing.* Wiley.

Fávero, M., Cruz, N., Moreira, D., Del Campo, A., & Sousa-Gomes, V. (2024). Violence in intimate relationships: Symptomatology and motivation for change. *Psychological Trauma: Theory, Research, Practice, and Policy, 16*(3), 462–469. https://doi.org /10.1037/tra0001471

Fishbein, R. (2023, September 8). *Everyone is setting boundaries. Do they know what it means?* Washington Post. https://www.washingtonpost.com/wellness/2023/09/08 /setting-boundaries-therapy-words/

Frances, A. (2012, December 5). *DSM-5 is a guide, not a bible: Simply ignore its 10 worst changes.* Psychiatric Times. https://www.psychiatrictimes.com/view/dsm-5-guide -not-biblesimply-ignore-its-10-worst-changes

Frances, A. (2013). *Saving normal: An insider's revolt against out-of-control psychiatric diagnosis, DSM-5, Big Pharma, and the medicalization of ordinary life.* William Morrow.

Freud, S. (1923). The infantile genital organization (An interpolation into the theory of sexuality). In J. Strachey (Ed.), *The standard edition of the complete psychological works of Sigmund Freud: The ego and the id and other works* (Vol. 19, pp. 139–146). The Hogarth Press.

Freud, S. (1925). Some psychical consequences of the anatomical distinction between the sexes. In J. Strachey (Ed.), *The standard edition of the complete psychological works of Sigmund Freud: The ego and the id and other works* (Vol. 19, pp. 241–258). The Hogarth Press.

Freud, S. (1975). *Cocaine papers.* Plume.

Greenberg, L. S., & Johnson, S. M. (1988). *Emotionally focused therapy for couples.* Guilford Press.

Gottman, J. M., & Gottman, J. S. (2008). Gottman method couple therapy. In A. S. Gurman (Ed.), *Clinical handbook of couple therapy* (4th ed., pp. 138–164). Guilford Press.

Gottman, J. M., & Silver, N. (2015). *The seven principles for making marriage work: A practical guide from the country's foremost relationship expert* (Rev. ed.). Harmony.

Hardy, M. S., & Calhoun, L. G. (1997). Psychological distress and the 'medical student syndrome' in abnormal psychology students. *Teaching of Psychology, 24*(3), 192–193. https://doi.org/10.1207/s15328023top2403_10

Hassan, S. (1988). *Combatting cult mind control: The #1 best-selling guide to protection, rescue, and recovery from destructive cults.* Park Street Press.

Bibliography

Hill, D., & Scott, H. (2019). Climbing the corporate ladder: Desired leadership skills and successful psychopaths. *Journal of Financial Crime, 26*(3), 881–896. https://doi.org /10.1108/JFC-11-2018-0117

Holdwick, D. J., Jr., Hilsenroth, M. J., Castlebury, F. D., & Blais, M. A. (1998). Identifying the unique and common characteristics among the DSM-IV antisocial, borderline, and narcissistic personality disorders. *Comprehensive Psychiatry, 39*(5), 277–286. https:// doi.org/10.1016/S0010-440X(98)90036-0

Hudek-Knezevic, J., Kardum, I., & Banov, K. (2023). The effects of the dark triad personality traits on health protective behaviours: Dyadic approach on self-reports and partner-reports. *Psychology & Health, 38*(8), 987–1005. ttps://doi.org/10.1080 /08870446.2021.1998497

Jee, H. J., Cho, C. H., Lee, Y. J., Choi, N., An, H., & Lee, H. J. (2017). Solar radiation increases suicide rate after adjusting for other climate factors in South Korea. *Acta Psychiatrica Scandinavica, 135*(3), 219–227. https://doi.org/10.1111/acps.12676

Johnson, S., & Brubacher, L. (2016). Clarifying the negative cycle in emotionally focused couple therapy (EFT). In G. R. Weeks, S. T. Fife, & C. M. Peterson (Eds.), *Techniques for the couple therapist: Essential interventions from the experts* (pp. 92–96). Routledge.

Kardum, I., Hudek-Knezevic, J., Mehić, N., & Banov Trošelj, K. (2024). The dark triad traits and relationship satisfaction: Dyadic response surface analysis. *Journal of Personality, 92*(4), 931–947. https://doi.org/10.1111/jopy.12857

Klein, W., Li, S., & Wood, S. (2023). A qualitative analysis of gaslighting in romantic relationships. *Personal Relationships, 30*(4), 1316–1340. https://doi.org/10.1111 /pere.12510

Lee, H. J., Kim, L., Joe, S. H., & Suh, K. Y. (2002). Effects of season and climate on the first manic episode of bipolar affective disorder in Korea. *Psychiatry Research, 113*(1–2), 151–159. https://doi.org/10.1016/S0165-1781(02)00237-8

Logan, M. H. (2018). Stockholm syndrome: Held hostage by the one you love. *Violence and Gender, 5*(2), 67–69. https://doi.org/10.1089/vio.2017.0076

Loring, M. T. (1998). *Emotional abuse: The trauma and the treatment.* Jossey-Bass.

Möller, H.-J. (2014). The consequences of DSM-5 for psychiatric diagnosis and psychopharmacotherapy. *International Journal of Psychiatry in Clinical Practice, 18*(2), 78–85. https://doi.org/10.3109/13651501.2014.890228

Ociskova, M., Prasko, J., Hodny, F., Holubova, M., Vanek, J., Minarikova, K., Nesnidal, V., Sollar, T., Slepecky, M., & Kantor, K. (2023). Black & white relations: Intimate relationships of patients with borderline personality disorder. *Neuro Endocrinology Letters, 44*(5), 321–331.

O'Leary, K. D. (2015). Psychological abuse: A variable deserving critical attention in domestic violence. In R. D. Maiuro (Ed.), *Perspectives on verbal and psychological abuse* (pp. 23–42). Springer Publishing Company.

Pagura, J., Stein, M. B., Bolton, J. M., Cox, B. J., Grant, B., & Sareen, J. (2010). Comorbidity of borderline personality disorder and posttraumatic stress disorder in the US population. *Journal of Psychiatric Research, 44*(16), 1190–1198. https://doi.org /10.1016/j.jpsychires.2010.04.016

They're Not Gaslighting You

Powers, A., Petri, J. M., Sleep, C., Mekawi, Y., Lathan, E. C., Shebuski, K., Bradley, B., & Fani, N. (2022). Distinguishing PTSD, complex PTSD, and borderline personality disorder using exploratory structural equation modeling in a trauma-exposed urban sample. *Journal of Anxiety Disorders, 88*, Article 102558. https://doi.org/10.1016/j.janxdis.2022.102558

Scheiderer, E. M., Wood, P. K., & Trull, T. J. (2015). The comorbidity of borderline personality disorder and posttraumatic stress disorder: Revisiting the prevalence and associations in a general population sample. *Borderline Personality Disorder and Emotion Dysregulation, 2*(1), Article 11. https://doi.org/10.1186/s40479-015-0032-y

Schusdek, A. (1965). Freud on cocaine. *The Psychoanalytic Quarterly, 34*(3), 406–412. https://doi.org/10.1080/21674086.1965.11926355

Shen, H., Zhang, L., Xu, C., Zhu, J., Chen, M., & Fang, Y. (2018). Analysis of misdiagnosis of bipolar disorder in an outpatient setting. *Shanghai Archives of Psychiatry, 30*(2), 93–101. https://doi.org/10.11919/j.issn.1002-0829.217080

Strutzenberg, C. C., Wiersma-Mosley, J. D., Jozkowski, K. N., & Becnel, J. N. (2017). Love-bombing: A narcissistic approach to relationship formation. *Discovery, The Student Journal of Dale Bumpers College of Agricultural, Food and Life Sciences, 18*(1), 81–89. https://scholarworks.uark.edu/discoverymag/vol18/iss1/14

Talitman, E. (1996). *Predictors of outcome in emotionally focused marital therapy* [Doctoral dissertation, University of Ottawa]. University of Ottawa Digital Archive. https://ruor.uottawa.ca/server/api/core/bitstreams/a84469b8-2701-4249-945d-c03eb99b140f/content

Tan, K., Ingram, S. H., Lau, L. A. S. L., & South, S. C. (2022). Borderline personality traits and romantic relationship dissolution. *Journal of Personality Disorders, 36*(2), 183–200. https://doi.org/10.1521/pedi_2021_35_533

Walker, L. (1979). *The battered woman.* Harper & Row.

Weiss, B., Lavner, J. A., & Miller, J. D. (2018). Self- and partner-reported psychopathic traits' relations with couples' communication, marital satisfaction trajectories, and divorce in a longitudinal sample. *Personality Disorders: Theory, Research, and Treatment, 9*(3), 239–249. https://doi.org/10.1037/per0000233

Young, G. (2016). *Unifying causality and psychology.* Springer.

Zeigler, H. V., Hicks, P., & Brosch, N. (2024). Narcissism and romantic relationship functioning: The mediating role of the desire for power. *Personal Relationships, 31*(3), 734–757. https://doi.org/10.1111/pere.12551

Acknowledgments

I have to start by thanking my husband, Lucas. I actually think I made a lot of great choices in my twenties but you, my love, are undoubtedly the best one. I'm so glad that we finally noticed each other at the birthday party, that we've worked through our hard times, and that we've built this wonderful life together. Our marriage is one of my greatest sources of pride, not because it's perfect, but because it's perfect to me. We love, we laugh, we struggle, we persevere, and we grow. It's all I could ask for in a partner. Thank you for believing in my dreams and doing whatever you can to help them become realities—watching our girls while I write on weekends, brainstorming title ideas, talking me down from my irrational anxiety spirals—and just generally being supportive in all the right ways. I don't want to walk through this world with anyone but you.

Next, I want to thank my children, Maple and Wilde. Having you inspired me to contribute something that makes this world better, knowing it's a world you'll have to live in. I hope that when you're older, you find relationships that are meaningful and rich with love and growth, like what I have with your dad. And thank you for sleeping until 6:30 a.m. most mornings, giving me time to write.

I'm grateful for family members who were a part of this from the start. Robert and Anne Eccles and Charlotte Hamill, I know I made you talk about this book a lot, and I appreciate your support (and patience!). Char, please don't count how many texts I sent asking for ideas and opinions; it was your sisterly duty. Thank you for reading it and for your feedback. Robert and Anne—"the parental unit," as we, your children, like to call you—thank you for instilling in me a belief that I can do absolutely anything if I put my mind to it (but also that I don't *have* to). Mom, thank you for reading the draft! You were the first official person to read this book, and it means a lot to me. Dad, I feel like I owe my career success to you in so many ways. You've always believed in and supported me.

To my amazing in-laws, Sylvia Balderrama and John Morley, thank you for everything. For being supportive through it all: newborn phases, kitchen constructions, job changes. Thank you for watching my kids when they're sick or on holidays, for taking care of Cliff, and most of all, for creating Lucas. I won the in-law jackpot, and I know it.

To Bailey Hanek, my best friend, thank you for everything. This book has two parents, and you were one of them. It wouldn't exist without your contribution. We've had our own share of struggles, but you're a forever friend. No matter how dark things get, we'll find our way to the other side together. Only you and I know much is behind that statement. I love you, I'm grateful for you, and I'm keeping you no matter what.

Katherine Chase, I can't thank you enough for your love and support. I treasure and count on your relentless enthusiasm. This book was born from Bailey and me—and you, my friend, were the midwife. You were an unwavering bridge, and I'll never forget it.

Rebecca Eudy, having you throughout this process has made it so much more delightful. Thank you for the countless hours of talking through chapter organization, refining ideas, commiserating, and celebrating our milestones. I liked writing a book at the same time as you; let's always do it that way, okay?

Thank you to the amazing team at PESI: Kayla Church, Chelsea Thompson, Jenessa Jackson, Karsyn Morse, Jenny Miller, design team, and everyone else who touched this project. I'm forever grateful that you said yes to this book and worked with me to publish it as soon as possible. Thank you for your tireless efforts to make it what it is.

To my alma mater, William James College, thank you for giving me a wonderful education and clinical training and for supporting my work

Acknowledgments

to this day. Nick Covino and Julia Clement, thank you for giving me extended access to the library. I'm a very appreciative alum!

I can't write acknowledgments without expressing my love for my toy poodle, Clifford. Cliff, you've been there from the start . . . before Lucas, even! You sat on my lap while I wrote my dissertation, and ten years later, you sat in your bed in my office while I wrote this book. You're my little apricot rock, and I love you.

Curse Word Club (you know who you are), thank you for all you contributed to this book. Thank you for enduring my frenzied obsession with this topic, and not only enduring it but adding to it and growing my passion for it. Laura Morley, you've built an amazing community of friends, and I'm thankful I get the benefit of knowing them. I'm also just generally thankful I have you in my life.

You're all sociopaths, of course. But I love you dearly. ∎

About the Author

Isabelle Morley, PsyD, is a clinical psychologist and EFT-certified couples therapist (emotionally focused therapy). She is a contributing author to Psychology Today in her blog *Love Them or Leave Them*, where she analyzes on-screen romantic relationships. She is also the co-host of *Rom-Com Rescue*, a podcast that teaches life and love lessons from romantic comedies. Dr. Morley is frequently sought out by journalists for expert commentary on topics such as relationships, couples therapy, and reality television, and has been featured in *The New Yorker*, *The Boston Globe*, *Business Insider*, *Vox*, and *Verywell Mind*, among others. In philanthropic work, Dr. Morley is a founding board member of the Unscripted Cast Advocacy Network (UCAN) Foundation, a nonprofit organization that supports reality TV cast members in accessing mental health and legal support and advocates for industry change.

She received a bachelor of arts from Tufts University. As part of her major in peace and justice studies, she focused on interpersonal conflict resolution and wrote her capstone project on the evolutionary justification and modern-day use of forgiveness and revenge in relationships following significant transgressions. She earned her doctor of psychology degree from William James College in 2015. Her doctoral research explored young adults' perspectives on hookup culture and its impact on their ability to form meaningful romantic relationships. Dr. Morley started specializing in couples therapy early in her career, working with couples and pursuing additional education and training in many forms of couples therapy, including the Gottman Method, EFT, and relational life therapy. She worked at two group practices and served as a site director of a national mental health group before starting her private practice in 2021, where she provides therapy and intensives to couples. She lives and works in the Boston area.